THE FANTASTIC HORIZON

THE FANTASTIC HORIZON

Essays and Reviews

by

Darrell Schweitzer

THE BORGO PRESS

An Imprint of Wildside Press LLC

MMIX

*I.O. Evans Studies in the Philosophy
and Criticism of Literature*
ISSN 0271-9061

Number Forty-One

FIRST EDITION

CONTENTS

REVIEWS

WRITING ADVICE

ACKNOWLEDGMENTS

The essays in this book first appeared in the following publications:

"Introduction" appears here for the first time.

"Middle Earth Revisited; or, Back There Again" first appeared in *The New York Review of Science Fiction* #165, May 2002. Copyright © 2002 by Dragon Press.

"J. R. R. Tolkien as a Horror Writer" first appeared in slightly different form as part of "The Eyrie" in *Weird Tales* #328, Summer 2002, copyright © 2002 by Terminus Publishing Co.

"Of Worms and Hobbits, Cabbages and Kings, Not to Mention Heaps of Slaughtered Peasants" first appeared in slightly different form as part of "The Eyrie" in *Weird Tales* #340, June-July 2006, copyright © 2006 by Wildside Press.

"What Does a Story Mean?" first appeared in slightly different form as part of "The Eyrie" in *Weird Tales* #336, December 2004, copyright © 2004 by Terminus Publishing Co.

"Myth America" first appeared in slightly different form as part of "The Eyrie" in *Weird Tales* #330, Winter 2002-2003, copyright © 2002 by Terminus Publishing Co.

"Who Killed Horror? The Murder on the Orient Express Solution" first appeared in slightly different form as part of "The Eyrie" in *Weird Tales* #334, January-February 2004, copyright © 2004 by Terminus Publishing Co.

"Of Dream Research, Nyucks, Knuckleheads, the Intentional Fallacy, Biographical Criticism and Even More Nyucks" first appeared in slightly different form as part of "The Eyrie" in *Weird Tales* #342, October-November 2006, copyright © 2006 by Wildside Press.

"Fantasy and Tradition; or, Hey, Is That My Genre You're Stepping On?" first appeared in *The New York Review of Science Fiction* #199, Mach 2005. Copyright © 2005 by Dragon Press.

"Epic and Fantasy in Epic Fantasy (The Good Parts Version)" first appeared in *The New York Review of Science Fiction* #195, November 2004. Copyright © 2004 by Dragon Press.

"The Uses of Fantasy" first appeared in *The New York Review of Science Fiction* #175, March 2003. Copyright © 2003 by Dragon

INTRODUCTION

I should call this, perhaps, *Ponderings and Pontifications*? The book you are holding is a sequel to the 1998 volume *Windows of the Imagination.* Continuing the architectural motif, I might have called it *Doors of Discovery,* save that (thankfully) my editor, Robert Reginald, suggested the present title, which is much better.

This accumulation of essays, reviews, and a couple of speeches contains my best non-fiction of the past nine years or so. I have felt my literary gears shifting as I age, and have turned more toward commentary, as a continuing exploration of the fantastic fiction to which I have devoted a good deal of my life. Here are articles about, or touching on, J. R. R. Tolkien, Lord Dunsany, H. P. Lovecraft, pulp magazines, writing and editing, the aesthetics of fantasy, and even what happens to bibliomaniacs when they die.

These are pieces written for a variety of reasons, without a totally coordinated agenda, although I think that, as a whole, they have one. They're about what I do and why I think it is important. There is even the suggestion (in the last two, particularly) that you can do it too.

Beyond that, I just hope you find these pieces entertaining. Some have been revised slightly to make sense in this context. The pieces which were once embedded in *Weird Tales* editorials have been stripped of the editorial "we." Otherwise I have not revised them to update the topical references—a fool's game anyway, and something which can ultimate destroy the interesting context in which one's essayistic observations were first made.

Truth in advertising does require that more recently than the "Don't Give Up Your Dreams" speech was delivered, the publisher of *Weird Tales* shifted me from actually editing the magazine to writing columns and features for it. So, aside from my DAW Books anthology, *The Secret History of Vampires* (about to appear as I write this), I am not, at present, a fiction editor, although I have been one for almost twenty years. I am still a literary agent, in a low-key way, managing a few estates. I am mostly a *writer*, of fiction and non-fiction, with, I hope, something to say which you want to read.

Nothing more needs to be said by way of introduction.

—Darrell Schweitzer
April 3, 2007

I.

Middle Earth Revisited; or, Back There Again

I.

I've returned to Tolkien country recently, and stayed a while, but as a tourist. So hold the "you can't go home again" comments, sage observations, and the like. I never lived in Middle Earth. I visited once before. Then I went back. It being the custom to begin essays like this with a bit of What Tolkien Meant In My Life, if Karen Haber's *Meditations on Middle Earth* (St. Martin's, 2001) is any indication, I will volunteer the information that I first read *The Lord of the Rings* in college, when I was twenty, but the work did not give me the vast rush of revelation that it did to most twenty-year-olds in 1972. There are whole schools of criticism built on the idea that your experience with a book depends as much on who you are as what's on the printed page, and I have to admit, with the experience of going back to Tolkien almost thirty years later, that this is certainly true.

In 1972 I was way ahead of my classmates. For most Baby Boomers, Tolkien hit them with the force of a biblical vision, because they had never encountered *any* imaginative literature before. Certainly it wasn't taught in the schools. In fact it was actively discouraged in the schools. The English teachers I had were firm ideological adherents of the view that "realism" and "literature" were synonyms, that "serious" writing is about life as it is lived, and anything else is either for small children, or subliterary trash and for morons and perverts. They skirted around Shakespeare's *The Tempest*, which surely provides us with the greatest archetype of a wizard prior to Gandalf, and Poe's "The Masque of the Red Death"—which could be explained away as allegory, as could anything in Hawthorne. We had little exposure to medieval literature. *Everyman*,

13

of course, was allegory and therefore safe. *Beowulf* was the product of a very different time, and not examined in any detail.

So for most readers *The Lord of the Rings* was, aside from a few folksy fables, the first fantasy they had ever seen. It blew them away.

But I was different, by 1972. I had been in fandom since 1968. I was friendly with the de Camps and with Lin Carter, who was then editing the epochal Ballantine Adult Fantasy Adult Fantasy Series. My friends and I had long talks with Lin about fantasy at conventions. I was already reading Lord Dunsany, James Branch Cabell, Robert E. Howard, C. L. Moore, and even William Morris. That I hadn't ever read *The Lord of the Rings* was becoming a bit of a guilty secret.

And I was already writing fantasy. If you're curious to read a story of mine written prior to any encounter with Tolkien, look up "The Story of Obbok," as reprinted in Marvin Kaye's rather unfortunately titled *Don't Open This Book!* (Guild America, 1998). Open it. Read it. I actually "sold" that story to Lin Carter for an anthology in the Ballantine Adult Fantasy Series that never appeared. I wrote it when I was nineteen, in 1971. When I brought it into a creative writing class, my classmates compared it to Tolkien, naturally enough, having no other point of reference. The professor had no idea of what to make of it. (It's an obvious pastiche of Dunsany.)

When I finally *did* read *The Lord of the Rings,* Tolkien had my attention. I didn't read anything else but schoolbooks and newspapers for two months. I didn't write any fiction. I came away very impressed, but the Trilogy had very little immediate influence on me. The scale was all wrong. I was not one of those student writers with a closet full of unfinished, sprawling epics, probably because I didn't have the stamina to write something that long which I knew would never be published. If I was going to make it into print, it would have to be with short work. (I still hold to this. If you can't write ten pages of professional prose, you can't write a thousand. Save your epics until you have proven, by sales of shorter works, that you're writing at a publishable level.)

Tolkien isn't a very good model for budding short story writers. Besides, by the time I read him, my formative influences were already in place. I can make a halfway plausible claim to being the last, or certainly the youngest pre-Tolkien fantasy writer still active.

II.

When I returned to Middle Earth again recently, it was a changed country, because I was a changed traveler. I knew my Anglo-Saxon literature by now, Professor Tolkien's field, though I'd only read it in translation. Still, I knew that the term "Middle Earth" comes from Caedmon's hymn:

Then this middle-earth the Master of mankind,
The Lord eternal, afterwards adorned....

I understood the source of the BANG-BANG! BANG-BANG! alliterative rhythm of much of Tolkien's verse. And I was familiar with the one great utterance which echoes above all else in Old English literature and perfectly encapsulates the Anglo-Saxon heroic ethic. It's from "The Battle of Maldon" (about which, more later):

Thought shall be the harder, heart the keener,
courage the greater, as our might lessens.

So I journeyed again into Middle Earth carrying a lot of baggage I didn't have the first time, and also with a certain unease. I found, in the first few chapters of *The Fellowship of the Ring,* that cuteness is still a problem. I hadn't liked the first chapter very much at twenty, and when recommending the Trilogy to people ever after, I always described the first chapter as something you have to force your way through to get to the good parts. There is definitely a tone problem. The word "twee," which was probably not in my vocabulary at age twenty, now springs to mind.

Certainly *The Lord of the Rings* began in the nursery, as a "fairy story," to use Tolkien's term, and the adult reader may squirm just a little bit when we encounter the sentient fox, or when the storyteller breaks in, like an adult interrupting into a bed-time story, to reassure us that the horses are all right. And Tolkien makes a profound mistake in just five words, on page 36 of the standard Houghton-Mifflin edition of *Fellowship,* when the firework dragon "passed like an express train." This completely punctures the illusion of the story. There are no express trains in Middle Earth. We are drawn completely out of the proper frame of reference. (Fortunately the book, like its characters, grows and matures. The blunder is not repeated.)

I begin to have irreverent thoughts and doubts. Do they have sex in Middle Earth? The hobbits remind me of pre-adolescent boys, interested in exciting tales of adventure, but not yet in girls. In fact there don't seem to *be* many females in Middle Earth. That Tom Bombadil lives with a Mistress Goldberry comes as a bit of a shock.

What I remembered from my first reading was that the first chapter was a bit of a chore, but that the narrative darkened and deepened wonderfully in the second, as the back-story began to fill in and we first heard of the Dark Lord Sauron and of the epic history of the Ring itself. This time around, knowing that back-story, I find the tone problem continues, if to a lesser degree, for quite a while. I am not entirely reassured until chapter 5, when Frodo and Sam cross the Brandywine on the ferry, look back and see on the dock they have just left:

> ...a figure: it looked like a dark black bundle left be-
> hind. But as they looked it seemed to move this way
> and that, as if searching the ground. It then crawled,
> or went crouching, back into the gloom beyond the
> lamps. (p. 109)

If we overlook the redundancy of the word "dark" (there can be *light* black?), that is an image worthy of M.R. James. Tolkien has a considerable talent for supernatural apparitions of the creepiest sort. Under slightly different circumstances, he might have been a great ghost-story writer.

Even beyond chapter five, the story meanders. I note that Peter Jackson, in his very intelligent abridgement of the storyline in his film *The Lord of the Rings: The Fellowship of the Ring,* left out Tom Bombadil, the Old Forest, the Barrow Wight, and, thankfully, almost all of the songs. Tolkien was opposed to film adaptations of his work, mostly because he was terrified of what Walt Disney or someone influenced by Disney might do. All those songs would have, indeed, Disneyfied the whole film, so Jackson was wise to have omitted them. Some of the blame has to rest on Tolkien, though, that early on in *The Fellowship of the Ring* (book, not film) I was half afraid some hobbit would break out into "Bippety-boppety-boo!"

Of course it may be that I have such evil thoughts because Michael Moorcock, like Wormtongue, has been whispering in my ear for so long. Among the baggage I carry into Middle Earth on my second visit is the memory of having read Moorcock's pamphlet *Epic Pooh,* which he expanded into a chapter of his book *Wizardry and Wild Romance* (1987). It has long been Moorcock's view that *The Lord of the Rings* should be sent back to the nursery where it belongs and is "*Winnie the Pooh* posing as an epic."

Of course Tolkien has had his detractors all along, the most famous (or infamous) of whom is Edmund Wilson, whose "Oo, Those Awful Orcs" may now be found Alida Becker's *A Tolkien Treasury*, the inclusion of which may be compared to a severed head stuck on a spike over a castle gate. Wilson's very presence in such a book is the surest indication that he has lost the battle. (The same thing happened again when his "Tales of the Marvelous and Ridiculous," an attempted demolition of Lovecraft, appeared in S.T. Joshi's *H. P. Lovecraft: Four Decades of Criticism* in 1980.) One almost feels sorry for Edmund Wilson. Very likely his name will be kept alive by the very writers he tried to consign to oblivion; but he will be remembered as a fool.

Then again, maybe he deserves to be. When he tells us that "Dr. Tolkien has little skill at narrative and no instinct for literary form," and crows about how his seven-year-old daughter understood *The Lord of the Rings* perfectly, we can only sigh and say, yes, very likely she understood it better than he did, and could have returned to it at a later age to find the surprising depths her daddy never suspected.

Wilson, of course, was blinded by that same Protestant Work Ethic of Literature I encountered in high school and college. If it's imaginative, it is certainly frivolous and not really literature. If you enjoy it, it's probably wicked. "Serious" equals realistic. Anything fantastic after, perhaps, Mark Twain's "The Mysterious Stranger" (1916) must be excluded from the canon, and Twain's fantasy is only allowed in because he was Mark Twain. The rest is to be kept away by such watchdogs as Edmund Wilson, who was deeply suspicious of anything popular. He also tried to wipe out the mystery field ("Who Cares Who Killed Roger Ackroyd?") and in particular, Dashiell Hammett ("Duh toast of duh intellectuals," sneered Wilson). He lost those fights too. Mysteries flourish. Hammett is in Library of America. Wilson rots on his spike over the castle gate. We can dismiss him with contempt.

It may be generally observed that critics are not at their best when trying to tell millions of people of several generations why they should not have enjoyed their favorite books. Mark Twain actually did it with "Fenimore Cooper's Literary Offenses." Few will ever read Cooper quite the same way again. I cannot think of another example.

You can't so easily dismiss Moorcock, certainly not on the charge of being unimaginative. He is one of the most important fantasy writers of our time. A treatise on fantasy, by such a figure, has to be taken seriously. Yet in a letter in the January 2002 *Locus* Moorcock is clearly out of line:

> While I agree that Prof Hobbit has produced a vast raft of clones, I suspect he has had very little influence on literary fiction in any language, whereas the likes of Philip K. Dick and other American "pulp" writers continue to have considerable influence on writers who could be said to make up the British literary establishment. I suspect time will show that *The Lord of the Rings* has about as much effect on the history of literature as *Gone with the Wind.*

Never mind literary establishments. I am sure that Michael Moorcock, of all people, would agree that they exist to be overthrown. Otherwise the statement is patently ridiculous, and implies an insult to some very fine writers indeed (Gene Wolfe, Ursula Le Guin, Peter Beagle, probably John Crowley) who have indeed absorbed Tolkien's influence without producing clones. I am unaware of any continuing series of Margaret Mitchell conferences, any body of Margaret Mitchell critical scholarship to match the shelves and shelves of books about Tolkien. Forty-eight years after the publication of *The Fellowship of the Ring,* we finally have a decent Tolkien movie, but certainly his success cannot be attributed to a film, as Margaret Mitchell's can be. Had there not been the famous movie, would *Gone With the Wind* be any more remembered today than other costume best-sellers of the late '30s, such, as say, Hervey Allen's *Anthony Adverse*? As far as I know, the only significant book written in response to *Gone with the Wind* was *The Wind Done Gone.* Not the same at all.

Meanwhile, with a certain irony of timing, Tom Shippey has released his provocatively entitled *J. R. R. Tolkien, Author of the Century,* which makes the case that Tolkien is the central figure in twentieth-century literature.

I think the truth is somewhere in between. *The Lord of the Rings* was certainly the most important fantasy since *Alice's Adventures Underground.* Does that make Lewis Carroll the most important figure in nineteenth-century literature? But we have to admit that the *publication* of *The Lord of the Rings* may well have been the pivotal event in twentieth-century literature, at least in English. Fantasy, which had been the normal mode of literary expression since the beginning of civilization, had been temporarily banished to the nursery for ideological reasons. Meanwhile, during the Dark Years of the Reign of Realism, great works of fantasy continued to appear, *Jurgen* (1919), *The Worm Ouroboros* (1922), *The King of Elfland's Daughter* (1924), all the way up to *The Broken Sword,* which came out the same year as *The Fellowship of the Ring* (1954), but, aside for the briefly notorious *Jurgen,* these were by and large part of an underground literature, written by eccentrics, and read only by a few. Then, with the mass-market publication of *The Lord of the Rings* in the 1960's, fantasy came racing back, as the tide over flat sand.

If we are to sum up literature since the 1960s in one phrase, it might be "the fantastic dominant." It goes far beyond Tolkien. Mark Helprin, John Gardner, A. S. Byatt, Sylvia Townsend Warner—pick your own names—have all written "literary" fiction which either directly embraces or at least addresses the fantastic. You must look back to Tolkien to understand why this is possible, when it would not have been in, say, 1935. (Stories about *elves* in *The New Yorker*?) It is very hard to deny that Tolkien's influence has been vast, and terrifically liberating.

That Michael Moorcock doesn't like *The Lord of the Rings* is his business. If we read *Wizardry and Wild Romance*, we get the impression that part of his objection to Tolkien is one of taste. Tolkien lacks irony, and Moorcock finds a lack of irony a grievous fault in any writer. But the deeper objections seem to be political. Tolkien is conservative, even reactionary, if you read him a certain way. He seems to turn his back on the twentieth century. Tom Shippey argues that Tolkien is very much a part of the twentieth century, of that generation traumatized by World War I, who just took a different course from his contemporary, Ernest Hemingway, by rejecting modernism. Tolkien is saying that, aesthetically at least, the twentieth century has it all wrong. And who is to say that the reigning aesthetic is the correct one, or the only possible one?

But Moorcock faults Tolkien for the very attitudes which made World War I possible in the first place. Some of this may be lost on American readers, but we can get the gist:

> It was best-selling novelists, like Warwick Deeping, who, after the First World War, adapted the sentimental myths (particularly the myth of Sacrifice) which made war bearable (and helped ensure that we should be able to bear future wars), providing us with the wretched ethic of passive "decency" and self-

sacrifice, by which we are able to console ourselves in our moral apathy.... Moderation was the rule and it is moderation which ruins Tolkien's fantasy and causes it to fail as genuine romance. The little hills and woods of that Surrey of the mind, the Shire, are "safe," but the wild landscapes everywhere beyond the Shire are "dangerous." Experience of life itself is dangerous. *The Lord of the Rings* is a pernicious confirmation of the values of the morally bankrupt middle-class. Their cowardly, Home Counties habits are primarily responsible for the problems England now faces. (p. 124-25)

That Moorcock prefers The *Gormenghast* Trilogy is not at all surprising. Peake actually is, line by line, a better stylist. There is nothing in *The Lord of the Rings* as stunningly lyrical as the opening pages of *Titus Alone*. But, more significantly, in Peake we see the Tolkien fantasy turned inside out. Tolkien's characters yearn for the good old days of the heroic past. They worship tradition. Peake's characters are buried alive by it. *The Lord of the Rings* is about the acceptance of tradition and responsibility. *Titus Groan et al.* are about rebellion.

III.

Let me respectfully beg to differ and offer up some subversive thoughts:
There is something to be said for tradition and responsibility.
Tolkien's lack of irony may be his greatest strength.
The Lord of the Rings is not *Winnie the Pooh* posing as an epic, but *Winnie the Pooh* genuinely evolving into an epic, and that's a lot more interesting.
What I found when revisiting Tolkien country after all these years is pretty much the same thing Michael Swanwick did (see "A Changeling Returns' in *Meditations on Middle Earth*). It's a sadder, wiser place than we remembered. *The Lord of the Rings* refutes Moorcock's objections. It does not reject the experience of life. What it tells us is that growing up might be scary, as any child or anyone who remembers childhood knows, but you *can't* remain in the nursery (or the Shire) forever. If you try, the evils of the world will come and get you anyway. Once you have grown up, as Frodo has by the end of *The Return of the King*, you can't go back to the

nursery either. It is a different place. You are different. You don't fit anymore. We observe this in real life all the time. Uncharitably, we might say that we see this in Science Fiction and Fantasy fandom a little more often than is comfortable: people who try to avoid growing up, who never embrace responsibility and try to keep adolescence going forever, merely end up as arrested-development cases, stunted, unhappy, and unfulfilled. (Early on I learned the phrase, "Classic Fannish Ne'er-Do-Well.")

The adult returning to *The Lord of the Rings* discovers that it is a book about loss. John Clute and John Grant have coined the term "thinning" in *The Encyclopedia of Fantasy*. Middle Earth is thinning. The magic is going away. Soon it will be a squalid medieval realm of knights and peasants. There won't be any elves anymore.

Swanwick writes that as an adult he finds *The Lord of the Rings* "the saddest book in the world. This is a tale in which everyone is in the process of losing everything they most hold dear."

Indeed, now I find *The Lord of the Rings* to be about loss and coping with loss. Tolkien seems a bit reluctant to let go of his characters, to admit that anyone but the spear-carriers can actually die. I remember that upon my first reading, I had the uneasy sense that the author would always pull strings, always get the good guys out of a tough spot, and that ultimately there was no real danger. I had given up on E. E. Smith's Lensman series largely for that reason a few years earlier.

Now I find that Frodo suffers far more than I remembered. The first time around, it was the death of Boromir at the beginning of *The Two Towers*, which restored the faltering sense of suspense. This time it didn't seem to matter as much. It's Frodo's story. He is the one who is crushed by the burden of the Quest. Now, as after my first reading, I linger in the appendices of *The Return of the King,* absorbing additional bits of the back-story, scanning through "The Tale of Years." In the chronology we find that Frodo missed out on most of what he must have wanted in his life. He went directly from adolescence into old age. Like his uncle Bilbo and like Gollum, the two others who bore the One Ring the longest, he never marries and leaves no descendants. He comes back from the quest, honored to be sure, but like a war veteran suffering from Post-Traumatic Stress Syndrome, he cannot get his life together. His health fails. Two years after the fall of Sauron, Frodo and the now decrepit Bilbo leave Middle Earth forever.

We might mention in passing that going down to the Grey Havens, boarding an Elfish vessel, and sailing out to the West is a Middle Earth variant on death, available to only a select few. Many of the heroes, King Theoden and the like, rest under mounds. Going into the West is rather like being raised to Olympus. It removes the hero entirely beyond human (or Hobbit) ken, into the realm of legend. But even the other Ring-Bearers merely die. Gandalf, who is a supernatural being who has been in Middle Earth for thousands of years, goes away. After sufficient thinning, dead Middle-Earthers rot in the mud like anybody else.

I understand now why there is no formal religion in Middle Earth. This is, I think, an important point, because Tolkien was all his life deeply religious. (A further part of Michael Moorcock's quarrel with him.) Lin Carter didn't get it, for all he may have written *Tolkien: A Look Behind the Lord of the Rings.* He used to rail at some length about the "error" Tolkien made by not having temples, priests, and assorted cults in Middle Earth.

Those will come later, as the Fourth Age progresses. But in earlier times, even during the time of the War of the Ring, the peoples of Middle Earth are in too close contact with the divine to need formal religion. If there are unfallen beings walking among you, even if they're becoming fewer, if you can actually talk to angelic messengers and wonder-workers (like Gandalf, or even the still fearsomely impressive fallen angel, Saruman) if you can actually *see* the forbidden shores of Heaven, as was once possible from the hilltops of Numenor, then who needs to go to church? We only do that when the numinous has become invisible.

I think that's the core of the fantasy for Tolkien. He was writing about a time and place where the numinous is still in the world, as is described in the early books of the Bible, when there are giants in the earth, burning bushes talk, visions come, and miracles commonly happen. But miracles don't happen anymore, at least not out in the open for everyone to see. The world has undergone thinning. We remember the former times in myths. This transition, Tolkien is telling us, is inevitable. It is a cultural growing-up.

While *The Lord of the Rings* is not an overtly Christian book, the way most by his colleague C. S. Lewis are overtly Christian, but no one can write a serious story, much less a life-work without having his beliefs come through. (The great mass of Tolkien's *legendarium* is a life-work; he worked on it throughout almost his entire adulthood, to express what he had learned and experienced in life.)

Remember that this is a book written by a devout, highly-educated Catholic. Theology has to slip in somewhere. The main theological thread that I find is one of free will. As long as we're in Eden, as long as there are angels to watch over us and miracles happen every day, then we don't really need free will. We don't mature. We remain in the nursery. That is why the angels (or wizards) have to go away, why the thinning must take place.

For without free will, it is impossible to be truly heroic. I find that now I am most interested in, and moved by, Tolkien's concepts of heroism.

Certainly the Ring itself is a brilliant invention, which brings everything into focus. There is much in *The Lord of the Rings* which Tolkien transmits from earlier traditions, and if anybody knew traditions, it was Tolkien. Remember, too, that this is an author who reverses the usual literary orthodoxy that English literature starts getting interesting about the time of Chaucer. Tolkien held that English literature *ceased* to be interesting about then.

But the Ring is something new, an evil, supernatural object which seems to have a mind of its own, which no one can master because it draws out the evil in even the most innocent people. The idea of an epic quest to *get rid* of something is itself quite novel. Not surprisingly, when Terry Brooks and successors reduced the quest fantasy into a formula and started serving up McTolkiens, the Ring was the first ingredient that had to be removed.

Frodo, in an act of free will, must take the Ring. Meanwhile, it eats away at him, slowly corrupting him as he travels toward Mount Doom. This again is a completely fresh idea, that the good guy has to complete his mission before he ceases to be good. If Frodo had yielded to the Ring's allure, or even dawdled, he might have become another Saruman at the very least. (When Edmund Wilson complains that "the hero has no serious temptations," we hope his seven-year-old daughter will explain it to him.)

The Lord of the Rings really soars in the latter parts, as darkness closes in, and Frodo's journey becomes one of non-stop horror and misery. This is where Tolkien is both very, very old-fashioned and downright revolutionary. He is able to bring back into literature, unashamedly, with no irony whatsoever, values which we had thought lost in the twentieth century. He achieves an epic sense. There are passages which are genuinely *noble,* which is not something any of Tolkien's contemporaries would have dared to attempt. Some of the descriptions of the siege of Gondor and the diversion before the Black Gate achieve a kind of prose battle-poetry, which Homer would have understood. That descriptions of mass-killing can deliver such an aesthetic buzz may give one pause, and is certainly worth examining, but that's what poets have always been good at. That is arguably what poetry was invented for. Tolkien is a poet in the Homeric sense, not in his actual verse, which tends toward jingles (and a pretty good pastiche of an Anglo-Saxon elegy here and there), but in his prose storytelling. The medium is different, but he doing a very old, old thing. Naomi Mitcheson was right in comparing *The Lord of the Rings* to Malory. The description of the death of Arthur, and how Sir Bedivere had to throw the sword Excalibur back into the lake (so that the heroic age passes away, and England undergoes thinning) is one of the few passages in English prior to Tolkien that rises to his best level.

What Tolkien celebrates, of course, is not death and destruction, but heroism. His appeal is his suggestion, without irony, in a cynical and disillusioned time, that genuine heroism is possible and sacrifice can be worthwhile. This is more than a sentimental myth. It's something that few in our time have dared to address.

Tolkien's idea of heroism brings us back to those lines from "The Battle of Maldon":

Thought shall be the harder, heart the keener,
courage the greater, as our might lessens.

The poem was written in the tenth century, shortly after a battle with the Vikings in Essex. Significantly, it is not about the glories of chopping the enemy's head off, but about *defeat.* The English lost the battle largely because their leader Byrhtnoth suffered from *offermod*, which means "overweening pride." The poem, which celebrates the bravery of the warriors who died beside their lord, does not call followers to blind, fanatic allegiance. It is actually a *criticism* of that very same lord, who failed to hold up his end of the heroic code. It seems that the Vikings had landed on a little island in the river Blackwater, and could only wade across a few at a time, at a narrow spot, to the shore where the English militia waited. Byrhtnoth, rather than take advantage of this, decided it would be more sporting, and his victory more glorious, if he allowed the Vikings to cross, then took them on "fairly" as if this were a football match. The English were slaughtered, and Byrhtnoth died. This kind of frivolous wasting of men's lives is not what real heroism is supposed to be about. Byrhtnoth is stupid. His men, however, are heroic for standing by him. His retainer, who speaks the above lines, sounds like a Tolkien character (one of Theoden's retainers?) when he goes on:

I am old in age, I will not hence,
but I purpose to lie by the side of my lord,

by the man so dearly loved.

Of course Tolkien knew this poem. He even wrote a sequel to it, "The Homecoming of Beorhtnoth Beorhthelm's Son," which is an eerie playlet for voices, about two Saxons, one old, the other a youth, trying to find the leader's body on the battlefield in the dark. (We know from history that the Vikings carried off the head, and Byrhtnoth/Beorhtnoth was buried with a wax ball atop his shoulders.) The poem is very much about the cost of heroic action. Tolkien, after all, had been through one of the greatest and most pointless slaughters of the twentieth century, the Battle of the Somme. (British commander, Field Marshall Douglas Haig, lost 40,000 men in an afternoon and thought that not at all excessive, so he did it again.) Tolkien remarked once that when he was twenty-one, he had many friends. When he was twenty-six (*i.e.*, after the war) only one of them was left alive. He himself would doubtless have perished if he hadn't been saved by a fortuitous bout of trench fever.

So Tolkien knows what he's talking about. He has been there. He saw the blood of heroes wasted by a bemedalled moron, but this didn't make the soldiers any less heroic. If anything, like those at Maldon, it made them more so. He is still able to see a certain purity in the acts of heroes, and convey it through his prose. You might argue, as Moorcock seems to, that this is (in more senses than one) bloody foolishness, but Tolkien would doubtless reply, gravely, that it is not. There are times when heroic sacrifices actually matter. The Battle of the Somme was not one of them. General Haig was infinitely worse—and stupider—than Byrhtnoth. But possibly Allied soldiers entering the German concentration camps at the end of World War II felt that their sacrifices had been worth it.

Certainly a heroic code like that in *Beowulf,* Christian on the surface but even older and deeper, is at the core of Tolkien's beliefs, and of *The Lord of the Rings.* Its idealism appeals in what we generally perceive as a morally bankrupt time. It offers consolation (a loaded word with Tolkien, who wrote about it extensively in "On Fairy Stories"), but not (as many of Tolkien's detractors have charged) the comfort of the nursery, or anything but the most grim sort of comfort. Tolkien is telling us that some difficult and painful things are actually worthwhile.

It occurs to me, from the perspective of twenty-nine years, that the another difference between The *Gormenghast* books and *The Lord of the Rings* is that when Titus Groan, at the end of the second volume, says, in essence, "Screw you all!" and leaves, this is the rebellion of an adolescent. Frodo Baggins, as childlike as he seems at the beginning, evolves into a more mature character. To be fair, if Peake had lived, he would have written more books about Titus and let him grow up. But Tolkien knows you can't just run away from your problems. They will follow and overtake you unless you actually *do* something about them.

IV.

It's quite clear that Tolkien isn't going away. *The Hobbit* has been continuously in print for more than sixty-five years and *The Lord of the Rings* in its entirety for more than forty-six. Interest in them shows no sign of dying down. The Peter Jackson film as caused a spike in sales, to be sure, into the millions per year (according to *Locus*) rather than the mere hundreds of thousands. Clearly these works have the first hallmarks of true classics of literature. They can appeal strongly to generations yet unborn at the time of their composition. They appeal for their emotional intensity, their idealism, and for their universality.

This last may be the key. When the works of James Joyce or Henry James or Marcel Proust, important as they are, have fallen into the domain of a handful of scholars—when they are as esoteric as *Piers Plowman*—Tolkien will still be widely comprehensible and widely read. This is not to say that Tolkien is a greater writer than any of those three (or William Langland for that matter) but that he is likely to be read longer. The books which transcend the time in which they were written tend to be the ones which have mythic power, which present archetypes in broad, colorful strokes. *Dracula,* for instance. Not a "great" book, but very likely an immortal one. *The Lord of the Rings* clearly has an appeal to readers far removed from Tolkien in both time and geography.

This means, of course, that Michael Moorcock has lost the fight, and is virtually the last, lonely voice decrying Tolkien. We have to respect his views, which are honestly arrived at and sincerely held. He has too much integrity to give up, turn around, and join the winners. So we acknowledge him, but then go on, and hope that his head doesn't end up (figuratively) on a spike. Will he be remembered in a hundred years as anything other than a Tolkien detractor? I hope so.

Edmund Wilson, of course, deserves no better.

I make a series of further observations about *The Lord of the Rings,* upon rereading it:

1) Far from having no influence on literature and culture, *The Lord of the Rings* has had such pervasive influence it can now evoke the *Hamlet* Syndrome. Even as many lines from *Hamlet* have become part of the language, so that someone coming to the play for the first time reacts, "Oh, *that's* where that comes from," Tolkien's images and ideas (but not particularly his language; it's hard to come up with a "famous line" from *The Lord of the Rings*) are now everywhere, so that it is very hard for anyone to come at the material totally fresh, the way readers did in the 1950's or 1960's. The Peter Jackson film will accelerate this process.

2) There aren't a lot of women in this story. We're trained, post-Feminism, to notice how older writers depict women. Tolkien generally doesn't. But then, neither does Homer through much of the *Iliad,* except where women are objects of loot for the heroes to squabble over. I count three named women in *Beowulf,* and the only one who gets to say anything is Wealhtheow, Hrothgar's queen, who seeks protection for her sons.

Tolkien actually presents us with more women than most epic writers. It is true that Galadriel is basically an apparition, like the Lady of the Lake in Malory, and Arwen just sits on a pedestal at a feast. (Her story is explored a little more in one of the appendices.) The most surprising female character, whom I had completely forgotten from my prior reading, is the heroic Eowyn, who chafes against the traditional role of women in epics. When asked what she fears, replies that she is not afraid of pain or death, but of "A cage. To stay behind bars, until use and old age accept them." (*Return of the King,* p. 58)

3) Tolkien's dialogue can be stiff, particularly when people start lapsing into *thee* and *thou* and talking in potted High Heroic. But this is only a nuisance, because the narrative really *is* heroic and we accept the dialogue as a convention. Still, Frodo and Sam talk more naturally among themselves than do the lords of Rohan and Gondor.

4) I agree entirely with my younger self on one point. I have never been satisfied with the climax of the story. That Gollum manages to *slip* and topple into Mount Doom, Ring in hand, strikes me as awfully fortuitous, and Tolkien is a bit overfond of convenient cavalry-to-the-rescue deliverances at the darkest hour anyway. This can only be described as contrived, or Catholic: Free will alone cannot achieve salvation, but the hand of God can deliver it.

I mean, what if there had been a ledge five feet below? What then? What if Frodo, in pain, just having had his finger bitten off, had struck out at Gollum, either in blind rage, in an attempt to regain the Ring, or with murderous intent and *pushed* him to his death?

27

Would he ever have been able to sort that one out? He was, after all, corrupted by the Ring to the point that he was ready to abandon his mission. Could good have been accomplished by such an "evil" act?

5) I also see that, quite unlike many of the generic fantasies that followed it, *The Lord of the Rings* maintains a solid sense of physical reality. We always know *where* we are in the story. If there were not maps provided, I am sure most readers would attempt to draw them. Tolkien was a tireless walker, who knew and loved the English countryside. He can convey a great feeling of the outdoors.

He also understood the need for realism in fantasy. Somewhere he expressed contempt for the sort of medieval romance in which the knight sets out on a quest "without so much as a cake in hand." (A sound observation. Many years ago an editor wrote to me, "Your hero keeps crossing these incredibly barren landscapes. What does he eat? Medieval space food sticks?")

Tolkien's characters expend a good deal of effort and concern over supplies. This heightens the sense of hopelessness in Frodo and Sam's final trek to Mount Doom. They are crossing a desert. They have enough food and water to get there, but not to return. They don't expect to return.

6) The back-story goes on forever, into the remote depths of time. *The Silmarillion* is so vast in scale that the entire story of *The Lord of the Rings* is included in it in less than a page. You can delve into this as far as you care to go. Middle Earth is the most completely imagined secondary world ever created in literature. Despite all of Tolkien's literary flaws, we are, in his works, in the presence of greatness.

I confess I still skip over the purely linguistic appendices.

7) I am also reassured by people closer to the college scene than I am these days, that the party line on fantastic literature is beginning to shift, as professors who anathematized it are replaced by their former students. When I was in school, my teachers had never heard of Dunsany, they had certainly not read Tolkien (or Vonnegut, or *Dune*, or *Stranger in a Strange Land*, to name other surprisingly durable "campus fads" of my generation), but a few of the older ones, who got their education in the 1930's, had been programmed to despise James Branch Cabell, and could still manifest a vestigal response to that name. I predict that within a few years, the Ivory Tower will rediscover Cabell, at least in a small way. Meanwhile Tolkien is a solidly respectable scholarly subject, if the number of works about him by professors coming out from Greenwood Press is any indication.

The Scouring of Academe continues apace.

v.

In the end there are some people who still can't get it. They never will.

I have a friend who, unable to see the attraction of much fantasy and of Tolkien in particular, asked me in all sincerity, "What is the appeal of myth anyway?"

After some hesitation, I gave him the only answer I could think of, which is, "If you have to ask, you cannot be told."

Maybe a great philosopher can handle a question like that, on the order of "What is beauty and why should we care?" Some things are otherwise too basic for words. It is like describing color to the blind, music to the deaf. If someone cannot be stirred by the soul's music, then they cannot feel the grandeur of an epic. Homer and Shakespeare must be just noise to them. (From my friend's testimony, this seems to be so.) Such a person cannot make the journey to Middle Earth, at twenty, forty-nine, or ever. That is really too bad. We shake our heads sadly and go on without them.

Edmund Wilson deserves far less sympathy. His head belongs on that spike. We pass it by and look away.

And the road goes ever on and on.

WORKS CITED

Becker, Alida (ed.) *A Tolkien Treasury.* Courage Books/The Running Press, 1989.

Carter, Lin. *Tolkien: a Look Behind the Lord of the Rings.* Ballantine Books, 1969.

Clute, John, and Grant, John. *The Encyclopedia of Fantasy.* St Martin's press, 1997.

Gordon, M. A. (ed.) *Anglo-Saxon Poetry.* Dent/Dutton: Everyman's Library, 1970. Contains "The Battle of Maldon." "Caedmon's Hymn" is quoted in the introduction.

Haber, Karen (ed.) *Meditations on Middle Earth.* St. Martin's Press, 2001.

Moorcock, Michael. *Wizardry and Wild Romance.* Victor Gollancz Ltd., 1987.

Tolkien, J. R. R. *The Fellowship of the Ring, The Two Towers,* and *The Return of the King.* Houghton Mifflin, 2nd edition, 1965. Various printings.

Tolkien, J. R. R. *Poems and Stories.* George Allen & Unwin, 1980.

Contains "The Homecoming of Beorhtnoth Beorhthelm's Son," "On Fairy Stories," etc.

Swanwick, Michael. "A Changeling Returns." In *Meditations on Middle Earth.*

Wilson, Edmund. "Oo, Those Awful Orcs" in *A Tolkien Treasury.*

AMUSING AFTERTHOUGHT

After a panel at a Readercon, Moorcock said to me, of Tolkien's trilogy, "I was so disappointed when I read it that I traded away my first editions for a bunch of *Planet Stories* with Leigh Brackett in them."

"But—but—" I sputtered. "Do you know how much those were *worth?* You could have gotten an *entire run* of *Planet Stories* for them!"

"Nevertheless, I think I got the better deal," Moorcock said.

This is yet more proof of Moorcock's integrity. He was thinking of art, not commerce.

II.

J. R. R. TOLKIEN AS A HORROR WRITER

I've had occasion to reread *The Lord of the Rings* recently, for the first time in twenty-nine years, and this, combined with the recent, very successful Peter Jackson film of *The Lord of the Rings: The Fellowship of the Ring,* has caused me to give J. R. R. Tolkien and all he represents (and spawned) a major re-evaluation. The end result was in an essay for *The New York Review of Science Fiction.* I will not repeat my conclusions here, save to say that I did not find Tolkien's work, as Michael Moorcock (nowadays *the* leading Tolkien detractor) put it, "*Winnie the Pooh* posing as an epic," but instead Winnie the Pooh *evolving into* an epic, which s a lot more interesting. It is a story that moves from childhood into maturity, from sweetness and light into suffering and darkness, and is ultimately about the process of that movement.

But it also occurs to me that Tolkien was a damned good horror writer. The darkness in his work is essential to its success. Peter Jackson sensed that, and the reason his film version is so successful (other than its very intelligent abridgement of the sometimes meandering storyline) is precisely that Jackson concentrated on the horror elements, not the cuteness. His film has a more uniform, scarier tone than, particularly, the first volume of Tolkien's trilogy.

Tolkien a horror writer? There are doubtless many horror fans out there scratching their heads about now. Isn't Tolkien about sweet elves and cute hobbits and mythopoeic something-or-other set in never-never land? What's that got to do with horror?

For the answer, see my essay, "Horror Beyond New Jersey," in *Windows of the Imagination.* It has always been my contention—and part of the agenda of *Weird Tales* as long as I was editing it—that horror is an emotional tone, not a setting or a frame of reference, or even any sort of specific content. (Admittedly, for *Weird*

Tales I would prefer to achieve that emotional tone of horror through fantastic or supernatural content, but we recognize that this is not the only way to do it. Poe's "The Pit and the Pendulum" or Richard Connell's "The Most Dangerous Game" are definitely classics of horror, but not fantastic.)

That being so, there is no reason why horror has to be restricted to the parameters of popular horror-genre paperbacks. A horror story doesn't have to be set in the present, or in any place within the experience of the reader. A horror story should be possible even if set in ancient Egypt, or medieval France, or a primordial continent in the prehistorical past, or millions of years hence, or even on the planet Mars. I am aware that some masters of the horror form, notably M. R. James, disagreed on this specific point. James felt that a ghostly tale set long ago might be exciting and romantic, but the reader feels that *anything* could happen in, say, the twelfth century, so that the reader will never get the *this could happen to me* sort of creeps from a story in a remote setting.

My only answer to that is that in *Weird Tales* in my time Keith Taylor achieved quite effective horror with stories set in Egypt 4000 years ago, and as for all those other settings, Clark Ashton Smith did them all in the pages of *Weird Tales* in the 1930s, with his tales of Averoigne, Hyperborea, Zothique, and the vaults of Yoth Vombis.

So horror can happen in Middle Earth too, and, rereading Tolkien, I find that it does. A very nice moment occurs in chapter five of *The Fellowship of the Ring* when Frodo and Sam have crossed the Brandywine on a ferry, and Frodo looks back at the dock on the opposite shore, from which they embarked a few minutes before. He sees something that "looked like a dark black bundle left behind," only it begins to move, crawling about for a second before it vanishes into the darkness beyond the lantern light.

M.R. James could have written that, and it seems that if things had worked out just a little bit differently, Tolkien might have become a practitioner of the traditional English ghost story, of which James was the greatest exponent. James was a generation older than Tolkien. The two had similar academic and antiquarian backgrounds. It's easy to imagine that there-but-for-fortune, Tolkien might have attended the right school and been one of the boys to whom James first told his famous ghost stories, which might have inspired Tolkien to go and do likewise.

Certainly Tolkien had a talent for conjuring spooks, such as his famous Balrog, or the Lord of the Nazgul who rides in through the broken gate of Gondor (in chapter four of *The Return of the King*) to confront Gandalf and very likely defeat him, had not the Riders of

Rohan come to the rescue just then. One can argue that Tolkien was overfond of bringing the cavalry to the rescue, but the potency of the image remains, as does the potency of that "bundle" on the dock or much which is left to the imagination in the haunted mines of Moria.

And certainly the Ring itself is a wonderfully horrific invention, an object which draws out the evil in anyone's nature, so that the story's quest is a race to get rid of the thing before the hero is too corrupted to care.

Now there is much of the fairy tale in Tolkien, and many have objected that his bugaboos (the Nazgul, *et al.*) get chased away too easily. I argue that the *real* struggle, the battle Frodo experiences within himself, to save his own soul before the Ring devours him, doesn't go away so easily, and this is the stuff of genuine horror. Stephen King's Jack Torrance undergoes a similar ordeal in *The Shining* (in the novel, not so much in either of the film versions) as he has to make one last effort to save his family before the Overlook Hotel can turn him into Something Else.

Horror can happen in the Third Age of Middle Earth or in the 1970s in Colorado. But it's the same and Tolkien had a knack for it.

In generic terms, Tolkien was writing something closer to what we now call "sword & sorcery," which goes in a different part of the bookstore than books published as "horror." But it seems to us that sword & sorcery, to be any good, almost requires a horror element. Otherwise it becomes a kind of lackluster pseudo-historical fiction, about the politics of imaginary kingdoms, with maybe a little magic thrown in. Robert E. Howard instinctively summoned up the most potent horrors he could in "Worms of the Earth," "The Valley of the Worm," and the better Conan stories. He knew, as Tolkien did, that not only can a horror story happen far away in time and space, but that a genuinely heroic hero (be he Frodo Baggins of Conan of Cimmeria) needs something genuinely horrific to square off against. This was why H. P. Lovecraft admired Howard. Surely it wasn't for the sword-swinging and furious action, but for the atmospheric descriptions of elder (and eldritch) evils from the dawn of time.

Would Lovecraft have admired Tolkien? The two were very far apart in philosophical outlook, to be sure, and Tolkien had a different aesthetic agenda. Lovecraft would probably have had trouble with cuter and sunnier parts of *The Fellowship of the Ring,* particularly the first couple of chapters, but he would doubtless have found some of the later sections enormously potent.

Because they are. Because Tolkien, when he put his mind to it, was a horror writer.

III.

OF WORMS AND HOBBITS, CABBAGES AND KINGS, NOT TO MENTION HEAPS OF SLAUGHTERED PEASANTS

So I finally finished reading E. R. Eddison's classic fantasy novel, *The Worm Ouroboros* (1926). It took almost thirty years to do so. The last time I tried reading it, I found it a bit tough going, though enjoyed what I read. Then I put the book aside, and somehow never got back to it. While this may not seem to be much of an endorsement, I do endorse it. There are some works that have to be taken at their own pace. Milton's *Paradise Lost* is not something you're going to zip through either, but that does not diminish its greatness.

Lest anybody not know what I am talking about, a brief summary is in order. *The Worm Ouroboros* is one of four fantasy novels written by Eric Rucker Eddison (1882-1945) and by far his most accessible. We know that H. P. Lovecraft bought a copy remaindered for a quarter in the late '20s, and praised its "magnificently poetic" imagery and vivid scenes in letters to Donald Wandrei. Clark Ashton Smith wrote in a letter to August Derleth, "I like it better than anything I have read in seven epochs," and that the book left him with "a tremendous impression of imaginative fervor and reality." Fritz Leiber, Michael Moorcock, L. Sprague de Camp, and many others have all written of the book's virtues. It became one of the great classics of pre-Tolkien fantasy, one of the first books to be reprinted in mass-market paperback in the 1960s when word went out in the industry to "find another Trilogy." (Tangentially, *The Worm* is related to Eddison's other three novels, which form the genuine *Zimiamvian Trilogy*.) Its own merits aside, the chief importance of *The Worm Ouroboros* may well be that it is one of the first heroic fantasies set in a completely self-contained world, complete

35

with a chronological appendix. It points the way to Tolkien's *The Lord of the Rings.*

The story is one of war, adventure, and sorcery of the clash of kingdoms and the utter destruction of one of them, set on the planet Mercury.

The setting is the first of the books problems, or eccentricities, perhaps one should say. Above all else, Eddison was an *eccentric* writer, who cared not a whit for current critical fashion, and wrote what he had to write in his own way. His books are a product of his inner dream-life, and echo the real world only remotely. So he set his story on Mercury, but not even the planet known to astronomers of the 1920s. It is not a world of burning, eternal day and frozen, eternal night, with one side locked toward the sun, as Mercury was thought to be at the time, but remarkably, but an earthlike place with oceans and glaciers, a moon in the sky, and "Irish yews" growing in a garden. Nevertheless, a viewpoint character, Lessingham, dreams that he is taken to Mercury in a chariot pulled by a hippogriff. This serves as an invocation, such as you would expect at the front of an epic. It removes the reader from the here-and-now into the realm of gods, heroes, and magic. As such, it works very well, but on a literal level, it makes, one must admit, little sense. The argument that the setting is symbolic, that the world is the Mercury of *astrology,* does not, for all the decidedly "mercurial" behavior of the characters, really hold up.

This epic is written in a suitably epic style, archaic and Elizabethan which, for many readers, is doubtless the chief barrier accessibility. The sort of reader who wants to skim a story just for "what happens" will be lost here. *The Worm Ouroboros* is a prose symphony, read for the music of its language. This is not something which the average writer (as Ursula Le Guin points out in her seminal essay, "From Elfland to Poughkeepsie") would dare try to emulate. But parts of it are breathtakingly beautiful. You'd have to be pretty deaf to the charms of fantasy if you don't feel a chill from passages like this:

> In the still night were flames seen, and flying forms dim in the moonlit air; and in moonless nights unstarred, moans heard and gibbering accents: prodigies beside their beds, and ridings in the sky, and fleshless fingers plucking at Juss unseen when he went forth to make question of the night. (Chapter 12)

What an ear this writer has! What a difference between "He went out of a midnight stroll" and "he went forth to make question of the night." The book is full of such phrases, as when the heroes behold an apparently unclimbable mountain which they must climb standing "in tremendous silence, death-pale against the sky."

One of Eddison's further eccentricities is that he chose to name the nations of his imaginary Mercury after supernatural creatures found on Earth, without paying any attention to the connotations. While the major combatants, Witchland and Demonland, have a certain *gravitas*, Impland, Pixyland, Goblinland, and the rest really do not. The reader has to take them in stride, and just accept the entire story on its own terms.

The characters are all larger than life, difficult to relate to, utterly aristocratic in their outlooks, though readers have always been drawn to the enigmatic Lord Gro, the doomed romantic and perpetual traitor, whose perspective looks beyond good and evil to the realization that all is vanity and dust. (He has the bad habit of always switching to the losing side.)

There is a magnificent demon-conjuring in Chapter Four. I was mightily impressed with this when I began the book about 1975, about the same time I was writing *The White Isle.* The conjuring scene in *The White Isle* undoubtedly owes much to Eddison, even has his work echoes through many other writers. The great mountain-climbing sequences in the middle of the book are clearly replayed in Fritz Leiber's Fafhrd and Gray Mouser novella, "Stardock."

But the real problem with the book, the one even its admirers chew over endlessly, and the reason I am writing now about a 1926 novel, classic or otherwise, is in the ending, and ultimately in E. R. Eddison's expressed attitudes about life and particularly about war.

The theoretical, even moral problem can be stated bluntly: is it possible for a great work of literature, exquisitely crafted though it may be, to be, on some level at least, complete rubbish?

Eddison was of the same generation as J. R. R. Tolkien. Tolkien was ten years younger, which may help explain why Tolkien found himself in the trenches of the First World War while Eddison remained in a safe, civil-service job. Tolkien had a horrible time in the war. Virtually everyone he knew in the army was killed. The only reason he survived what may have been the most ghastly conflict in the history of warfare, the Battle of the Somme, was that he fortuitously came down with trench-fever. (Everybody else in his unit died.) He remarked that prior to the war he had many friends, but afterwards only one of them was still alive.

The Lord of the Rings is very much a novel about people who have no desire to kill anybody caught up in a necessary, but still terrible war. The attitude of his characters is that one may regret that such a thing happened in one's lifetime, but still there is duty, and some things are worth fighting for. But Tolkien never denies the cost. Frodo comes back from his quest with what in modern terms might be described as post-traumatic stress. His wound never heals. He lingers for four years, writes his book, then sails off for the West—*i.e.*, dies. He is crushed by the experience. He certainly wasn't seeking, nor did he value, military "glory."

But if the four hobbits, sitting around in the tavern afterwards, reminiscing about their adventures, had suddenly said, "Gee! That was fun! *Let's do it again!*" and then magically turned back time until Sauron menaced Middle Earth all over again, you would throw the entire trilogy across the room in disgust. Admit it, you would. Such a conclusion would be *so* false, a complete betrayal of everything that went before....

Yet that is exactly how *The Worm Ouroboros* ends. After all that smiting and slaughter, the heroes are feeling useless. They can only gaze longingly at their swords and shields, now hanging decoratively on the walls. They can only recount their adventures so many times. Finally, to their great relief, a miracle is worked, and the story begins again, the form of the book itself being that of the *ouroboros,* the "worm" (*i.e.*, serpent) that swallows its tail and symbolizes eternity. You or I or Tolkien (or his hobbits) would regard warfare without end as our idea of hell, but Eddison's characters think this conclusion is just fine.

Is this merely the difference between a writer who has been to war (Tolkien) and one who hasn't? As Michael Moorcock and James Cawthorn wrote in their entry on *The Worm Ouroboros* in *Fantasy: the 100 Best Books,* "Eddison writes of battle and slaughter with an enthusiasm which suggests a frustrated swashbuckler behind the neat civilian exterior. We can only thank Fate that he was assigned to the Board of Trade and not the War Office."

At the same time, Moorcock and Cawthorn note how Eddison's youthful imagination was gripped by Icelandic sagas. We must remember that to the pagan Norse, the reward of a virtuous and heroic life was that you went to Valhalla and fought all day, suffering wounds, even getting killed, over and over again in endless strife. True, the wounds were healed and you spent all night getting drunk in Odin's mead-hall, but the following morning you had to get up and do it *again, and again...*until doomsday (Ragnarok) when the gods and their warriors would all perish in one last battle against the forces of darkness. Casual homicide was a Viking's idea of fun. Rape and pillage of strangers was his idea of taking a vacation. A similar attitude shows through in Homer, although in, particularly the *Odyssey,* there is some sense of the cost. (Nevertheless, Odysseus upon his homecoming, having lost his entire crew and his treasure and supposedly gained wisdom, doesn't merely tell the suitors, "Party's over. Get out and don't take the silverware." He drenches Ithaca in blood.)

So we have to avoid being too provincial in our attitudes. *The Worm Ouroboros* is a problem book. Is it ultimately sanguinary nonsense, or is it an authentic expression of another time, place, and morality? Vikings would have appreciated it, or ancient Greeks, or even the nobles and kings of the Renaissance, who regarded warfare as something of a sport and peasants as disposable as packing-material. Eddison's outlook is decidedly feudal. This doesn't merely mean that peasants are supposed to die for their lords and keep mum about it. It's more complicated than that. Recall the conversation Shakespeare's Henry the Fifth has with a soldier—the man's individual conscience is how own, but his duty is to his king. The ideal feudal lord, too, has a duty to his men. This is vividly articulated in Eddison's twenty-sixth chapter ("The Battle of Krothering Side") as a wounded peasant soldier, home from the wars, extols the virtues of his commander who goes to great lengths to make sure that the men are well-fed, well-armed, and well-led. Their lives may be lost in battle, but they are valued, and not expended frivolously.

This is the one point where *The Worm Ouroboros* really connects to the modern reader, and seems fully human for all its strangeness. So, is the novel just the daydream of a frustrated swashbuckler who didn't know anything about warfare, or is it an authentic expression of the high, heroic ethos of feudal Mercury?

In some sense, at its core, a fantasy novel, to be a great fantasy novel, has to be true. Is *The Worm Ouroboros* "true" on its own terms, and is that enough?

IV.

WHAT DOES A STORY "MEAN"?

There's an article in that classic reference work, *Uncle John's Bathroom Reader* (compiled by the Bathroom Readers' Institute, and published by St. Martin's Press in 1988), which outlines the more or less absurd theory that L. Frank Baum's *The Wonderful Wizard of Oz* is "really" a political allegory, all about late nineteenth-century Populism, the gold standard, and William Jennings Bryan, who appears in the book as the Cowardly Lion, all oratorical roar and nothing else. Allegedly, when Bryan's run for the US presidency in 1896 failed, Baum was inspired to write the book. Bryan felt that the little people (Munchkins) were being oppressed by the gold standard and that all would be well if the country shifted to a silver standard, which would make money plentiful. Dorothy's house kills the Wicked Witch of the East (eastern bankers), frees the Munchkins, and then she and her companions depart on the Yellow Brick (gold standard) to the Emerald City (Washington) where she confronts the Wizard (president), who is a humbug who hides behind a false image.

To which most readers today, particularly the younger ones, might say, *Huh?*

But wait, there's more. How about this? I was on a panel at Capclave once, called "Twisted Tolkien," which was devoted to new and different interpretations of *The Lord of the Rings.* For instance, I began by putting on my Commie Hat (a Chinese "Mao cap" with a red star in the appropriate place—actually a Soviet Cub Scouts pin, with a heroic, flaming profile bust of Lenin in the middle) and begin as follows, assuming a fake Russian accent:

"Comrades! Clearly *The Lord of the Rings* glorifies the revolt of the oppressed masses against the sniveling bourgeoisie hobbits and disgusting Gondorian and Elvish running-dog lackeys of decadent divine-right monarchy. The heroic Orcs, representing the working class, struggle for freedom, while all ends in tragedy because Samwise, a downtrodden proletarian if ever there was one, but whose revolutionary indoctrination has been insufficient, fails to understand the need to push Frodo into the fiery pit, take the ring away from him, and turn it over to the Glorious Leader Sauron, who is of course more equal than his fellow Central Committee members, Saruman and the Ringwraiths."

I then turned the hat around backwards and did the Libertarian version:

"The War of the Ring is wasteful and unnecessary. Let the *market* take care of it. Allow free competition, unhampered by government interference, and if the people want Good, they will choose Good."

There was also a Freudian version. There's this *ring*, you see, which is penetrated, and this *sword* which is broken but restored... need anyone say more?

Several more interpretations later, someone piped up, "But of course you cannot appreciate *The Lord of the Rings* until you have read it in the original Klingon." Much laughter followed. The Klingon version (possibly intended as an opera) also seems to be about heroic Orcs, who regain their honor by embracing death in the last, glorious battle after the destruction of Sauron, rather than surrendering to weak and honorless humans and Elves.

This is very much reminiscent of the commentary to the restored Klingon translation of *Hamlet* put out by the Klingon Language Institute...but I won't go into that here.

The serious question raised is this: What does a story *mean* and who knows it?

If you take seriously Deconstruction, Post-Structuralism, and other academic fads of recent decades—and I do not—then the answer would have to be that *nobody* does, except maybe the critic whose revolutionary indoctrination has been correct...er, I mean someone who has mastered the arcane code-language of this sort of criticism and now isn't able to speak to anybody else. (Do you know what happens when the Mafia discovers Deconstruction? They make you an offer you can't understand.)

Well, never mind that. I will grant that there is such a thing as subtextual or even unconscious meaning. Did Bram Stoker really understand the sexual dynamic of *Dracula*? Recall Tim Powers's witty remark in the interview I did with him in *Weird Tales* #229 that the book is not so much about the oppression of Victorian women as "about a guy who lives forever by drinking blood. Don't take my word for it. Read the book. It is." At the same time, is it possible that the power of this book (which continues to fascinate when most of Stoker's other work is no more than a curiosity today, stems precisely from its ability to tap into the subconscious fears, dreams, and desires of millions of people?

For that matter, for all Tolkien explicitly denied that *The Lord of the Rings* is allegory, it is hard to deny that the great, epic War of the Ring against the forces of darkness echoes the twentieth century's two world wars. Tolkien himself was a veteran of the Battle of the Somme, perhaps the most terrible and grueling military encounter in history. Just about everybody he knew in the army was killed. He only survived because he was lucky enough to be invalidated out in the nick of time with trench fever. (For more about this, see *Tolkien and the Great War* by John Garth, Houghton Mifflin, 2003.)

Allegory or not, surely *The Lord of the Rings* resonated with many people because they associated with it some of the same emotional response they had from experiencing (or at least reading about) the Free World's vast struggle to remain free in the face of the gathering Shadow of the Dark Lord in the East, whether that Dark Lord might be the Kaiser, Hitler, or Stalin. Likewise, a lot of people have seen vampirism as a metaphor for forbidden sexuality, and for underground lifestyles. These things fit, and resonate, whether the author had them in mind or not.

Sometimes an author can deliberately put a meaning into a story and it fades away with time. I have a copy of James Branch Cabell's *Figures of Earth,* in which, where the Redeemer of Poictesme, Dom Manuel, starts rallying his followers with the slogan, "Mum with Manuel," someone has written in the margin, "Cool with Coolidge." This was a contemporary joke of the time, which the modern reader is better off without. The Cabell books are more self-contained and timeless without 1920s' in-jokes.

Otherwise, I tend to think that a story means what the author says it means. There may be broader emotional associations, but, unless we were to discover some letter or diary in which L. Frank Baum says, "Yes, *The Wizard of Oz* is about William Jennings Bryan and the gold standard," we are amused by that piece in *Uncle John's Bathroom Reader,* but not really convinced by it.

The problem of literary interpretation is complex. Whenever somebody says they have the One Answer, as the Deconstructionists seem to (inasmuch as anyone can understand them), I get very suspicious. Certainly there are pitfalls to be avoided. It *is* possible to read entirely too much into a story, particularly if you try to discover the opinions of the author in the actions of his characters.

V.

MYTH AMERICA

I recently read and very much enjoyed Neil Gaiman's *American Gods* (Morrow, 2001, 465 p.), which is already so well-known that it is hardly necessary to formally review it. The book is both a critical and popular success very well, sweeping all before it, having already won a Stoker Award (from the Horror Writers of America) and a Hugo (from the World Science Fiction Convention). It is also a likely bet to have won a World Fantasy Award by the time you read this. [It did—DS.] That the same book could be nominated for or win so many different awards is just a hint of its appeal. Suffice it to say this is an extremely well-written, imaginative book which has my highest recommendation.

But what makes it the subject of this essay is that it's one of those not-very-common attempts to produce a myth—even a mythic epic—for North America and especially for the United States. There are echoes of everything from Roger Zelazny to Homer in this book. It's about a rootless man with a mysterious past who finds himself in the employ of "Mr. Wednesday" (*i.e.*, Woden/Odin) on behalf of the old gods of Europe and Asia, who have been transplanted to the New World but didn't quite take root there. These gods are opposed by the new gods of America: gods of television, high-tech, commerce, automobiles, etc. A big smash-up is coming, a "war," which may be the undoing of all. Tricksters abound, not the least of whom is our hero, who does coin-tricks with a favorite "coin" which may actually be (on some level) the Moon, taken down out of the sky. This is the kind of book where spirits and apparitions about, the dead don't stay dead, but that the gods and demons all assume particularly modern guises. Odin, down on his luck, does confidence scams and robs ATM machines. More than once we found ourselves thinking of, in particular, Zelazny's "The Last Defender of Camelot," which is also about tarnished remnants of the legendary past working out their differences in the present.

What I particularly appreciate is Gaiman's sense of the vastness of the American land. There are lots of roadside details. One reads much about the House on the Rock in Wisconsin and Rock City, on Lookout Mountain in Georgia. The irony is that Mr. Gaiman, an Englishman now resident in the Midwest, has, in more senses than one, conjured up the spirit of America better than most American writers could.

A myth is a story which tells the hearers *who they are*. It is culture-defining, as opposed to a legend, which is merely a colorful story about some local person or place. America has lots of legends, but not very many myths. We can be grateful to Mr. Gaiman for evoking the latter.

Of course American writers have been writing about America in fantasy since the very beginning. Washington Irving started out with the same thing Gaiman is doing, transplanting German and other European material into the new country, in his case, the Hudson Valley. "Rip Van Winkle" has European antecedents. So does William Austin's "Peter Rugg, the Missing Man" (1824) which is a landlubber's Flying Dutchman story, about a man under a curse, condemned to drive the roads forever without reaching Boston. (Surely many commuters feel that way. You will recall the old song "Did He Ever Return?" about someone lost in the labyrinth of the Boston subways.) Nathaniel Hawthorne found a uniquely American brand of the fantastic in his stories of Puritan New England. The Puritans' experience in America was distinctly *not* European; they saw themselves as the lone upholders of the Light, perched on the edge of a vast, unknown continent of Darkness, rather like the first men on another planet. Therefore "Young Goodman Brown" becomes a uniquely American story, as much about the unknown as it is about guilt or Devil-fears.

Edgar Allan Poe did not write about America very much. His stories looked back to Europe. "A Cask of Amontillado" is set in Europe. "The Masque of the Red Death" takes place in a medieval European Never-Neverland.

It might be argued that there is something too practical and everyday, too prosaic in the American character for the creation of myth. America has nothing as grand and sweeping as the story of King Arthur. Instead we have a lot of funny stories about Mike Finn and Davy Crockett. We have a great deal of (still replicating) folklore about regional hauntings, monsters, and wonders, but rarely does the American literary imagination seem to take in the Big Picture. Longfellow's *Hiawatha* is purely artificial, the work of a man trying to imagine the innermost workings of a culture which not his own. His epic tends to be ridiculed, or at least not taken very seriously. Its distinctive meter, taken from yet another artificial (Finnish) epic, *The Kalevala*, is a common mode for parody.

One thinks of other comic, "epic" novels, such as Vincent McHugh's *Caleb Catlum's America* (1936), but there, again, the mythic impulse has been laughed away. It has given way to the Tall Tale. Stephen Vincent Benét tried to create a non-fantastic epic with *John Brown's Body*, a veritable American *Iliad*, but that seems to have faded from the forefront of American literary consciousness. Too bad. Benét was a great poet and prose-writer, and he should be more widely reprinted. He wrote some of the best American fantasies, "The Devil and Daniel Webster" and some others, and he gave hints that he could have written the great, mythic epic of the United States if only he had lived longer and literary fashion had supported such an endeavor.

How remarkable then that Neil Gaiman, an outsider, has come as close to putting it all together as anyone.

VI.

WHO KILLED HORROR? THE *MURDER ON THE ORIENT EXPRESS* SOLUTION

The April 2003 issue of that most admirable British science fiction and fantasy magazines, *Interzone*, which contains a column by a favorite commentator, Gary Westfahl, with the arresting title of "Who *Didn't* Kill Horror?"

I had to read that right away. I was poised to write a *Weird Tales* editorial about something else, but could only push the other editorial idea forward an issue or two.

Who killed Horror? Those of us old enough (or historically cognizant enough) to remember the 1961 Hugo Awards know that there actually was a publication called *Who Killed Science Fiction?* which won a Hugo for Best Fanzine that year. Yet Science Fiction isn't dead, is it? Westfahl doesn't think so. Nor does the editor of *Interzone*, obviously, but that is a discussion for another time and place.

Horror has been reported dead many times. "Who Killed Horror?" panels have been mainstays at conventions for at least a decade by now, ever since...they *found the body?* Or did they?

To the point, Westfahl concludes:

> ...in confronting what happened to horror, we arrive at a conclusion rarely observed in the literature of detective fiction: the detective eliminates all the obvious suspects and announces to the interested parties, "Something much more complicated than a simple murder is going on here, so we must launch a thoroughgoing investigation of the various factors that might have contributed to the victim's death." In sum, determining who—if anybody—killed horror

> does not demand the services of police officers or de-
> tectives to find a perpetrator; instead it requires a
> doctor of forensic medicine who is prepared to con-
> duct an extensive autopsy and diligently search for
> the true cause or causes of death. On the basis of my
> cursory examinations, such a figure in the field of
> horror has not yet emerged. (p. 51)

But at the same time, the unstated subtext of Westfahl's article is the *Murder on the Orient Express* solution. Sorry if this is a spoiler, but the novel and the film derived from it are now so famous that most people know the ending, that, Agatha Christie, in the course of systematically breaking the "rules" of detective fiction one by one, finally went over the top and did a novel in which *everybody* participated in the murder, all the suspects, several hangers-on, and probably a few people nobody bothered to notice.

Westfahl doesn't succeed in eliminating *any* of the usual suspects, pointing out that, when horror was making lots of money, it was only natural that more writers, including less talented ones, would flock to the field, and that publishers were not about to say, "Well this isn't very good, so, for the sake of the integrity of the field, we'll publish something less profitable."

For a time readers tolerated the results. Then they didn't. But other fields have undergone this sort of boom/flood-of-crud/bust cycle, including, most obviously, science fiction, which was at the bottom of a collapse when *Who Killed Science Fiction?* came out.

It is very helpful for Westfahl to question the accepted wisdom on this matter. I'd like to ask a few more questions:

Is the victim really dead?

Here's an anecdote. Back in the 1980s, when I began to sell stories to magazines like *Night Cry* and *The Horror Show,* I was given a bit of career advice by a very respected editor of the time.

"Re-invent yourself," he said. "Disown everything you have done up till now. Cut all connections with science fiction, fantasy, fandom, conventions, and fanzines and become a new person, a Hor-ror Writer, whose career will be much more profitable. Dress differently. And oh, by the way, grow a moustache."

Well, I didn't. For one thing, I was reluctant to disown everything I'd written up to that time, maybe out of sheer egotism. (I am still not at all embarrassed by *The Shattered Goddess* or the Tom O'Bedlam stories.) I also didn't like the idea of turning one's back on old friends and associates merely for career advantage. Hey, this is *my* tribe. I am a part of it and it is a part of me. There might also be the objection that a moustache would mar such boyish good looks as I allegedly still possessed in those days, or become a repository for week-old soup, but the more serious point is that if I *had* taken that editor's advice, I might have found myself on the proverbial (or metaphorical) bread-line with the rest of the ex-horror writers. Instead, I went on to write *The Mask of the Sorcerer* and the other Sekenre stories, more Tom O'Bedlam, and quite a bit else which has pleased at least some readers.

There might have been short-term career advantage to total re-invention as a horror writer. It worked for Dean Koontz, didn't it? I might have had a couple good years in horror's mid-list around 1988, but by the early '90s, something catastrophic had clearly happened to the horror field. Those black-covered books with the demonic children embossed drop of blood visible through the show-through outer cover were disappearing. With them went, frequently, the entire horror section in major bookstores. Publishing houses which used to have major horror lines and full-time horror editors now didn't.

The field imploded, largely collapsing down to the small-press or near vanity-press level, where one could become a "big name" with a print-on-demand novel that sold four hundred copies. The first sign was something I noted at the time in one of my *Weird Tales* editorials, the attempt to remove the supernatural elements from horror fiction and repackage it as "Dark Suspense." Ramsey Campbell, in the interview I did with him for *H. P. Lovecraft's Magazine of Horror* #1, discusses this candidly. He was told by his publishers in no uncertain terms that ghostlies didn't sell and he should remake himself in the image of Thomas Harris of *The Silence of the Lambs* fame. It was an astonishing thing to demand of an author who'd written more first-rate supernatural horror fiction than anybody, ever.

Fortunately Campbell survived, and his career continues apace. Fortunately *Weird Tales* survived, and is now the equivalent of a still-living denizen of the Jurassic, rather like a shark or a ginkgo tree which existed in pretty much the same form when dinosaurs ruled the Earth.

Many of the ex-horror writers didn't make it. One year at NE-Con (Northeast Regional Fantasy Convention, sort of a "summer camp for horror writers") this was particularly evident when *all* the freebie books by attending writers were media tie-in novels. That's where some of them went. Others (like Joe R. Lansdale) stayed in "dark suspense" and merged into the crime-fiction field. (Where

Lansdale is doing very well, thank you.) And a few, like Ramsey Campbell, are still writing what they always did. But it is impossible to deny that, if the field is not dead, it is at a low ebb, comparable to where science fiction was in 1960.

Yet we all continue to tap-dance around the question of who killed it. Publishing scuttlebutt has it that one very central, prominent mass-market horror imprint failed *so* badly, that with classic corporate logic, it was allowed to continue for the next five years with smaller and smaller budgets and print-runs, so accountants could spread the zillion-dollar loss out over several years, rather than take it all at once. When this was over, so was the field, as far as the Big Boys were concerned.

That's one more suspect to the long list, again reminding is of the ending of *Murder on the Orient Express.* But, not only did I not grow that moustache, I came away with a feeling of having missed the plane that crashed.

There *is* something to be said for versatility. In the corporate world of bestseller-or-die publishing, this may be faulted as lack of focus, but I for one am still happy to have the ability to move, with some degree of success, between fantasy, horror, science fiction, and various types of non-fiction when conditions warrant. The thing I most recently wrote for pay before doing this editorial was an article on Urban Legends for reference book to be published by Gale Research. Illustrous horror writers of the past, such as Fritz Leiber and Richard Matheson, have been well served by an ability to write more than just horror.

Had I been giving that advice to a young writer, circa 1986, we would have said, "Never mind the moustache. Yes, horror looks like it's getting big, so now is the time to write a horror novel. But don't get yourself so typed that you haven't got anything else to fall back on."

Was the victim ever alive?

Westfahl suggests, probably without 100% belief, that maybe "horror is a form of narrative, like westerns, pirate stories, and jungle adventures, that is by its nature becoming outdated, a problem that cannot be solved by superficial transformations to accommodate contemporary sensibilities." Perhaps, he goes on to say, it is a fad which cannot endure, like hula-hoops or pet rocks.

Surely Westfahl is just teasing us with this possibility, because he is a very knowledgeable critic, who is well aware that something identifiable as horror fiction has existed for centuries, and that the duration of hula-hoops and pet rocks is not even a blip on its timeline.

But there is a serious question here: *was horror* ever *viable as a commercial genre?* Of course there have been supernatural stories published for a very long time. Poe was active in the 1840s and hasn't been out of print since. *Dracula* has never been out of print since its first publication in 1897. *Weird Tales* has published horror fiction (but never been a 100% horror magazine) in all its incarnations over the past eighty years. But such classic horror novels as *The Haunting of Hill House* (1959) were published as "mainstream" novels.

But the first attempt to make horror into a *genre*, in the sense of a category of publishing with its own packaged "look," its own editors, imprints, and niche in the bookstore may have begun only about 1960 with a couple anthologies from Ace (*Macabre* and *More Macabre*) and, more significantly, by a series of Ballantine books, which had Richard Powers covers and a distinct design which told the reader that here was another of "those books." The line was a modest success. It included a couple of Sarban titles, one H. R. Wakefield, and Fritz Leiber's *Shadows With Eyes* (1962). I am not old enough to remember where these books were placed in stores, but it was probably in the science fiction section. There was certainly no horror section then, anymore than there had been in 1840 or 1897.

Toward the end of the 1960's Lin Carter invented a publishing category. In the wake of the huge success of *The Lord of the Rings* in paperback, he created the Ballantine Adult Fantasy Series. Most of the books were reprints, many dating back into the nineteenth century (and one, Beckford's *Vathek,* to the eighteenth), but they were Carter's attempt to build a canon, define a category and an audience, and create a new "kind" of book. Before that, fantasy books were published either as mainstream (*e.g., The Once and Future King*), as juveniles (the works of Alan Garner) or disguised as science fiction.

Carter's experiment worked. In fact it worked so hugely well that it completely absorbed the contemporary and more limited publishing phenomenon of Sword & Sorcery, which derived its content and imagery, not from Tolkien, but from Robert E. Howard.

Why didn't this work with horror, which tried to do the same thing with post-*Exorcist*, post-Stephen King supernatural fiction? Clearly it did not. Entirely too great an edifice was built on too small a foundation, and it came crashing down.

This is not to suggest a definite solution. Westfahl is right that the matter will take more study and a careful autopsy. But one could add to the roster of everybody-did-it suspects (and I haven't even *begun* to talk about the debasement of audience expectations due to the influence of slasher films) publishers, editors, and writers who define horror *too narrowly.*

Symptoms of this were visible long ago too. One of the other things one of the editors I knew back in the '80s told me, was that no matter how much he admired my horror fiction, he "couldn't read" stories set in the historical past, in imaginary lands, or on other planets. He certainly couldn't regard them as *horror,* for all I have consistently argued that a story about a man who comes back from the grave and crawls into bed with his wife (my "Going to the Mountain," in *Refugees from an Imaginary Country*) is still horror, whether set in contemporary New Jersey or in some ancient and fabulous land where gods still walk the Earth. Clark Ashton Smith stories are horrifying, whether set in the present day, in medieval Averoigne, pre-historic Hyperborea, or on the planet Mars. Can't I do that too?

This blurs definitions, a corporate publisher's salesman is going to object. You bet it does. I also think it's one of the reasons why *Weird Tales* is still here and that paperback line which so thunderously carried off the core of the horror category in the middle '90s is not. *Weird Tales* has always done its best to broaden the definition of what it will publish, not narrow it. My friends the horror editors of the '80s were very insistent that they didn't want horror fiction outside of a contemporary frame of reference. This seems to have applied to the whole field during the boom years. With such exceptions as Chelsea Quinn Yarbro's historical vampire novels (which are arguably selling as Romance, rather than horror), the rule seems to have always been that category horror could not be set prior to Victorian times.

One can only ask: how many post-King books about lower-middle-class families in supernatural peril does anybody want to read? Maybe what happened is that repetition set in, caused by over-narrow definitions and expectations on the part of both producers and consumers of horror, and everybody just got bored. Maybe the "field" was too narrow to *ever* have been successful. It was a chimera. Nobody killed it because it was never alive. Maybe we'll just have to go back to how things were from the beginnings of literature until about 1980, when horror and supernatural books and stories were published aplenty, but there was no "category" at all.

At least for a while. After all this *is* horror we're talking about, where things can't be trusted to stay dead, even things that have never, strictly speaking, been alive.

VII.

Of Dream Research, Nyucks, Knuckleheads, the Intentional Fallacy, Biographical Criticism, and Even More Nyucks

Very much in the spirit of the writer colleague who argued that the great thing about writing is that *anything* you do, unless you are snoring loudly, can never be called goofing off, but always "research"—and going further to insist that this colleague overlooked the whole area of dream research (which is very scientific)—I will shamelessly admit that I spent an afternoon in which I could have been writing a *Weird Tales* editorial visiting the Stoogeum, the world's greatest collection of Three Stooges memorabilia. It's quite an amazing place, a three-storey, really professional-quality museum located north of Philadelphia. This Edifice of Culture (which is undeniably more interesting than, say, the Cockroach Hall of Fame) would surely make it into *Roadside America* in an eye blink (or perhaps we should say eye poke) if it were open to the public more often, but it is a private institution owned by Mr. Gary Lassin of the Three Stooges Fanclub, and it is only open a few days a year, usually in connection with Stooge film events in the Philadelphia area. Philly is a very Stooge town, you know. Two of the six men who played in the Act were born there, Larry Fine and Curly-Joe DeRita, and certainly every tourist should view, not only such conventional high-points as the Philadelphia Art Museum and Independence Hall, but the gigantic Larry Fine mural at on South Street.

What, you may reasonably ask, has this amazing building full of Stooge posters, toys, original props and sound-effects devices, comic books, not to mention life-sized wax figures of Moe, Larry, and Curly (which help you appreciate that these guys were short, about five feet, four inches) and even a Stooge slot machine (with appropriate sound effects); where you can either sit and watch Stooge films in a luxurious theatre or view the collection *and* watch Stooge films because there is a large TV monitor in every room; have to do with *Weird Tales*? Can I possibly demonstrate that this digression is even remotely germane to our ostensible topics of horrific and fantastic literature, our pulp heritage, or *anything* I am supposed to be writing about?

Well, soitenly.

I might mention at this point that H. P. Lovecraft is not known to have ever seen a Stooges film, or even one of their early vaudeville acts with Ted Healy, nor does he mention "the boys" anywhere in his vast writings, even in the countless thousands of surviving letters (some of which are almost book-length), so this *could* be one of those rare editorials in which I Take the Pledge do not mention H. P. Lovecraft, but I'm afraid I'm inevitably going to fall off the wagon within a few paragraphs, so let me merely intone a suitably sepulchral "Nyuck, nyuck fhtagn" and proceed.

What all this got me thinking about in a slightly more serious frame of mind, is the whole question of writer, artist, actor, or Stooge biographies, and why people want to know something about the people who produce the stories we read, the films we watch, etc. Is the Work not enough? Doesn't it stand on its own?

Obviously not. The tendency has been apparent since ancient times, when more than one city in Asia used to offer tourist a glimpse of the alleged birthplace of Homer and there was, even then, much speculation on who the author of the *Iliad* and the *Odyssey* really was. Suetonius, the author of the famous *The Twelve Caesars* also wrote a book of *Lives of Grammarians and Rhetoricians,* which covers Terence,, Horace, Virgil, Persius, Lucan, and a (very fragmentary) bit of Pliny the Elder (classified as a rhetorician), and which is, basically, a collection of literary biographies.

Certainly if, in those days, someone could have displayed the very reed with which Homer wrote (it being a whole other subject whether Homer wrote at all, or had ever even *heard* of writing, but this is to digress; apologies) or his lyre, they would certainly have drawn a crowd of paying customers.

Philadelphia is not only a haven of Stooginess, but it's got an Edgar Allan Poe house, which Lovecraft *did* write about in his "Homes and Shrines of Poe." (There you go. I knew it would happen.... Cthulhu makes me do these things. My brain has been taken over, or possibly carried off to Yuggoth in a jar. I can't help it.) There is not a whole lot *in* the Poe house, but it is a place where he did actually live, and one of several where he allegedly wrote "The Raven"—shades of the multiple birthplaces of Homer.

It just seems to be a natural and universal desire to want to get close to and summon up some sense of the presence of writers, artists, and other performers after they are dead through places and artifacts associated with them. Probably the reason so many cranks try to "prove" that the plays of Shakespeare were written by the entire population of Elizabethan England *except* a certain gentleman from Stratford—other than the fact that he's the biggest target and nobody would get famous proving that Francis Bacon or the Queen or Sir Walter Raleigh or Attila the Hun wrote the works of Thomas Dekker, or even Beaumont and Fletcher—is that his biography, though more detailed than those of most of his fellow playwrights, is still much too sketchy for us to have any sense of the man himself. Was he an extrovert or introvert, bawdy or chaste, secretly a Catholic or a flag-waving arch-Protestant? If you read enough Shakespeare biographies you will discover that the he evolves over time, and each version is the product of the era that produced it—*i.e.*, the biographical Shakespeare is essentially a creation of later imagination.

And that will never do. We want to know the artist, not just experience the art. For weird-fiction aficionados, not to mention *Weird Tales* readers—and if that sounds like the famous lines, "Gentlemen! Gentlemen!" "Who came in?" I can only plead that it may take a while to recover from that Stoogeum visit—we have the perhaps fortune coincidence that through H. P. Lovecraft's 10,000 or so letters (many of them *very* long) and the memoirs and other first-hand material about him, which range (as you can see from Peter Cannon's Arkham House volume, *Lovecraft Remembered*), from 1915 to 1997, Lovecraft is perhaps the most thoroughly documented literary person of all time. Verily, if there was a three-day stretch in his life in which we don't know where he was, who he was with, what they talked about, and what flavor the ice cream was, that is the "lost period."

As artist-writer Jason Van Hollander has pointed out, for a lot of people in our field, Lovecraft is talismanic. It is remarkably easy to outlive Robert E. Howard, for instance. One doesn't want to make light of a great writer and the tragedy of his life, but all you have to do is *not* shoot yourself at the age of thirty. Yet, when you reach your forty-seventh birthday, you notice. You have outlived H. P. Lovecraft. (See my poem, "My Age," in *Groping Toward the Light*.)

Struggling writers and artists out there take encouragement from *his* struggle, knowing, as Lovecraft painfully did *not* know and would never have believed, that by maintaining the integrity and originality of his work to the point of counter-commercial obsessiveness, by refusing to become a conventional pulp writer of like so many of his colleagues, Lovecraft has left virtually all the pulp writers of his day (not to mention most of the literary writers) in his wake. That's why he's in Library of America before E. Hoffmann Price—or for that matter, Ernest Hemingway.

The more obsessed among us may even be preparing for their own fame, carefully preserving every draft, letter, and laundry-list for the benefit of future literary scholars. Daniel Pearlman wrote an extremely funny story on this tendency, entitled "The Best-Known Man in the World." It's not specifically in a Lovecraftian context, but it splendidly captures the vanity and absurdity of banking on your own posthumous success. (Seek out Pearlman's book, *The Best-Known Man in the World and Other Misfits,* Aardwolf Press, 2001. It's great stuff.)

It is inescapable, though, that our reading of an author's work is influenced and to some sense *completed* by some notion of who the author was. We don't just read "The Raven." We have a sense of Poe sitting in that dark room under the bust of Pallas, writing it. The personality of Lovecraft is behind all his works. "The Horror at Red Hook" is a story, but when we read it were are informed by the fact that this is a product of HPL's New York period.

Of course there is a whole school of academic criticism which rejects all this, which says texts are just texts, and that nobody wrote them, really; they somehow exist in space between the page and the reader and the printed page and that the "story" is a collaboration, continuously created, and if anybody brings up the naive and old-fashioned idea that the actual writer had any idea of what he was doing or what the story meant, this must be dismissed as the "intentional fallacy."

To which the only appropriate response is, "Phooey," and "Go soak your head in a bucket while reading the collected works of Jacques Laçan and gurgling 'woo-boo-woo-boo!' underwater." Fortunately such notions have had remarkably little impact on either the writing or reading of literature, because the Deconstructionists, Post-Structuralists, and that lot tend to write in a thick jargon which rapidly turns into gibberish, and on the rare occasion that one of them achieves momentary lucidity, their ideas seem just plain *silly,* worthy of a poke in the eye.

This is not to deny that a story by a writer about whom nothing is known has meaning, and that this is a somewhat different meaning from a story by someone as fantastically over-documented as

Lovecraft. A text by Mark Twain is one thing, Mark Twain on the stage delivering that text must have been quite another, not merely from the manner of his delivery or even his stage personality, but from the awareness on the part of his contemporaries that they shared the planet with this particular man and that he mattered.

It may well be that a living author, in effect, collaborates with his own text, and a dead author's memory collaborates with it *differently,* and this is filtered through culture, so, yes, the meaning of a text does change over time, but, I argue, it changes precisely because we try to reach out to the author himself. It is why we read author blurbs and dust jacket copy, to get a sense that, hey, there is *someone* behind the byline.

I wasn't weren't goofing off that afternoon I went to the Stoogeum afternoon. It was all research. Nyuck-nyuck.

VIII.

FANTASY AND TRADITION; OR, HEY, IS THAT MY GENRE YOU'RE STEPPING ON?

A Speech Delivered at the Philadelphia Free Library,
October 25, 2004

I have not yet read Susanna Clarke's *Jonathan Strange & Mr. Norrell*, though I would like to, and have heard very good reports about it, but I must take exception to the ignorant review which was in, alas, *The Philadelphia Inquirer*, which said, in effect, hey, prior to this fantasy was read by geeks with tattoos and piercings and a walkman blaring in both ears, but now, for the first time ever (or nearly so), here is a fantasy novel which is *LITERATURE* and may be read by adults.

I believe this would be news to the readers of Tolkien and C. S. Lewis in the 1950s, to readers of Lord Dunsany and James Branch Cabell in the Teens and Twenties, to readers (or spectators) William Shakespeare's archetypal fantasy, *The Tempest*, circa 1615, or even the audience for Lucius Apuleius's *The Golden Ass* in the reign of Marcus Aurelius.

The secret has been out for sometime: Fantasy is not a new form of literature. If we define it as fiction about fantastic events which the reader reads with the understanding that it is all made up, a fable or adventure yarn or whatever, then we cut ourselves free from tangled questions about the *Iliad* and the book of *Exodus* and *Gilgamesh* all that—narratives which were intended to be believed—and still fantasy has been around for a long time. *The Golden Ass*, written somewhere around 160-180 A.D. is not only self-consciously made-up, but it is almost post-modern metafiction, devoting a good deal of its energies to questions of what is real and what is not, how do we tell the difference, and the matter of the un-

59

reliable narrator. It is a vast liar-paradox of a book, whose first line of dialogue may be translated from baroque, Clark Ashton Smith Latin as, "Stop all this outrageous lying!" The tone is then set by the story of a traveler who, with a companion, stopped at an inn in witch-haunted Thessaly, and was horrified to awaken in the middle of the night to behold a gaggle of levitating witches, like a sinister black cloud floating in through the window to hover above his room-mate's bed. They slit the poor fellow's throat, reach down inside, snatch out his heart, and leave a sponge in its place. As in any nightmare, the worst thing happens next. The witches discover that the traveler is observing him. Outraged, they flip over his bed, urinate on him, and leave.

The following morning, the traveler, smelling somewhat the worse for wear one imagines, sneaks out very early and saddles his horse. No one will believe his story. He'll surely be arrested for murder. But who should he meet in the stable, but his friend, apparently alive and well.

They set out on their journey. The tension between reality and unreality—was it a dream? Is the man still alive or some kind of ghost?—will be familiar to any reader of Robert Aickman or Philip K. Dick. It becomes unbearable until the two of them stop by a stream to drink, and the sponge gets soaked, falls out, and the companion dies. Wilder and wilder episodes pile on top of one another as the book progresses. The main story is about how Lucius, the narrator, identified with the author (who was in real life tried and acquitted for witchcraft—his defense speech still exists), visits a Thessalian household, seduces the maid, learns from her that the mistress anoints herself with magic oil at night and turns into an owl, and resolves to try this himself. But he screws it up and is transformed, quite deservedly, into an ass. He spends the rest of the book trying to regain human shape. When at last he is able to convince someone of his plight, this doesn't help. He becomes a novelty. A depraved woman wants to have sex with him and arranges for him to be brought to her perfumed, richly-decorated bedroom, until at the—if you will excuse the phrase—climax of the book the ass-man leaps out the window, runs down to the beach, calls on the goddess Isis, has a vision and gets religion in the last chapter, which of course makes the entire book, with its many frivolous, terrifying, and racy episodes entirely moral, edifying, and worthy of the time of serious-minded persons. Daniel Defoe employed a similar narrative strategy in *Moll Flanders* sixteen centuries later.

In other words, *The Golden Ass* is a comic-philosophical fantasy novel, which has a great deal in common with, say, the works of Terry Pratchett. Of course such works do not spring fully-grown from the forehead of a single writer. Undoubtedly Apuleius was drawing on earlier examples, possibly a vast literature of ancient fantasy novels, now entirely lost. A tradition. A genre.

This will only come as a shock to that reviewer in *The Philadelphia Inquirer*.

What may come as a shock to general readers—and a lot of literature professors—who have never thought much about it is this: *there are no non-genre books*, at least not anymore. Books are published and sold according to two strategies. Either it is a *brand-name* book, identifiable as a Kurt Vonnegut novel or a Stephen King novel or a Thomas Pynchon novel, or whatever, or else it is a *genre* book, meaning that it is published and sold on the basis, not of the author's name, but on what kind of book it is. A mystery. A western. Science fiction. An imaginary world fantasy according to the Tolkien model. A novel of rebellious youth on the cutting edge of whatever they're cutting this week. This last is one of the really old chestnuts. It accounts for everything from *The Rampant Age* by Robert Spencer Carr in the 1920s to (with varying degrees of accuracy) *The Great Gatsby*, *The Catcher in the Rye*, to any number of 1950s paperbacks about juvenile delinquents, to the works of Brad Easton Ellis, to whoever has inevitably followed him into that niche.

Some genres come and go. The aforementioned juvenile delinquent novels were big stuff in the '50s, particularly in paperback. As any collector of vintage paperbacks knows, '50s juvie novels had a distinct look, with repeating iconography: the black leather jackets, the switchblades, and, inevitably, a cigarette dangling loosely from the sneering lips of a tough hood and, usually, one of the girls.

The Lost Race novel, the story about the lost city inhabited by survivors of ancient Atlantis or wherever, completely cut off from modern civilization and maintaining its ancient lifestyle and supernatural wonders in a volcanic valley in Darkest Africa (or wherever), began more or less with H. Rider Haggard in the nineteenth century and died out somewhere in the early-twentieth, although there are still sporadic revivals. But there used to be hundreds of these books. The problem was, as the world became more and more explored, finding places to lose the lost city. Edgar Rice Burroughs solved that one deftly in 1911 by moving the whole business to Mars, where he could also have four-armed warriors and egg-laying princesses. He created a new genre, the interplanetary romance, which was the dominant model into at least the 1930s, when science fiction, which had gained genre-awareness in specialized pulp magazines, began to evolve in other directions. You can still find late, degenerate interplanetary romances, written in imitation of Edgar Rice Burroughs, being published well into the 1970s.

Another example of a forgotten genre is the "road book," which exists at least in publishing lore, if no longer in the mind of the public. When Jack Kerouac's *On the Road* became such a hit, there was a fashion for other books about rootless young drifters discovering America, the meaning of life, and their inner selves while thumbing their noses at authority. The film *Easy Rider* was a reflection of this genre. But somewhere along the line "road books" stopped selling, and there were no more of them.

Now, here is the challenging question: Is genre awareness a good thing or a bad thing? If somebody sat down and said, "I'm going to write a 'road book'," rather than just unselfconsciously baring his soul in the midst of a travel novel, would that make for a better or worse performance?

Let me suggest that the conscious genre writer has an advantage. The fantasy writer, the science fiction writer, or whatever is like the anthropologist gazing in on the island paradise of the Literary Establishment, or Mainstream, or the Halls of Academe, or whatever you want to call it, where the benighted natives still think that their quaint customs and folkways are the *only* ways, the established laws of the universe, instead of one of many possible paths of literary endeavor. That is why mainstream literary novels are sometimes published with the words "a novel" on the cover. Of course the latest Discworld book is a novel too, as is *The Lord of the Rings* (which only broken into three volumes for the publisher's convenience; the archetypal trilogy, ironically, isn't one).

But the literature professor, the *Philadelphia Inquirer* reviewer, and several mainstream novelists I have met don't know that. They lack broader perspective. They think their little island is the whole world. They don't know that "the novel," as they pompously describe it, is a genre label. John Updike is a genre writer. He has even ventured outside his familiar genre into science fiction and fantasy on occasion. *The Witches of Eastwick* has a lot in common with Apuleius.

The latest Philip Roth novel *The Plot Against America* is an alternate history, a work in an established genre that includes such classics as Keith Roberts's *Pavane* and Ward Moore's *Bring the Jubilee*, not to mention any number of Harry Turtledove novels, and even such archaic curiosities as *When William Came* by Saki, which was published before the First World War and is about Kaiser

Wilhelm conquering England. As yet I have not read the Roth book. But I heard him interviewed about it on National Public Radio. It *sounds* like a good book, more personal in focus than most alternate histories. It's about Roth's own childhood and his imagining how his own family would have fared in a sinister, subtly anti-Semitic America in which Charles Lindbergh became president in 1940 and the United States remained neutral during World War II.

But nowhere in the radio show did either Roth or the interviewer let on that there has ever been a book like this before, or that it belongs to a recognized genre. He is getting amazed reviews from mainstream sources. He is wowing the primitives, re-inventing the wheel.

We have to admit that while such "mainstream wander-ins," as science fiction fans arrogantly call such books, are indeed often primitive and dated—for example, Walter Moseley's cyberpunk novel, which seems to come out of an alternate universe in which William Gibson never happened—some of the others knock over the standard genre product for ninepins. Think of Bernard Wolfe's *Limbo*, George Orwell's *Nineteen Eighty-Four*, Gore Vidal's *Messiah*, all great science fiction novels, considerably better than the Ace Doubles of the same period.

Oh yes, I was supposed to be talking about fantasy. Think of *Portrait of Jennie* by Robert Nathan, *Grendel* and *Freddy's Book* (but nothing else) by John Gardner, *The Wandering Unicorn* by Manuel Mujica-Láinez, all of which are infinitely superior to one more generic fantasy novel following the post-Tolkien pattern wittily described by Brian Aldiss as "three cub-scouts and a moron defeat Hitler." (There is another strange cliché in such books, which I discovered by accident when reviewing three random titles for one of my columns. In two out of three, the Fellowship of the Good Guys, on a Quest, deep into enemy territory, menaced on all sides by nameless unspeakables or unspeakable namelessnesses, stop in the middle of the woods at night and *light a roaring campfire* with no concern for how far the light might carry. In other words, outdoorsy novels by writers who have never been there.)

Literary and critical provincialism works both ways. It enlightens no one. The bastion or island or ivory tower of Serious Literature, is, let us face it, gazed upon with envy by "genre" types, who may enjoy higher sales and have a larger readership and even a better shot at literary immortality the darlings of the Literary Establishment. Be honest now: Any writer who doesn't in his heart of hearts want his works to be presented to generations of students as classics or reviewed reverentially in *The New Yorker* or *The New*

York Times Book Review and won't admit it at least when you get a few drinks into him or otherwise remove inhibitions is, very likely, either a very good liar or a little bit nuts. Even Frederick Faust, the great pulp writer of many pseudonyms, best known as Max Brand, the author of countless westerns and the Doctor Kildare series, yearned for literary respectability. A disciplined professional, he devoted part of his day to the steady production of pulp fiction. But he also set aside time in which he locked himself away and wrote what was intended to be exquisite and profound poetry. *With a quill pen.* Edgar Rice Burroughs wanted respectability too. He made repeated attempts at social realism, and even tried to one-up Robert Graves (whose *I, Claudius* was a big hit at the time) with *I Am A Barbarian*, which actually did rise above the level of the routine Burroughs product of about 1940 (by which time he was cranking out inferior, late Tarzans and Mars books). It's a fast-moving inside story of Julio-Claudian politics, told from the point of view of a slave and boyhood companion of Caligula, a novel filled with genuine wit, some almost Monty-Pythoneseque, grotesque comedy (including a crucifixion scene which recalls *The Life of Brian*), and eccentric characterizations. But it didn't make it as a serious novel, probably because Burroughs couldn't bring himself to depict the depravities of the adult Caligula. Burroughs lost heart, wrapped up the book in a hurry, and it was never published in his lifetime.

Yes, we want literary respectability, even as we hold the Literary Establishment in contempt. It is a curiously schizophrenic attitude, which causes some genre writers, who find themselves dismissed as "sci-fi" to refer to the enemy as "SeriLit" or even "LiFi." We hear a lot of rationalizations about being "just paid entertainers." This is the standard defense mechanism for writers of L. Sprague de Camp's generation, writers who got their start in the pulps of the Depression and developed an impenetrable shell of "I'm just a working stiff, not an artist." For some of them, including, I fear, my old friend Sprague, this was limiting. It hobbled their aspirations. For others, like Fritz Leiber, or, late in life, Henry Kuttner, very likely it did not.

But, anyway, calling the other guy names may be amusing but it doesn't accomplish very much. It is at best a minor tool of satirical discourse.

For the mainstream, literary establishment provincials, I have this to say. It's a quote, possibly apocryphal, allegedly uttered by one of the most senior people in New York publishing. He (or she) supposedly said, "Only fantasy is commercial. Everything else, including mainstream, is cult fiction."

That does put the "serious literary" or "LiFi" novelist in his place, but I also have to reply, let us not be ridiculous. The largest genre of all is *romance*, something everybody likes to look down upon, even as it outsells everything else. We like to imagine that one day a literary encyclopedia will have an entry that reads: "Hemingway, Ernest. A minor contemporary of Tolkien limited by his inability to achieve broader thematic range and appeal."

But it's just as likely to read: "A minor contemporary of Daphne du Maurier...."

For the Fantasy writer who thinks he is the center of the world literature, let me tell you when I heard the crack of doom.

It was the 1974 or 1975 Lunacon. Lin Carter had just been fired as he editor of the Ballantine Adult Fantasy Series and was replaced by Lester del Rey. At that point we knew del Rey as a Golden Age science fiction writer, the author of "Helen O'Loy" and "Nerves." As a critical polemicist, he was a staunch opponent of the New Wave. He had edited some short-lived digests in the early 1950s, including one quite good one, *Fantasy Fiction.*

What would he do as a fantasy book editor? The audience wanted to know. Del Rey was addressing a large auditorium full of people, virtually the entire attendance of the convention. (This was in the days of one-track programming.) People started to ask him about the sort of writers he was looking for and would publish. Since our awareness of fantasy, as a distinct genre, was quite a recent development—somehow the oldest form of literature, from which everything else branched off, did not become a distinct publishing category with its own label on the spine of a paperback until 1969—the examples were taken from the Ballantine Adult Fantasy Series.

Would del Rey publish a latter-day Ernest Bramah, author of the Kai Lung series?

No, absolutely not.

How about Lord Dunsany?

"Yes," del Rey said, "but I would tell him he didn't need all that fancy style to tell a good story."

I won't say my jaw dropped, but that's the equivalent of saying, "Well, Mister Shakespeare, *Hamlet* has a nifty plot, but why do you need all this distracting poetry?"

("It's a generic convention," Shakespeare would answer.)

I understood at that point what was completely borne out by his later performance. Lester del Rey was purely a pulp editor, who saw fiction as product, perhaps as a device for conveying interesting ideas, but with no awareness whatever of its subtler and richer effects. Indeed, he once said to me in an interview that if he could paid as much to do wiring diagrams as write fiction, he would do wiring diagrams. He had no artistic sensibilities at all. Here was that Depression-era, writer-as-working-stiff attitude at its very worst. It had left his soul a dried-out husk.

Oh yes, the Clap of Doom. You were waiting for that. Lester del Rey then went on at some length and with great enthusiasm about a hot new writer and a great new book he was about to publish. He was talking about Terry Brooks and *The Sword of Shannara*, which, del Rey assured us, would change the fantasy field forever.

Alas, he was right. Twenty years of darkness followed. Epic or mythic fantasy, which had previously held some reasonable claim to literary respectability, which could aspire to artistic ambition without being laughed at—far better to be seen as a brilliant, if poorly-understood eccentric, like a Tolkien or a Peake or a T. H. White—suddenly became generic product, very much like (as selling more like) despised romance novels. Medieval Harlequins, with elves. In bug-crushing trilogies.

This certainly had a major impact on the career of every fantasy writer alive today, particularly the ones who were a couple years either side of twenty and just starting out as Lester del Rey was speaking. We do not remember him fondly or honor his name. Instead we admire and salute the writers who somehow broke through the del Rey mold. As someone remarked in this context, no system of oppression is totally complete. Fantasy may have been established as formulaic junk in the minds of the publishing world, the public, and the critical establishment (*even* within the science fiction critical establishment), but it was still possible for John Crowley to publish *Little, Big*, for Ellen Kushner and Tanith Lee and Michael Swanwick and Charles de Lint and Greer Ilene Gilman to do genuinely ambitious, even (particularly in Gilman's case) difficult and demanding work within the fantasy field. Not, I note, for Del Rey Books. But they did it. They're ones we take our hats off to. (And, to be fair, even Del Rey published a couple of good novels by Phyllis Eisenstein and Tim Powers.)

What I conclude is that no form of literature should be dismissed. The realistic novel has its place, even the much-maligned novel of academia and adultery. The romance novel has its place. So does the western. When somebody tells you "poetry is dead" or "the theater is dead," the answer must always be, "No, as long as artists of ability do serious, sincerely-imagined work within it, it is not dead. Anything else is a problem of marketing."

The epic or romantic fantasy, which has been with us since before the beginnings of writing and which is distinguished by its ability address mythic concerns directly—not metaphorically, as James Joyce's *Ulysses* or the plays of Eugene O'Neil, but head on, with the gods brought on stage if necessary—also has its place in the vast dream which is literature. It is a very important place.

But Fantasy is also a genre. If it was ever possible for a writer to "invent" fantasy, that time has passed. Anyone writing such fiction today is doing so in the inescapable presence of predecessors, even as a subset of fantasy, Arthurian fiction, has been tied to its roots for the past thousand years. Tolkien is likewise inescapable. You may accept him, or reject him as Michael Moorcock has, but anything you write, in some sense, is very likely to be part of a dialogue with him.

But of course when Shakespeare was writing *Hamlet* he was working within the confines of the Jacobean revenge tragedy. Apuleius was working within the genre of what he called "the Milesian tale," which had become synonymous with racy stories, almost pornography, but was, in his hands at least, a whole lot more. (That may be why his example survived and so many others didn't.) The mainstream writer looks back on precedents too, perhaps to Henry James, or Henry Fielding, or Daniel Defoe. But his is a more modern form. His roots aren't quite as deep. The fantasy writer looks back to Tolkien, but hopefully further back, to *The Tempest*, to *Sir Gawain and the Green Knight*, and maybe even to Apuleius and Homer.

All any of us can do is try to escape the Lester del Reys of this world, try to produce work that matters, at least to the writer, rather than tired formula work which matters only to accountants.

Yeah, it's genre. At this stage of civilization, everything is. There may come a time when it becomes decadent, as late classical writing did—hundreds of years after Apuleius, in the days of Sidonius Apollinaris and Nonnos of Panopolis, in which the height of "fine" writing was to cram in as many mythical allusions as possible as obscurely as possible to hide the fact that the writer had nothing to say.

If that happens, some rebellious genius will have to throw away the accumulated conventions of centuries and start over.

But I don't think it has happened yet. Good, even great work is still possible, as long as fantasy, like any other type of writing, responds not only to previous writings, but from life itself. The fresh input comes from the times in which we live. Even as James Branch Cabell was uniquely a writer of the Twenties, Terry Pratchett is uniquely a writer of now. How long either will last is a crap-shoot. It depends on how well the contents of their books just happen to match the concerns of readers yet unborn.

So we just do our best and muddle through. As for the Literary Establishment, there's nothing you can do about them. Maybe one day they'll venture out of their little preserve to find out what the excitement is about.

IX.

EPIC AND FANTASY IN EPIC FANTASY (THE GOOD PARTS VERSION)

I.

Alec Austin's "Quality in Epic Fantasy" in *NYRSF* #185 reminds me of one of those frustrating manuscripts editors often get, which are pretty good as far as they go, but stop just as they begin to approach what they're actually about. What Mr. Austin has to say is perfectly sound and sensible, but he has not quite managed to reach the beginning of the topic.

Now I shall digress.

II.

My wife has gotten me hooked on a Korean television serial, something halfway between an Asian *I, Claudius* and a soap opera. It's called *Age of Warriors*, and to most American viewers it might as well be taking place in an imaginary time and place. From what I've been able to figure out from the occasional hints dropped in the subtitles, including one very useful expository lump, we are in Korea circa A.D. 1100, about a century before Genghis Khan, when the once-mighty Sung (or Song) Dynasty of China has lost its grip on the northern half of that country. The Southern Sung persists, exotic and far away, the land of expensive silk. Northern China has broken up into "barbarian" states, each with their own court and emperor. Jin and Khitai have been mentioned. Koryu (Korea) is such a minor power that it is tributary to one of these fragmentary "empires," Jin. A major plot thread has to do with getting the Jin ruler's approval for the newly-installed Koryu emperor, or else knocking off his envoy and starting a war.

Things are not going well in the land of Koryu. It seems the previous emperor, a decadent coward of the Nero or Caligula type and wholly under the spell of a courtesan with the unlikely (to us) name of Muby, has been deposed by at least four factions of the military. But this is one of those polite, Asiatic revolutions where rebels rise up in the name of loyalty, alleging to *preserve* the imperial house. The empress dowager has been forced to substitute a wimpy son for the wicked one. (A third son, who might have had some backbone, mysteriously vanished).

Against this background we meet three career soldiers who, in their youth, sacrificed a horse together, drank its blood, and swore that all should live and die as brothers, with honor. This vow is getting increasingly difficult to keep. All three are generals now, each with their own agendas. Everybody seems to betray everybody else at least once an episode. There are sporadic battles and assassination attempts. Everybody glares and utters growlly *"Hmm..."* sounds a lot. Since half the cast seems to be named Yi, a prophecy that Yi will become emperor only adds to the confusion. The deposed emperor is still on the loose. One of the sworn-brother generals is in bed with Muby. The very corruption they all took up arms to remove seems to be coming back.

It's great stuff, very colorful and dramatic, occasionally quite touching, all about courage, honor, ambition, the loss of ideals. Shakespeare could have made plays out of this material. *Star Trek* fans can't help but notice how Klingon-like it all is.

But, other than one odd moment in which the portraits in the Hall of Merit Subjects winked at the camera (an effect done with animation; meaning probably lost in cross-cultural translation) *Age of Warriors* is not fantasy, nor would it be improved by being fantasy. It doesn't need any sorcery to go along with all that intrigue and swordplay. Its *themes* do not demand fantastic content.

What bothers me about the Alec Austin article is that it stops short of addressing what epic fantasy is actually *about*. It is *not* about the politics of imaginary kingdoms. If you want a story of pride, power, and intrigue, with rulers being murdered and deposed, villains plotting, castles stormed, etc. there's plenty of that in real history. If you want a grand, melancholy, heroic tragedy, pick up Constance Head's *Imperial Twilight: The Palaiologos Dynasty and the Decline of Byzantium* (Nelson-Hall, 1977). It's got everything. Have fun. You could spin a dozen novels out of it. Your grand theme will be the destructiveness of ambition, with a sub-theme of the tempering effects of family ties and mercy, as you'll notice that after fighting among themselves for 200 years, the Palaiologoi may have completely destroyed their own empire, despite which *none of them killed another*—except for one ghastly accident in a back alley in the fourteenth century. John V was deposed, in sequence, by his father's best friend, his own son, and his grandson, and died in possession of his throne. *That's* quite a story.

It's also obvious that you could get quite a lot of exciting story material out of the history of medieval Korea.

But I am not interested in *faux*-history in a fantasy novel. I got bored with Guy Gavriel Kay's *Sarantine Mosaic* quite quickly. It's Byzantium with the names changed. That's like tennis with the net down. If you want to write about history, write about history. Do it honestly. (The same applies in science fiction. I am not fond of Mike Resnick's Africa-on-other-planets novels either. I'd like to see Mike write a real book about Africa on Earth.)

III.

All the things Austin brings up are perfectly valid. In an epic fantasy novel the characters should avoid anachronistic language like "Yo dude!" and the narrative itself should avoid imagery and metaphor outside of the frame of reference of the story. "The dragon roared like an express train" doesn't work in an setting where there are no express trains.

Furthermore, what Mark Twain called (in his "Fenimore Cooper's Literary Offenses") "crass stupidities" should not be foisted upon the reader. It is useful to know why nobody can wield a fifty-pound sword, why a horse cannot gallop all day, and how the people who live in castles are actually fed. Most of the obvious problems are deftly dealt with in Poul Anderson's essential essay, "On Thud and Blunder." Diana Wynne-Jones's *A Tough Guide to Fantasyland* should also be read by all practitioners in this field, as an examination of conscience.

Consistency, in general, is a good idea. If your hero wields a broadsword and wears only a fur jockstrap, either he stole the sword from more advanced folks or else he is an exhibitionistic lunatic. The technology which produces broadswords also produces armor.

There's another of my favorites, which came to my attention once when I reviewed three generic fantasy novels together. In two of them, within the first forty pages, the Fellowship of the Good Guys, deep in enemy country and hotly pursued by Evil Awful Big Nasty Things, stops to cook supper around a *campfire*. One wonders: have these writers ever been in the woods at night? Do they have any idea why three on a match is unlucky?

So I suppose it's another bit of sound advice for epic fantasy writers that you should not write about the outdoors unless you have actually been there.

IV.

But all this sage advice applies just as well to writers of historical novels. What Alec Austin barely touches upon are the two *essential* ingredients to any Epic Fantasy. They are "Epic" and "Fantasy."

My high school English teacher, Mr. Bowen, a diehard Modernist who despised imaginative fiction and would probably be horrified to learn the effect of his teachings on me, gave me a very clear idea of what an epic is, quite early. It's more than something that's just big, big, BIG! It has specific conventions. I think we were talking about the ridicule of these conventions in Alexander Pope's mock-epic, "The Rape fo the Lock," but there they were. You start out with an invocation to the Powers, the Muse or the gods. There's an epic hero, who goes on an epic journey, for something that really matters. There is a descent into the underworld. And so on. The course of the story defines a culture. Part of the purpose of the *Iliad* is to explain to the Greeks in the audience *who they are.* The catalogue of ships was thus very important to the hearers, because everybody could point out their ancestors and towns and define themselves thereby. This tends to be lost on modern cultures, though with some accuracy it has been said that the Civil War is the American *Iliad.* A lot of Americans point to their Civil War ancestors. (I am descended through my mother's grandmother from the Confederate Cavalry raider John Hunt Morgan. This was a deep, dark secret when she was growing up in Ohio, because Union sympathies prevailed, but there it is. The contemporaneous ancestor on my father's side was a draft-dodger.)

Definition in an epic is more than just political or anthropological. *Beowulf* defines, to the Anglo-Saxons, where men stand in relation to God and Fate, what duties are owed to one's lord, and so on. An epic is about the hero confronting the universe and his place in it.

When I wrote my first novel, *The White Isle* about 1975 (published, 1980, revised 1990), I was very consciously writing an epic. There's even an invocation, like the *Hwaet!* in *Beowulf,* followed by a funeral, war, romance, death-of-the-beloved, a journey to the End of The Earth (which was flat and had an edge), a descent into the land of the dead, a confrontation with the god of death...and then things *knowingly* took a strange, new course, because the actual premise of the book was *what if the epic hero fails to live up to his role?* What if Beowulf had been just a little too selfish and screwed up?

My point is simply this: *The Lord of the Rings* is not about Gondorian politics, the intriguing of Denethor to prevent the return of the rightful king and the loss of his own job, nor does it stand or fall on logistical details (though Tolkien, to his credit, is well aware of the questing hero's need for supplies), or (in the movie version at least) the eternal mystery of why Legolas the Elf never runs out of arrows. No, it's about the magic ring and its effect on the bearers, about deep evil from the dawn of time, and the intrusion of numinous beings into human affairs. Similarly, Ursula Le Guin's *A Wizard of Earthsea* is all-well-and-good as *faux*-anthropology about island cultures, but it becomes something more interesting when Ged calls up a spirit from the land of the dead, which then haunts him as a literal "shadow of pride," and which, in the end, he must absorb into himself. If I may cite another example from my own effusions, I didn't write *The Shattered Goddess,* set a million years hence, as a speculation on the future of technology-turned-into-magic. I started with the vast corpse of the Earth's last divinity, fallen from the sky and now buried under a mountain, where random miracles and magic still sputter off the sacred Bones like the last sparks of a dying fire. That's a myth-image, which defines the condition of the characters in their universe. The setting itself, an antique, crumbling city at the end of time is also a myth-image, though I at least took care to place it on a river and have cultivated fields in the surrounding countryside.

This remains the crux of the matter. What you do in epic or mythic fantasy is avoid crass stupidities in the realistic details and then get on with what the story is *actually about.* Sometimes, as in David Lindsay's *A Voyage to Arcturus,* the question of realistic detail is pretty much sidestepped. It is useless to try to work out the ecology of Lindsay's planet, or to explain the physical transformations the hero undergoes in biological terms. It's a gnostic allegory. These are mystical transformations. Something similar, but a lot more orthodox, is going on in C. S. Lewis's *Out of the Silent Planet* and *Perelandra,* which, despite their interplanetary trappings, are mythic, epic fantasies.

Only once in a great do we get a genuine, mythic epic in science fiction—Gene Wolfe's infinitely rich *The Book of the New Sun* is the outstanding example. But ultimately the mythic element—never mind the dictionary definitions of myth—is a kind of "buzz." You feel it, or else you can't, and if you can't, no amount of explaining will ever make it so.

This is what an epic fantasy good. It is what defines "quality" in the form. One writes fantasy in order to address elements of myth *directly,* not just metaphorically as a mainstream novel—*Ulysses,* for example—could do. It's not about statecraft or how to ride a horse or the ecology of dragons. It's about Fate, about pushing beyond the limits of human experience to confront the gods and demand an explanation for the world's pain, about shaping the world or unmaking it.

The subject-matter is supernatural, mystical, and religious. It's about letting primal dream-stuff become concrete. *A Wizard of Earthsea* may ultimately teach you something about sailing boats, but it is that phantom self, manifesting itself nearer and near to where Ged has just been or is about to arrive, which makes the book resonate deeply in our psyche.

So, yes, I agree with everything Alec Austin says, but if you're not interested in *more* than that, why not just write an honest historical?

X.

THE USES OF FANTASY, WHICH MIGHT ALSO BE ENTITLED: HOW TO BE A FANTASY WRITER IN ONE EASY LESSON (WITH NUMEROUS SUB-LESSONS OF NO VAST DIFFICULTY)

A Speech Delivered at The Write Stuff, the Greater Lehigh Valley Writers Conference, April 28, 2001

I.

Okay, this is the part of the conference where you are expecting me to perform miracles. Apparitions, conjurations, and perhaps a dragon are in order. But I am not going to channel your great Aunt Millie from the Beyond and tell you all sorts of amazing things about yourself that you didn't even know until I sneakily coaxed them out of you. *That* sort of supernaturalism works according to extremely old and well-known principles, and is perhaps more the province of crime fiction.

What I want to talk about is Fantasy, the fiction of the unreal. This has been around for a long time too, although it is not as old as what I have described above. The credo of any fantasy writer was ably stated by the second-century writer Lucian of Samosata (author of the "True History," which is anything but, and involves a flight to the moon, and an adventure on cheese islands in an ocean of milk), who prefaced his fabulations thus:

> The one and only truth you'll hear from me is that I *am* lying.... I am writing about things I neither saw, nor heard from another soul, things which don't

exist and couldn't possibly exist. So readers beware: don't believe any of it.

Not inappropriately, Lucian also wrote a piece called "Alexander the Quack Prophet," an exposé of a fake medium and cult-founder, whose activities are not at all strange to modern readers, though some of the specific details and techniques may have changed.

So if you have come to write about your true psychic experiences or how you were given a nasty rectal exam by little grey men aboard a flying saucer, you are in the wrong class. We are all acknowledged liars here.

We distinguish fantasy from mythology by Lucian's explicit contract between himself and his readers. The story is openly admitted to be made up. The works of Homer, or *Genesis*, or the *Bhagavad-Gita* are mythology. They were intended, on some level, to be believed, and, indeed, there are still people who believe them, though the tribe of Homeric fundamentalists, who insist the Indian Ocean is landlocked because the Poet said so, must be vanishingly small by now. But Lucian never expected to be believed, nor did his near contemporary, Lucius Apuleius, whose *The Golden Ass* may be a bit more episodic than most modern editors will stand for, but is otherwise an excellent fantasy novel in the modern sense. It is a story. It is made up, containing things which are not true, and which the author does not claim to be true. A man cannot be changed into a donkey through the misapplication of magic potions. Levitating witches do not drift into a traveler's hotel room and cut out his heart, replacing it with a sponge so that he doesn't even know he's dead until the following morning when he drinks water and the sponge gets wet and falls out. That doesn't happen in real life.

Fantasy distinguishes itself from other forms of fiction by these explicitly unreal elements, which are not "symbolic," hallucinatory, or fraudulent within the context of the story. There used to exist a species of "weird menace" pulp fiction in which, after scantily-clad ladies endured numerous dire perils and the threat of the Fate Worse Than Death, the Spectral Shape always turned out to be a murderer under a sheet or Mad Uncle Elmo in a monster costume. However ridiculous the situations in many of those stories, this is not what we mean by fantasy, and not what Lucian and Apuleius meant by it either. It is not what Shakespeare meant when he was writing *The Tempest*, or what Tolkien intended by *The Lord of the Rings*. It's nothing I would ever do, except as a joke. I did, after all, once compose a limerick in homage to the spirit of those 1930s "weird menace" pulps:

A killer, who howled at the moon,
exclaimed, on dark night in June,
"Indulge in trite rhymes,
concerning my crimes,
and I'll scrape out your brains with a spoon!"

If you're looking for the poetry workshop, I think you're in the wrong room.

II.

We *all* have a capacity for fantasy. I think that much is inborn. While the Human Genome Project may be over (sort of: they haven't so much deciphered the Book of Life as worked out the table of contents), we still haven't identified the gene for imagination. Nevertheless, you all have imagination. In many people, it is suppressed. We have, particularly in this country, what I call the Protestant Work Ethic of Literature, which holds that only Realism of the grimmest sort may considered Real, Serious Literature, and everything else is frivolous, for children, or, worse yet, *genre*, which means "escapism" and might well give you cooties. God forbid that you actually *enjoy* what you read. That is probably a sin. (The Protestant Work Ethic of Literature eerily echoes the doctrines of Socialist Realism. The Puritan is a close cousin to the Stalinist.)

You were taught this by your English teacher in school. (That is surely one of the first demonstrations, for bright children at least, that much of what adults tell you is suspect.) Such ideology still prevails in mainstream critical circles in *The New York Times Book Review*, and in much of American publishing, which is why John Updike is taken very seriously indeed and, say, Gene Wolfe is not. It has nothing to do with the quality of their writing.

We can blame a lot of this on Henry James (who was not above a ghost story or two in his less stuffy moments), about whom Oscar Wilde once quipped that Mr. Henry James wrote fiction as if it were a painful duty.

As someone else once said, the only people opposed to escapism are jailers.

So, cast wide the prison doors. Escape. Don't be afraid. Throw off the official ideology of Henry James and the mainstream establishment and your high-school English teacher.

I can't actually tell you how. I *hope* I don't need to give you permission. The imagination is, I believe, inborn. It can only be nurtured. Everyone has it, except possibly for a few psychotics or sociopaths, who have lost their humanity. It is as basic as that, as essential as dreaming.

"But what is fantasy *for*?" the uninitiated continue to ask.

"All art," said Wilde, "is quite useless." That is to say, don't look for the answer in simple notions of utility. What is the "use" if the *Pieta* or Leonardo's *The Madonna of the Rocks* or of music by Mozart? What is the "use" of *A Midsummer Night's Dream*?

Fantasy does have some discernable "uses."

It entertains, which is the key to doing anything else in literature. If you cannot hold your audience, nothing else matters. Shakespeare entertains. Even *Finnegans Wake* must entertain *somebody* or else it would not remain in print. Just remember that "entertainment" is a very broad concept, and that which entertains need not be mindless.

At its most utilitarian, fantasy can be allegory or satire. Most of the fantasies of Mark Twain are satires, as are those of Lucian of Samosata. The fantasist uses the imagination to produce caricatures, to highlight some absurdity in human behavior. George Orwell's *Animal Farm* is a very great fantasy and a very great satire, as is Jonathan Swift's *Gulliver's Travels*.

Fantasy can, only incidentally, change the world. It does so as any literature does, but providing images which become the common property of all and influence the thinking of mankind. Swift's work is full of such images. His war between the Big Enders and the Little Enders (factions which disagree over which end of the egg to break) illuminates for all of us a certain sort of human behavior, and has, perhaps, caused a few politicians somewhere (we can only hope) to pause before starting a war over trivial matters.

Isaac Asimov was very proud of the fact that as a science fiction writer, he had changed the world. (Science fiction is, for purposes of the present discussion, a subset of fantasy, the difference being that in SF the unreal element of the story could, we at least pretend, become possible someday and is amenable to human reason.) He had added the word "robotics" to the language. His Three Laws of Robotics have had a profound effect on how robots are actually built. Many leading roboticists have chosen their field of endeavor precisely because they grew up reading the works of Isaac Asimov.

But that is only incidental. Asimov wasn't thinking to change the world when he wrote his first robot story at age twenty. If you deliberately set out to change the world, chances are you're going to fail, and not write very good fantasy either. The uses of the imagination are more subtle than that.

At its most boring, fantasy can be used for allegorical instruction. I never cared very much for *Everyman*, much less *The Pilgrim's Progress*, and I suspect you wouldn't either. Even medieval miracle plays got away from that sort of thing as fast as possible, and started to develop slapstick comedy routines about the difficult wife of Noah who didn't want to get aboard the Ark, and so on.

I think we need to come back to the idea of fantasy as delight. That is the gateway to everything else. Ursula Le Guin, a very great fantasy writer indeed, argues in her 1974 essay, "Why Are Americans Afraid of Dragons?" that the truest answer to the question of the use of fantasy is that it gives pleasure and delight.

The Protestant Work Ethicist cringes.

The "next truest answer," says Le Guin, which will also fail to satisfy the Protestant Work Ethicist (or the Stalinist), is that "the use of imaginative fiction is to deepen your understanding of your world, your fellow men, and your own feelings, and your destiny."

Both are fine answers, but frankly I think the second one is more enlightening. There *are* after all people who derive pleasure and delight from things the rest of us might not enjoy at all, or even approve of. A miser derives pleasure and delight from counting money. A sadist does so by inflicting pain on others. There may well be someone out there who is really *into* watching paint dry.

Later on in the same essay, Le Guin gets to the heart of the matter:

> ...fantasy is true, of course. It isn't factual, but it is true. Children know that. Adults know it too, and that is precisely why many of them are afraid of fantasy. They know that its truth challenges, even threatens, all that is false, all that is phony, unnecessary, and trivial in the life they have let themselves be forced into living. They're afraid of dragons because they're afraid of freedom.

Again remember that only jailers are opposed to escape.

What then is fantasy *for*? It's for writing about the big issues. It's where you go when you want to write about courage, honor, memory, identity, power, forgiveness, free will vs. predestination, and so forth. (Most of these themes you'll find in *The Tempest* or any great fantasy.) It is basically where you speak the things that are truer than merely factual. Its function is to produce those great images which inform all our thinking: Swift's Gulliver tied down by Lilliputians, Prospero drowning his book, Faustus making his bargain with Mephistopheles, Bilbo on his quest to Mount Doom, or even Le Guin's Wizard of Earthsea pridefully summoning the Shadow out of the land of the dead and dealing with the consequences.

III.

Now this is supposed to be a writers' conference, so I am expected to offer practical advice.

I cannot make you a fantasist anymore than I can make you a writer, but if you *are* one—and you know if you are, even if, perhaps, you are not yet willing to admit it—then I can erect some useful signposts. These are, to quote another great fantasist, the ghost-story writer M. R. James (no relation to Henry) to so much rules as "characteristics observed to accompany success."

The first is that you must learn by example. Literature is a culture you immerse yourself into. It is not at all "natural," in the sense that there are natural basketball players who just have the knack from the start. Possibly pro basketball players, remembering all the hours they've spent practicing, would vehemently disagree with that too. Certainly when I had a student once, who said he had read almost nothing, didn't care to read much of anything, and yet proposed to be a "natural" fiction writer, I could only shake my head sadly after I had recovered from my initial amazement.

If you're going to write fantasy, you have to read it. You have to read the good stuff too, not eighth-generation knockoffs of the Really Too Long to Read Trilogy or books based on role-playing games. Here is a list of names, by no means complete. You should explore the works of the following, just to check out the possibilities: J. R. R. Tolkien, Ursula Le Guin, Mervyn Peake, Avram Davidson, Lord Dunsany, John Collier, Peter S. Beagle, T. H. White, James Branch Cabell, Neil Gaiman, Edgar Allen Poe, Lucius Apuleius, L. Sprague de Camp and Fletcher Pratt, Franz Kafka, Jorge Luis Borges, H. Rider Haggard, Jonathan Swift, H. P. Lovecraft, Fritz Leiber, Harlan Ellison, Shirley Jackson, M. R. James, Jonathan Carroll, Lewis Carroll (no relation), J. G. Ballard, and, last but not least, William Shakespeare. That's only a beginning, but it should keep you busy for a season or two.

The next observation is that good writing is good writing by any standard. In some of the genres (techno-thrillers, detective fiction, westerns, romance, science fiction, heroic fantasy) there is a tendency to make excuses for bad writing as long as the content of the story is what the reader is hoping for all along, be it spies, murder, cowboys, meeting Mr. Right, alien planets, or muscle-bound swordsmen smiting eldritch monstrosities amid the haunted, cyclopean ruins of old Atlantis.

This will never do. You have to know what point of view is, how to use language, how to set and pace a scene, how to introduce needed information into he story without stopping to lecture—in short, you need all the tricks *any* writer needs. This is why a course on writing fantastic fiction sounds, once you get beyond the introductory lecture, very much like a course on writing fiction generally. Think of *story* as being a vast tree. You have to work your way up the trunk first. Specialization only occurs in the branches. If you don't get that high, it doesn't matter whether you're writing about dragons or adultery on a college campus. And—this is a point a lot of would-be writers have a lot of trouble with—if you haven't mastered the basics, when you send your story to an editor, you will never get to the point where such factors as individual opinion, taste, or editorial policy come into play.

The fantasy writer needs a copy of *The Elements of Style* on the shelf in the office like anyone else.

Further, paradoxically, it is important to remember that in fantasy, more than in other sorts of fiction, you need some element of realism. That does not merely mean that your knight, riding off to slay a dragon, must know something about horsemanship (and you should know something about the discomforts of wearing armor), but that you, as author, must take your imagination seriously for the course of the story. To a character living in Middle Earth, what we call the fantastic is part of everyday life. Make it so. Make it believable. Play around with the characters' "everybody knows" assumptions to change the rules of how the world works. The best way to learn to do this is by reading texts written from radically different cultural viewpoints. Observe how normal human emotions work in a context very different from our own. (Two of my favorites that I recommend are *The Lives of the Twelve Caesars* by Suetonius and *Magic and Mystery in Tibet* by Alexandra David-Neel.)

What you must *not* do is take the attitude, "Oh this is just fantasy, so anything can happen. I don't have to worry about the details." The late John Gardner, author of *Grendel*, doomed himself to a very minor place in the history of fantastic literature for just that reason. He punctured his fantasies over and over again with anachronistic, often irrelevant details, which remind the reader over and over again, "This is just a story. Don't take it seriously." So we don't. (Just between you and me, I think Gardner's one great book is not *Grendel* but *Freddy's Book*, which is about the very process of making things up and manages to take the imagination itself, if not the imagined, a lot more seriously than is usual for this author. *Freddy's Book* will be remembered in a couple generations by fantasy-specialist readers who will ask, "Did he ever write anything else?")

And, most importantly of all, fantasy has to touch down in the real world through the emotions of the characters. If your characters cannot experience the real pains, doubts, fears, passions, and longings of real human beings, then it doesn't matter how impressively your wizards intone their spells or how many neat details you can work into your haunted castle. Without real emotions, nothing works. Nothing matters.

My best-known book is called *The Mask of the Sorcerer*. You can get it from the Science Fiction Book Club. Jokingly, echoing Arthur Machen's claim that his *The Hill of Dreams* was "a *Robinson Crusoe* of the soul," I suggested that I was writing a *Huckleberry Finn* of the soul.

I wasn't quite kidding. It *is* a story about a boy uprooted from childhood and forced to take a jo`urney, in which he learns much and discovers what is important within himself. My hero is the son of a notorious, quite dreadful sorcerer, but, rather like the younger Corleone in *The Godfather*, he is the one the father has set aside to be "normal" and live outside of the family business. As in *The Godfather*, things don't work out that way. It seems that if you kill a sorcerer, you *become* that sorcerer. The sorcerer, and everyone *he* has ever murdered, and everyone *they* have ever murdered (though like diminishing echoes) come alive inside your head. You become a multiple personality. Your name is Legion, and most of the members are pretty sinister. Pressed by enemies, the father sacrifices his hopes for his son, and arranges patricide. Now the father is alive inside the boy's head, still pursued by those same enemies, and the boy must struggle to master sorcery so that he doesn't become a mere addition to someone else's collection. But he also has to struggle to *avoid* becoming what his father was. He has to maintain some sense of decency and self-worth, not to mention self-identity, despite everything. To make matters worse, he ceases to age. He will be physically fifteen forever, in this condition.

I hope it is too early to say that *The Mask of the Sorcerer* is my *magnum opus*, but it certainly was, as I was writing it, a book about everything. People who ask, "When are you going to write something *serious*?" do not deserve an answer.

This was a book about a boy who both fears and tries to love his father, but cannot understand him. It's about a father, drowning in his own vile career, who still loves his son, but selfishly sacrifices even that love. It's about fear of becoming something other than you want to be. My hero wants to be "normal." He wants to get this immediate trouble "over with" so he can get back to his "regular" life. But meanwhile his friends reject and fear him, and his predicament is all the more obvious as they physically mature and he doesn't.

Paradoxically, this is a book about growing up. The character has to come to terms with what he is, even as we do, as we age. We cannot cling to what we were at fifteen or twenty or thirty. Somewhere in middle age we look at ourselves and say, "This is what I have become." But we can't cling to middle age either. We keep on changing.

I had to attempt to make all that real, in order to make the book real. Love, or any kind of human connection, becomes problematic for my hapless hero, but the need for such a connection is made all the more poignant.

Without that kind of emotional grounding, with out the events in the story being that intimately personal and personally essential to the characters who experience them, then the magical conjurations, the shambling corpses (my book is rather thick with shambling corpses), the battle scenes, the eerie crocodile-headed messengers of the Death God, and everything else in the book simply do not matter. They are no more than pretty, painted backdrop for a play that fails to engage our interest.

If my book has any merit, that is why.

And so I have just told you everything I know about writing fantasy. Go and write some yourself. Thank you.

XI.

DIAMONDS IN THE PULP-HEAP

I've been buying pulps on eBay of late. *Argosy* mostly, the celebrated weekly pulp magazine, which gave readers their regular dose of western, adventure, sport, detective, jungle, historical, and fantastic fiction for decades, and is now most remembered for its associations with Edgar Rice Burroughs and A. Merritt. One of the secrets of collecting in our field is that while old copies of *Weird Tales* or the Gernsback *Amazing* will dazzle the folks on eBay and go for absurd prices, the reverse can also be true. The 1930s *Argosy* that costs $35 at the Worldcon might go for $3.99 on eBay. At those prices you can have a "fishing expedition," buying issues at random for possibly unknown and certainly unfamous contents.

The level of writing *Argosy* is quite high. This will come as a revelation to some. Most of us in the science fiction field have read only stories from *science fiction* pulps, where, for a good deal of the 1920s, '30s, and even (in the lesser magazines at least) into the '40s, most of the writers were amateurs, whose command of prose style or narrative technique was, quite frankly, nowhere near the level of, say, a Max Brand western. *Argosy*, which paid better and more reliably than anything Hugo Gernsback ever touched his hand to, tended to hire professionals.

The absolute aristocrats of the pulps in those days were *Blue Book* and *Adventure*, which pretty much insisted, according to the tastes of the time, on realism. Authentic detail. Nothing too farfetched. The entertaining thing about *Argosy*, particularly toward the end of the '30s, was that its fiction could at times get a little crazy. Certainly if Indiana Jones had existed as a pulp-magazine character, he would have appeared in *Argosy*, alongside Peter the Brazen, Singapore Sammy, and No-Shirt McGee. There were any number of stories about pith-helmeted heroes finding wondrous things in crumbling temples amid dense jungles.

Argosy published a good deal of outright science fiction, by Edgar Rice Burroughs, Ralph Milne Farley, Murray Leinster, Ray Cummings, and, toward the end of the period, Jack Williamson. There's also a lot of wild-and-wooly stuff like "Locusts from Asia" by Joel Townsley Rogers (April 17-24, 1937), of which I presently only have the first installment, which seems to be about fleets of ghostly German biplanes issuing forth from Tibet.

Then there's a good deal of what an only be described as alarmist fiction, published in the immediate run-up to World War II, in which America is menaced or even conquered by invading Asiatics or Fascists, with or without the help of traitors from within—rather like *Operator 5* only better written. (The cover blurb for "The Sun Sets at 5," the first part of a serial by Borden Chase, March 4, 1940, reads: "Smooth Kyle returns! To beat the Bunds and smash the Swastika, to make America safe for Americans.") Most extreme is a whole series by Arthur Leo Zagat about a post-holocaust Tarzan named Dikar who battles the Japanese in the ruins of the USA with bow-and-arrow while dressed in a loincloth. (Cover blurb for "Tomorrow," May 27, 1939: "Will your children walk in chains as slaves of the Yellow Horde?")

Argosy was like a television network, which reflected and played to the fears and dreams of its audience.

Intriguingly, toward the end of *Argosy*'s pulp existence (it turned into a largely non-fiction, slick, men's magazine in the mid-'40s) there appeared quite a few interesting short fantasies, which were less formulaic, and more literary that what you'd expect from the magazine that gave the world *The Insect Invasion* by Ray Cummings.

"Till Doomsday" by Richard Sale, featured on the cover of the March 9, 1940 issue, is a supernatural sea story about the Flying Dutchman. It wouldn't have been out of place in *Weird Tales*. (Except that Sale was an *Argosy* regular and *Argosy* paid better.)

My random delvings also turned up "The Devil in Hollywood" by Dale Clark (August 8, 1936). Startling. About an obsessive Hollywood director, clearly based on Erich Von Stroheim, who makes a film so decadent, so intense, that the Devil Himself appears in it. Quite a lot of sexual tension right below the surface of this one.

A bit less forgotten are a whole series of charming, *Unknown Worlds*-style fantasies by Robert Arthur, circa 1940. Some of these ("Postpaid to Paradise" etc.) were reprinted in *F&SF* in the early 1950s.

But the story that impressed me the most so far is in the September 3, 1938 issue. The cover shows a European man in an Arab headdress, scowling as he peeps around the arch of a stone doorway and aims a pistol: "Dale Harden follows—THE ROAD TO DAMASCUS."

Inside is something else again, "Karpen the Jew" by Robert Neal Leath, an unfamiliar byline. It's a powerfully written short story, which at first might make the modern reader a little queasy, because pulps were sometimes pretty bad about ethnic stereotyping. The narrator, a reporter, has made the acquaintance of Silverstein, the executioner at San Quentin. Silverstein comes to him in a condition of some shock, because he'd *tried* to execute Karpen the Jew in the gas chamber that morning, but the man just sat calmly and refused to die. Karpen was condemned for the apparently random killing a leading industrialist.

We soon get to meet Karpen, a powerfully built, bald-headed man of indeterminate age, who seems to have preternatural knowledge of what the narrator is thinking. His presence is decidedly *creepy,* and this creepiness is conveyed with great skill.

In case you haven't guessed, Karpen is in fact the Wandering Jew, condemned to deathlessness because he refused to grant Christ a moment's rest on the way to Calvary. Karpen has been spending the time, grimly, in the service of mankind, trying to prevent wars by killing those responsible for starting them. We are taken to a meeting of the German, Japanese, Italian, and Soviet ambassadors and an American steel magnate, who all agree, like gentlemen setting up a chess tournament, that it's time to start another war for their mutual benefit. The first three are, of course, Fascists. The Soviet dictator (not named) needs an external threat to distract his people from their suffering. The steel magnate (whom Karpen hurls out the window to his death by the time the scene is over) thinks it will be good for business. The story itself turns into an impassioned plea for peace, written, we must remember, in a darkening world, after *Kristallnacht*, and published a little before the Munich Conference.

The narrator was fourteen in 1918. He wore a Boy Scout uniform, sold war bonds, and waved a flag. He couldn't know what war is *really* about, Karpen tells him. Only the men ground to bits in the trenches could know that.

Karpen ultimately suggests that the way to end war is to make a law which forces every leader who agrees to participate in a war to actually go out and fight in it, regardless of his age or physical condition. Put the politicians in the way of machine-gun fire and there would be fewer wars. Of course this is completely naive. It isn't going to happen. Surely Leath knew that, as did his reporter character and as did Karpen the Jew, whose task, down the ages, may be hopeless. It's as quaint and pathetic a notion as the sort of conspiratorial belief that would *seriously* accept that World War II was about to consume tens of millions of lives because five men got together in a hotel room in San Francisco and agreed that it should.

But it's all the more heartfelt for that. What an amazing thing to find in *Argosy,* the magazine of two-fisted sailors, dead-shot cowboys, heroic French Foreign Legionaries, and Tarzan of the Apes.

This is a story that should be appreciated in context. It was reprinted once, in the first issue of *Famous Fantastic Mysteries*, a magazine created by the publisher of *Argosy* to recycle the magazine's rich lode of fantastic fiction for the growing, specialized, genre audience that bought *Astounding Science Fiction* or *Thrilling Wonder Stories.*

The September 1939 *Famous Fantastic Mysteries* would have gone on sale about the first of August, 1939, at which point no pulp story could have been more timely or urgent than "Karpen the Jew." By the time the issue went off-sale, Hitler had invaded Poland, and no story was more tragically dated.

It's still fascinating, as a message-in-a-bottle from a desperate time.

XII.

The Real Secret of 100% Formula Fiction

Fans, convention panelists, and even serious critics tend to speak disparagingly of the old-time SF pulps as being filled with "formula fiction"—the common cant of the highbrow critics of the day in condemning *all* pulp fiction—without, very likely, ever having read any of it.

What exactly *is* a formula story? What does it do? What does it not do? Did such things really exist in the bad old days? Do they still exist now?

To answer my next-to-last question first, yes, pulp formula fiction definitely existed. It might be useful to examine a genuine specimen.

On exhibit, then, is "Power Pit 13" by Edmond Hamilton, originally published in (and as far as I can tell never reprinted from) *Thrilling Adventures* for February 1938. It's a science-fiction story, published at a time when the Thrilling group of magazines had recently acquired Hugo Gernsback's failed *Wonder Stories* and redubbed it with that clunkiest of all (formulaic) titles, *Thrilling Wonder Stories*, so it would fit right in with *Thrilling Western*, *Thrilling Mystery*, and so on. The crossover is an obvious attempt to show readers of *Thrilling Adventure* what (largely familiar) delights awaited them in *Thrilling Wonder*. There is a plug for *TWS* at the end of the story.

All of the Thrilling magazines required formula fiction, much more so than most other pulps of the time. The formula was pretty much the same in all titles, so, indeed, a *Thrilling Adventures* reader could pick up *Thrilling Wonder Stories* without being too disoriented. That was, commercially, the whole point.

At the simplest level, a formula story was paint-by-the-numbers writing. It is not a rumor—there really *was* a product available in those days, which consisted of a series of cardboard wheels with which you could line up situations and characters and come up with completely "new" pulp stories, changing the hero from a sailor to a cowboy to a flying ace, or whatever, as needed. Today, software will do the same thing. Then as now, I suspect, such devices were more the province of the amateur rather than the working professional. A real pro could do that sort of thing in his head.

Consider "Power Pit 13." The characters are introduced in a purely formulaic manner:

> Smith Ballard hunched his powerful shoulders over his desk, gripping the radiophone crushingly in his big, calloused hands. The forty-year-old superintendent's granite-jawed face was hard as rock as he savagely jabbed the call-button.

A formula-pulp story introduces characters by physical description. Adjectives and adverbs are larded on as a kind of shorthand, to avoid the need for more detailed, or naturalistic description. Descriptions of jaws, which are either square or granite or both, to show strength of character, are pretty much *de rigueur*. We see here a distinct, standard pulp *style*, recognizable from a single paragraph. This is exactly what Lovecraft used to warn his correspondents against, arguing that if you habitually wrote this way, serious literary effort would become impossible. (Lovecraft's advice was not to read pulp magazines. He felt that he himself had been contaminated by them.)

Notice how unutterably *ancient* Superintendent Ballard is. He is, wow, *forty*, a veritable Methuselah in the eyes of *Thrilling Adventure*'s mostly teenaged readership, a grizzled veteran at whatever he is given to superintending.

The author must now introduce a younger cast. Family matters are seldom dealt with in pulp stories, which is one reason why so many pulp scientists seem to be widowers, with no one else to look after their beautiful daughters (a.k.a. Love Interest, the Prize for the hero at the end of the story). Superintendent Ballard is more of an engineer than a scientist, but sure enough, in the next paragraph:

> Behind him in the little office stood Jean Ballard, his daughter, a boyish figure in her khaki shirt and breeches.

But a "girl" can no more be the hero of a story like this than can a forty-year-old, so, right on cue in paragraph three we get:

> Her delicately tanned, sensitive face and fine
> grey eyes were strained with worry. Hovering in the
> background was Mark Leighton, supply-clerk, his
> dark young face sick with apprehension.

Not a square-jawed, blond-haired, blue-eyed sort. This guy obviously has problems, whereon hangs the tale.

"Power Pit 13" actually contains some quite interesting *ideas* for its time. It's about a wild and crazy concept—geothermal power. The Power Pit, of which Superintendent Ballard is in charge, is one of many sunk into the Earth's magma, from which infinite, and apparently economical power is drawn from the planet's molten subsurface. The science is admittedly dubious. The power station *itself* is fifteen miles underground, where technicians sit in cramped control rooms, "refrigerated by cooling machinery above." Wouldn't the energy expended keeping the place cool perhaps equal the amount of energy extracted of the operation?

But never mind that. There's even a second, quite interesting notion, though it is merely used to rev up the melodrama. This geothermal power is desperately needed to operate pumps which are all that prevent coastal cities from being flooded. Apparently the oceans have risen. Global warming? In any case, if the power-grid goes down, thousands might die. A crisis is at hand.

So, why isn't this story as famous as Lester del Rey's "Nerves" or Heinlein's "Blowups Happen," which appeared a few years later? It can't entirely be because they were published in *Astounding*, which science fiction readers and historians paid attention to, as opposed to *Thrilling Adventures* which they did not.

The answer is simply this: formula. It soon becomes apparent that for all Mark Leighton may yearn after Jean Ballard, her father disapproves. Not being sufficiently granite-jawed, young Mark is a bit of a wimp. (This may be the only emotional honesty in the whole story. Mark is the reader-identification character. The nerdy kid reading this is not a mineral-jawed, proto-Doc Savage. He is more like Mark.) The elder Ballard regards him with contempt because when Mark was in charge of the pit operations, a nasty "accident" happened, workers were killed, and it seemed to be Mark's fault, because he had incorrectly calculated stresses on some girders. That has brought on the current crisis. Workers are deserting their posts for fear the place is jinxed. Mark himself has the heebie-jeebies as a result of guilt over his experience, and cannot bring himself to descend into the pit.

I think you already know how this one is going to end. Any pulp-reader or television-watcher knows *perfectly well* how it's going to end. (Indeed, most of the pulp formulas moved over very neatly to television in the early '50s. So did many of the writers.)

If you think that young Mark will overcome his phobia, then redeem himself by saving the Power Pit, the father, and the daughter, and marry the daughter at the end, you *win a prize*, which is permission to skim to the end of the story. Yes, you have read this one before.

It's the old Disgraced Boyfriend plot. It could just as readily be about a cowboy who lost his nerve during a stampede, a sailor who wrecked a ship during a storm.... Reach for the plot wheel. That's what it was made for.

The rest of actual the idea-content of the story (the science-fiction part) hovers between sense-of-wondrous and a downright silly. No, Mark Leighton did *not* screw up. The girder collapsed and those men were killed because there is a race of humanoid beings living in the Earth's magma, who resent such intrusions into their environment. *They* cut through the girder with a diamond-toothed saw. They are silicon-based rather than carbon-based, a whole new order of living things, and obviously intelligent, despite which all our hero can do is blast some of them with tubes of liquid refrigerant while saving the father and getting the girl. The story has a couple of mildly exciting moments, but ends exactly where you expect it to. If this had been the one about the cowboy and the stampede, it would have to be revealed that our self-doubting hero's cattle-management skills were not faulty after all, but that rustlers (or another cowboy, who is his rival for the girl) spooked the herd. Same difference. The hero recovers his confidence, Proves Himself a Man, the Girl sobs in his manly arms, and things conclude with the traditional affirmation:

> The old man added anxiously, "Are you all right down there? Is this Leighton I am talking to?"
> "We're all right," Mark told him. "And you're talking to Leighton, yes,—*Engineer* Leighton!"

I bet that paid Edmond Hamilton's grocery bills for at least a week. Remember that the Thrilling group paid half a cent a word to most writers. The story is about 3000 words long, so that's fifteen bucks in an era when office workers would be glad to get fifteen dollars a week—*if* they had a job. So this little finger-exercise was worth a week's salary in real, working-stiff figures.

To be fair, Hamilton could be a much better writer when he chose. He wrote a great deal of formula fiction, his science fiction settling into four basic types: 1) the Mad Scientist Threatens the World with the Giant Blob story, 2) The Lone Hero defeats the Tur- tle-Men from the Moon story, 3) the generic space opera, and 4) Lost Race variants, usually featuring an international cast of charac- ters (including two-fisted Irishman) who discover the Incredible Se- cret of the Lost Valley. Later in his career, Hamilton dropped the mad scientist and the invading turtle-men and produced fairly re- spectable versions of the other two, *The Valley of Creation* (*Star- tling Stories*, 1948) and *The Star Kings* (*Amazing*, 1947), which had extended afterlives in book form. Indeed, *The Star Kings* is still in print. But what made Hamilton *good* was that he would, every once in a while, step outside of formula altogether and produce a story like "He That Hath Wings" or "What's It Like Out There?" Like his colleague and friend Jack Williamson, he continued to grow and change with the times, and so was still publishing into the late '60s. The collection *The Best of Edmond Hamilton* (Ballantine, 1977) is very much worth reading.

But he did a *lot* of formula work, like most pulp-writers. The question arises, why did he do it and why did magazines want it, when formula stories are, by their very nature, less satisfying. Once you know, "Oh yeah, the disgraced boyfriend again," you really *can* skim to the end and not miss anything.

The answer has to be that, for the writer, it was an easy way to crank out more and more stories faster than one could genuinely think and feel them into existence. There *is* some thought-content here, but what Hamilton did was take his novel ideas about geo- thermal power and subterranean races and plug them in to an al- ready-existing template. When science fiction got good, when the stories became worth rereading and reprinting, it did so precisely because writers began to abandon formula. Within less than ten years, the SF corpus would include such masterpieces as Kuttner- Moore's "Vintage Season" (1946) and Sturgeon's "Thunder and Roses" (1947) which have real characters and real emotions in them, not something you could get off a plot wheel.

Formula fiction was a boon for lazy writers, and the reason they got away with it has to be that lazy readers wanted it. A story like "Power Pit 13" might make you think, at least momentarily, but it won't make you *feel*. This is one of the reasons for all the modifiers and the physical descriptions. You're not going to genuinely experience the emotional tension between the three characters, so you have to be *told* about it. A non-formula story doesn't need to tag the characters with descriptions of complexions and jaw-lines. If they have personalities and real feelings, the reader will be able to tell them apart readily enough.

What we must conclude is that the formula story wasn't so much a substitute for "idea" content as it was a substitute for honest emotion. Certainly in the 1930s, most science-fiction readers (and pulp readers generally) felt threatened by honest emotion. "Thunder and Roses" in *Thrilling Wonder Stories* in 1938 would have been incomprehensible—and very unpopular. It had, after all, only been four years since the teenaged editor Charles Hornig had manfully turned down Stanley Weinbaum's *The Black Flame* from the bottom-of-the-bucket market *Wonder Stories* because the story was motivated by—gasp! horrors!—the emotional needs of the characters. "Our readers feel that love is a sign of weakness in a man," wrote Hornig, and very likely a lot of them did. *The Black Flame*, a ridiculously adolescent story today, was too "hot" to be published at the time, and only came out in 1939, in a wave of nostalgia three years after Weinbaum's death.

Yet even *The Black Flame* helped post-Gernsbackian science fiction grow up, by raising its level from something that might appeal to a nerdy twelve-year-old to something that might (seductively, even) intrigue a more emotionally-curious, if still insecure fourteen-year-old. *The Black Flame* helped pulp science-fiction *enter* adolescence. "Vintage Season" and "Thunder and Roses" helped it emerge into adulthood. Considering that all this happened in less than a decade, it must have been a dizzying development.

But "Power Pit 13" did no more than fill pages in a forgotten pulp-magazine, just one more formula story, a piece of shorthand, which saved the writer *and the reader* the trouble and emotional involvement of dealing with the real thing. This kind of stuff gave pulps—and the science fiction field—a reputation that took years to overcome.

And who is to say that formula fiction isn't still with us?

XIII.

What This Story Needs Is a Giant Gorilla: Thoughts on the Pleasures of Formula Fiction

The March 16, 1929 *Argosy* has a typical cowboy cover: our hero, in chaps, has apparently just had his horse shot out from under him, but, nevertheless having recovered his dignity with his Stetson in place, he crouches warily with six-shooter drawn. This illustrates "The Saga of Silver Bend" by J. E. Grinstead ("War in the Cattle Country!"). A little more promising for devotees of the fantastic is another story hyped on the same cover in even larger type, "The Gray God" by J. Allan Dunn ("Sea Seas Treasure!").

Dunn was one of those ubiquitous pulp generalists, now slightly remembered for *The Treasure of Atlantis,* which was reprinted by Centaur Press in 1971. The *Argosy* contents page blurb for "The Gray God" offers "Piracy and South Sea magic."

This novelette looks like the real deal, a genuine print ancestor of an Indiana Jones adventure and the sort of thing which the contemporary public, never having seen an actual pulp magazine, calls "pulp fiction." Does this image have any basis in reality? Consider:

Bob Stanton, two-fisted American adventurer, having found himself stranded in Fiji when a business venture evaporated, has barely held himself above the status of beach bum. He is broke and shabby, but furious when he overhears a tourist refer to him as "T.T.T., Typical Tropical Tramp," though he knows he is little more than that.

One of the first things we find reassuring about this story, other than that Dunn is, in every conventional sense, an extremely good writer with a fine eye for detail and a smooth narrative style, is that our hero is remarkably free of the sort of unquestioned racism often found in old-time pulp. He doesn't want to cheat his mixed-race landlady, knowing she has been patient and kind. He soon falls in with Cheung, a rich Chinese businessman, who could well have (in the hands of a lesser writer) turned into an Octopus of Evil, with tentacles (not to mention sinister agents) everywhere, but is actually an honest and honorable fellow. It is true that all the Chinese characters speak pidgin-English with a lot of "L"s in their words, and this may be politically incorrect by 2005 standards, but I cannot blame Dunn for his suggestion that Chinese who don't speak English very well might indeed sound like the one who reports, having questioned a black-skinned islander, "I saavy. All same I think Tiki talk plopeh."

That last word is "proper."

The aforementioned Tiki, a South Sea islander, stowed away on a vessel now docked in Suva, Fiji. He has become gravely ill, and cannot work to pay his way. As he lies shivering and helpless, the ship's mate attempts to beat him to death. Bob Stanton, who chances by, is so outraged by this wanton cruelty that he flattens the mate, rescues Tiki, nurses him back to health, and remarks that he has now acquired an embarrassingly grateful "man Friday."

But he has also made an enemy. The mate was in the employ of the insidious Loo Fong (ah, you were waiting for that....) a half-breed pirate and gangster, much feared in these parts.

Loo Fong is first encountered showing unwholesome interest in The Girl, a.k.a. Lucy Haines, a spunky lass who has journeyed all this way along to find her missing father, who disappeared on a mission for Cheung, involving a fortune in pearls hidden on the lost and fabled island of Motutabu, home of the equally fabled Gray God. Very likely Loo Fong had a hand in the disappearance.

Everything comes together quite neatly. Cheung hires Stanton, advancing him enough to pay off the landlady and buy some decent clothes. His mission is to sail to Motutabu, rescue the elder Haines if possible, and recover the pearls. Off he goes, accompanied by Lucy and Tiki, on a schooner crewed by very competent Chinese sailors who work for Cheung. The night before they leave, there is an attack by Loo Fong's assassins, but things otherwise proceed smoothly. It's a race to Motutabu, as the villain is also headed there.

On the way, Tiki sheds his fawning manner, which would have made him one of those embarrassing sidekicks of old-time fiction, whose function, as someone remarked, could just as readily be served by an intelligent dog. Instead, he regains his dignity. He speaks no English, but the schooner captain (who speaks English badly) is still able to draw out of him the garbled story of the haunted island and the wrathful Gray God. Tiki is in fact the exiled son of a local sorcerer who fell into disgrace with his people because of an earthquake and was killed. Presumably, Tiki Sr. failed to propitiate the god.

The sea-going details are nicely handled. Suspense mounts as the goal draws near. We see the awesome visage on the Gray God (which even Cheung warned our hero to avoid), carven out of the living rock, looming above the island of Motutabu. The elder Haines is discovered, wounded and barely alive after his own schooner was sunk and his crew was murdered by Loo Fong, who was on the island once before, but failed to find the pearls. Now Loo Fong obviously wants out heroes to lead him to the treasure.

The pirates arrive. The story builds toward its climax...and...and...there is a shootout. Cheung's Chinese sailors fight like disciplined infantrymen, but are driven up the mountain, to the very feet of the dread Gray God, where Tiki saves the day, when the secret of the God is revealed at last. Tiki activates one of those cleverly balanced stone mechanisms with which Lost Cities and Forbidden Temples are so often equipped, a bit of pavement flips over, and Loo Fong and a henchman are crushed. This "sacrifice" has now established Tiki has hereditary priest. He is content to stay on the island, having assumed a role of great dignity and importance in his own culture. Everybody else retires to civilization, with the pearls (which Haines had discovered and hidden). Boy gets girl. The end.

This story is interesting, in a literary-archeological sense, for its attitudes. At the same time it was published, Edgar Wallace's venomously racist "Sanders of the River" jungle series was hugely popular, even filmed. By comparison, Dunn was a crusading liberal. His hero Stanton seems to be willing to take people as individuals, good or bad. Loo Fong is rotten through and through, but Cheung is a decent and generous, the Chinese schooner captain is brave and true, and, more importantly, nobody belittles Tiki as a benighted savage. He is seen as an individual, and, at the end, as a clever and successful one.

Ultimately, despite its many virtues, the story wears thin. The narrative is quite gripping, but then Dunn can only serve up a gun-battle, a secret trapdoor, and a sack of pearls. Superficially exciting, but not *special*. What this story needs is a giant gorilla. It occurred to me while reading that the formula Dunn is using is not all that different from that of *King Kong*. The details are different, yes, but we respond in the same way to this story of a varied lot of characters with varied motives (and the required Love Interest) all pressing into the dangerous unknown to uncover the secret of, well, something. It could have been Skull Island, complete with dinosaurs and monster ape. Certainly by the time "The Gray God" appeared, jungle stories, and South Sea adventure stories, not to mention lost race and lost world stories, were a dime a dozen. The makers of *King Kong* certainly knew what they were doing. Once the foreground story has become overly familiar, you must *up the ante* if you are going to hold the audience's attention. Enter the giant gorilla who falls in for the Love Interest and follows her all the way back to New York where he dies swatting biplanes. There is a reason *King Kong* has become something approaching a cultural myth, and "The Gray God" might make an entertaining reprint, but is otherwise forgotten.

It's because Dunn, ultimately, did not deliver something extraordinary. This is what "pulp fiction" or any kind of "popular" fiction is *for.* It is a familiar, sugar-coated method for taking the reader quickly and efficiently somewhere else. But then it has to reveal something special. The detective novel which, after all the hugger-mugger and eccentric characters, ends on a lame, obvious solution to a routine crime, will be forgotten as soon as the book is closed. The space opera, which, upon uncovering the secret of the new planet can only produce (as *Star Trek* often did) a handful of people with funny noses who wear jumpsuits and speak platitudes, is sure to disappoint. If Shakespeare in *Hamlet* or Sophocles in *Oedipus Rex*, after trotting out the contemporary conventions of tragedy for their respective audiences, had then supplied nothing better than the previous version, we would not know their names today. Superior payoff is why *She* and *The Lost World* and a very few other books of that ilk retain their interest, when thousands of imitations are dust. It is why Tolkien will triumph over Terry Brooks.

In a sense, all fiction is formula fiction. There is a hook. The story starts on some point of interest, conflict, or tension. Characters are introduced. Something happens. But somewhere, usually near the end, if the story is to be memorable, it must *stop being formula fiction* and become unique. If the author has any compelling, personal vision, this is the place for it.

The rest is just stagecraft and empty motion. *The Time Machine* begins as a club-adventure story and rapidly turns into something else. *Dracula* is, and was described in its day, as a "mystery." It becomes something else. *The Left Hand of Darkness,* despite its somewhat contrived interplanetary setting, is awfully close to being another lost world novel, until we discover that there's something urgently different about the people our hero finds himself among.

That is what is really meant by "transcending genre." You must deliver the giant gorilla. J. Allan Dunn molders in the pulps because, by and large, he didn't.

XIV.

GIANT ANTS! ONE BAD STORY AND WHAT IT MEANS

The most salient characteristic of pulp fiction, or light fiction of any sort, is that it does not *challenge*. It affirms the prejudices of its readership, and as such gives us an idea of how the people of the time saw themselves and their world. Even the clichés are interesting. In fact, sometimes they are more interesting than the stories.

Good pulp fiction tends to have little flashes of reality in it, no matter how preposterous the plots. In my recent delvings into the Munsey magazines, *Argosy*, and the like—skipping the obvious material, like Edgar Rice Burroughs and A. Merritt that we already know about—I find numerous examples. The actual level of writing is pretty good, though these are obvious signs of haste. Nobody waxes poetic, though some of Max Brand's descriptions in the one western I read came close. But overall, the stories are told in a literate, efficient prose, with a lively, sometimes hyper-active sense of pacing.

Having just edited a mock pulp magazine, a "facsimile" of the April 1933 *Weird Trails the Magazine of Supernatural Cowboy Stories* for Wildside Press, I gravitated quickly to "Ghost Camp" by Donald Barr Chidsey (October 10, 1936), and was disappointed that it was not an actual eldritch cowboy yarn. (In real pulps, supernatural content in westerns was rare, almost a taboo, though *Argosy* published Robert E. Howard's "The Dead Remember" in 1936.) It's set in the present, about an old-time western bad man who used to run a crooked gambling hall in a gold-mining town. He was an anachronism even before he went to prison for plugging one owlhoot too many in "self defense," but now he's escaped, and the story itself is a blazing melodrama replete with a stashed fortune, a lost granddaughter, gangsters, and an impressive body count. But there's one moment that's real: the former king of this deserted town surveying his old domain in a moment of nostalgia, compared to a retired sea captain walking the decks one last time before his ship is broken up for scrap.

Likewise, "Goblin Trail" by one of the great pulp names, J. Allan Dunn (June 15, 1935) is completely over the top, ultimately about a lost volcanic valley in the Canadian arctic inhabited by mammoths and a lost race of Vikings, where a heroic Mountie must venture to Save The Girl from a Madman before the volcano destroys everything at the end of the story (the way such volcanoes always seem to.) There's a lot of "survival of the fittest" borderline racism in this one, but also a certain manly, heroic bond between white man and Eskimo, and seemingly authentic descriptions of the wilderness and how to stay alive there. Either Dunn studied *Nanook of the North* carefully or he'd seen somebody build an igloo, as the hero's faithful Eskimo companion does. Again, a little nugget of reality to anchor the fantasy.

I am considerably less convinced by "Creatures of the Ray" by James L. Aton (October 10, 1925). It's a giant insect story. An inquisitive young reporter is sent to interview the Scientist, Professor Gilreath, who is working on "something big" having to do with radium.

The professor is a typical Scientist. The hero knows the breed:

> I've interviewed more than one of our modern ultra-scientists, and I've found the top-notchers either as hairy as gorillas or else as bald as pumpkins. The gorillas are fiery but unsympathetic; the pumpkins are cold and unpitying. (p. 402)

It would seem that hirsuteness is a gauge of both morality and social grace. Professor Gilreath has neither. He's slugged any number of reporters nosing about his not-quite-secret laboratory (in rural Illinois), but, although he quickly sees through the hero's impersonation of "a brother scientist," he welcomes him as a witness to his greatest triumph:

> Scientist though I am, I have not outgrown certain primitive emotions; among them is the human longing for companionship in a supreme hour. I am yielding to that emotion. I welcome your companionship in this, the great hour of my life. (p. 403)

The Professor worked with radium until he discovered "that the feeble emanations of radium—is beta and gamma rays—were but suggestions of a great, new, all-penetrating, all powerful, yet perfectly controllable force or ray." He goes on a what the reporter finds to be tedious and incomprehensible length on such matters. Everybody knows that scientists talk gobbledygook beyond the comprehension of mere laymen, right? Certainly the Professor does, and doesn't bother to conceal his contempt for the rest of humanity.

That is probably why he plans to destroy the world. He could just turn his ray machine up all the way and annihilate everything for miles around (including a nearby town), but he's up to something more subtle. If he turns up the machine a little bit and leaves it on overnight, the radiation causes living things to get much bigger. Blades of grass grow like bamboo. Ants grow the size of horses, and it is the giant black ants the Professor is interested in. He hopes to communicate with them and help them wipe out mankind and build a utopia of civilized, intelligent ants. Soon the yard outside fills up with the skeletons of cattle, then people, even children, and other townspeople are enslaved by the ants, who apparently have learned to drain them of some blood, save the rest for later, and meanwhile use humans for forced labor. (This and one off-hand reference to Martians suggest the author is lifting a bit from *The War of the Worlds*.) The ants show an unholy interest in wheels, hinged doors, and the possibilities of machinery. This is all fine to the Professor, who proclaims that ants are a superior species, having "wonderful sense, none of man's silly conflicts and warfare, only peaceful communism and cooperation—a oneness of mind and soul that will make war forever impossible." (p. 408)

Never mind creeping bolshevism in the insect kingdom, it would seem that entomology is not the Professor's area of expertise. "They're fighting now!" the hero observes, and indeed they are, because some red ants have also been exposed to the rays and are now locked in ferocious battle with the Professor's pets. He rushes out—like numerous foolish or traitorous scientist types in the movies of subsequent decades—to "reason" with them and is promptly torn to bits. The reporter hero then turns the ray machine up all the way and annihilates everything, including the adjoining town and whatever inhabitants may have survived the ant onslaught. But it's all for the best. The world is saved.

Nobody believes the hero's story. There is a cover-up, about a disaster that destroyed the town, but then a colleague stops by.

"I'm off to Ann Arbor," he said. "Some professor at the college there claims he has a radium ray that will make things grow. I've got to get him."

"Go to it!" I growled. "Get him! Get him with a gun!"

And that's pretty close to what I meant. We've got to put a check on these scientific investigators—before some wild bird hits on the ultimate secret in his laboratory and blows up the earth. (p.409)

What's missing from this picture? Not much, except the beautiful girl to be rescued, who would come aboard when this formula was repeated over and over again in Ray Palmer's *Amazing* around 1940, and the somber intonation of "there are some things man was not meant to know," which comes from Hollywood films of the same period.

Otherwise, here we have in 1925, all the anti-science clichés of the 1950s movies fully developed, yet more proof of the old observation that Hollywood lags thirty years behind print science fiction. 1925 to 1955...that's about right. In October 1925, "science fiction" allegedly had not yet become a genre (the first issue of *Amazing* was about six months in the future), but many of its clichés had already hardened. Edmond Hamilton cranked out numerous variants of this one, usually for *Weird Tales*, just changing the menace each time. The caricature of the scientist as inhuman, amoral, and misanthropic was already, dismally, part of American popular culture long before anybody started worrying about atomic bombs. This is the Roaring Twenties, folks, not the Cold War Fifties with its more understandable jitters. Nowhere in any such stories is there any suggestion that the expansion of human knowledge might be a good thing.

Stories like "Creatures of the Ray" help us understand how science fiction was able to slide into the degraded condition of what I call the Great Retarded Period, circa 1926-36, when it was for the not only sub-literary but sub-pulp, completely cut off from any other sort of literature, after which slowly, painfully, under the guidance of John W. Campbell and other editors, SF writers were able to rediscover the basics of storytelling which most of the *Argosy* writers knew all along. "Creatures of the Ray" is decently written but has *no* flash of humanity or reality of the sort which momentarily redeem the above-mentioned Chidsey and Dunn stories.

It's all cheap sensationalism, reaffirming the still very popular idea—which has made millions for Michael Crichton—that using your brain hurts and is scary and likely dangerous.

Phooey. If I ever do an anthology of Munsey "fantastics" (as they were called, analogous to "westerns"), I'm not going to include "Creatures of the Ray." Yes, there was a whole school of pulp science fiction, of which this is a late example, a full generation before Gernsback. William Wallace Cook was writing about time-travel and a voyage to Mercury, in *Argosy,* as far back as 1905. A definite school. But it wasn't necessarily *good.* And it had been around long enough to start repeating itself and developing its own clichés.

XV.

Thinking About A. E. van Vogt's *Slan*

Slan by A. E. van Vogt. Orb/Tom Doherty Associates, 1998, trade
paper, 255 p.

"When you take aim at the king, you must kill him." Not only is
that sound advice for political assassins, but it applies to literature.
The story goes that a young Henry David Thoreau wrote a preten-
tious paper which tried to demolish Plato. He showed it to Emerson,
who gave him the sage advice.

What Emerson meant was that if a literary work has pleased,
moved, or informed readers not yet born when the book was written,
not to mention readers who died of old age before the would-be as-
sassin put pen to paper, then any demolition had better be awfully
convincing. It needs to show why the present critic is right and all
those other people are wrong. Mark Twain actually did it in "Fenimore Cooper's Literary Offenses." There have been other attempts
since, mostly unsuccessful. It doesn't pay to tell people why they
shouldn't enjoy something they already have enjoyed.

But I can think of one colleague who asked, in undisguised
tones of disgust, "How could *anyone* read van Vogt?"

Fortunately, he did not attempt a demolition, or he might have
paid the penalty for aiming at the king and missing.

At the outset, van Vogt takes some explaining. There is no
question that up to about 1950, he was one of the two or three most
popular writers in science fiction. There is no question, too, that
Slan was *the* SF novel of 1940. Not that it was a bad year. Other
works of note included E. E. Smith's *The Gray Lensman*, concluded
in the January *Astounding*, L. Ron Hubbard's *Final Blackout*, serialized April-June, Robert Heinlein's "If This Goes On—" (which was
actually more of a novella), February-March; and, outside of *Astounding*, Manly Wade Wellman's *Twice in Time* in the March *Star-*

tling Stories, a time-travel novel about Leonardo da Vinci which has enjoyed several printings over the years and still reads well. From the point of view of mainstream publishing, probably the top (and only) SF novel of 1940 was Herbert Best's *The Twenty-Fifth Hour*, which was actually published by Random House, but that one had the least impact of all. It was reprinted in *Famous Fantastic Mysteries* in 1946, and hasn't been seen since.

No doubt about it, in 1940, *Slan* and its creator ruled the roost. This story of persecuted supermen in a totalitarian future was indeed, as the blurbs on the Tor/Orb edition tell us, regarded for decades as one of the most essential science-fiction books.

Slan today has achieved (or suffered) a more curious fate. It's not a book you show to outsiders. It would be incomprehensible to a sophisticated adult unfamiliar with science fiction. It would, however, appeal to just about any twelve-year-old, and also to the most sophisticated and serious SF readers, who probably first read it at twelve, and now can go back to *Slan* and find both the same book, and something else entirely.

This is a masterpiece of the Golden Age, in more ways than one. It is *not* a juvenile in the usual sense of an adult writer trying to remember what it was like to be a kid and writing for kids. Instead, *Slan* reads like the work of a brilliant twelve-year-old trying to imagine how the world of older people works. He doesn't know, of course, any more about romantic quarrels than about secret councils of state in a dictatorship.

Here's big sister with her yucky would-be boyfriend:

> It struck her abruptly that there was no fazing this creature unless she could absolutely humiliate him.
> She snapped, "Beat it, you miserable dough-fleshed thing!"
> "Yaaah!" he said. And leaped for her. (p.97)

Then there's the memorable character of Granny, a drunken, scheming old woman who always speaks of herself in the 3rd person and acts just the way a child would expect such a character to act. And the setting itself, an Earth allegedly 600 years in the future, is more of a child's cartoon of 1940 than a future at all, for all there are spaceships and the cars go faster.

The plot is mostly a hugger-mugger of captures, escapes, and super-science gobbledygook. The science is unusually wonky, even for the period. A spaceship renders itself invisible by disintegrating light with atomic rays.

There are chalk cliffs on Mars. Logic lapses abound. One may reasonably ask why, if the hated slan supermen may be detected by the golden tendrils on their heads, hats aren't outlawed and extremely short hairstyles or even the bald-headed look aren't in fashion.

Never mind. It is similarly irrelevant that van Vogt fairly accurately describes a mainframe computer, which could be accounted prophecy in a normal SF novel. But this is not a normal SF novel. It is more a prose equivalent of *Invaders from Mars* or *The 5000 Fingers of Dr. T.* It is a child's nightmare, and, because all readers either are or have been children, it therefore touches something very universal.

Aiming at the king but refraining from pulling the trigger, we point to its archetypal qualities, which must surely have worked on the readers' unconscious in a way that very little SF of 1940 did. Indeed, very little SF of 1940 touched emotions at all. But here is a story which begins with a child separated from his mother and hounded almost to death by a screaming mob of adults. The mother is killed. The father is already dead, but, as in a fairy-tale, has left behind a legacy which the boy will one day understand, which will make him a "lord of irresistible power" (p. 155). Therefore the ugly duckling/child/exiled prince/persecuted genius grows up in the company of a cackling crone/witch/Granny and must live in dread of inferior enemies all around him and hide his special genius until he can grow up and can bring about a day of reckoning. When he does, he saves the world and gets the girl, who should have been dead, but is miraculously resurrected for the occasion. More than that, the person we thought was the arch-villain has turned out to be a secret agent of good, a power figure who has accepted and acknowledged the protagonist.

The cover of the Orb edition, which reproduces the original *Astounding* painting by Hubert Rogers, captures the spirit of the book very accurately. Our hero, aged about fifteen or sixteen at that point in the story, is shown with an almost androgynous face and a body like that of a champion weightlifter. It's exactly how a persecuted little boy would imagine himself when grown up. That there's a bulge in the figure's crotch and he's holding a very phallic atomic-energy weapon is probably irrelevant. The texture of this book is entirely pre-sexual, pre-adolescent.

This is not to say that A. E. van Vogt in 1940 (he was twenty-eight when the *Astounding* serial appeared) was an arrested development case, but that he had the remarkable ability to switch off his adult, logical mind entirely and dream on paper. He found a way into the subconscious which most SF writers of the period wouldn't have imagined or valued. Van Vogt wasn't a "neat idea" writer. He was a strange-feeling writer. This is why he appealed to such later prophets of the surreal and nightmarish as (in particular) Philip K. Dick. And he can, sometimes, produce a sense of genuine, helpless horror such as we experience in nightmares, particularly in the chapters told from the point of view of a slan girl being kept alive as an "experiment" by the architects of the genocide of her race. One thinks of a Jewish girl being raised by Hitler's inner circle, which may have occurred to van Vogt in that terrible year of 1940.

We have all had something like these dreams, and if we open ourselves up to van Vogt, we can have them again.

XVI.

Introduction to R. A. Lafferty's
The Fall of Rome

I've travelled quite a ways with this book, and maybe after many years I'm beginning to understand it.

What precisely *is* R. A. Lafferty's *The Fall of Rome* anyway?

It is of course the rarest of the books by Raphael Aloysius Lafferty. It was published by Doubleday in 1971. The first edition can easily command in excess of $100 on the used-book market.

Which tells us nothing, for our purposes here.

Lafferty was a unique voice in science fiction and fantasy from the 1960's into the 1980's. Born in 1914, a World War II veteran, he came to writing rather late, after he retired from the electrical supply business around 1960. At that point, as he described it in an interview I did with him in the 1980s (which may be found in the United Mythologies Press booklet, *Cranky Old Man from Tulsa*), he decided he might want to try something else, and so wrote a *Saturday Evening Post* story, a *Collier's* story, a western, a mystery, a science fiction story...and the science fiction story sold where the others didn't, and so the rest is history.

Which, for our purposes, tells us *almost* nothing.

Lafferty, subsequently, had a whirlwind career. He gained a strong cult following (particularly strong among fellow writers) some awards, and a long list of publication credits. Toward the end, as the corporate homogenization of American publishing accelerated, Lafferty became primarily an "underground" author, one who was too quirky, too unclassifiable to be published conventionally. A book like *Sindbad: The 13th Voyage,* if published in the late '60s, would have been an Ace Special and probably a Hugo finalist. By the late '80s, it was only viable in the small press. Happily, Wildside Press has that one, and many other Lafferty titles, back in print.

It isn't so much that Lafferty is a square peg who doesn't fit into a round hole; he is a Protean, ever amorphous peg who will *never* fit into anyone's hole. One can well imagine that if his experimental detective or western stories had sold in 1960, and his career had taken off in that direction, he would have been one of the strangest detective or western writers ever to come down the mean streets or dusty trail...and I think the results would have worked out about the same. Lafferty is one of those utterly unique writers who puts his own unique stamp on everything he does. His work contains mysteries (in the non-detective, more theological sense) which are not easily fathomed. He is like a Zen master, who keeps us entertained and befuddled at the same time, in hope that the befuddlement may someday lead to enlightenment. (Though one of the keys to understanding Lafferty is that he is not a Zen master, but a Catholic, very learned in theology and philosophy, history, and literature.)

All that being said, you would think, particularly if you had a copy of the first edition in your hands, that *The Fall of Rome* is pretty straightforward. It looks like, and was published as, a work of popular history, describing the events leading up to the sacking of Rome by the Visigoths in A.D. 410. The *Publishers Weekly* blurb reads, "Rousing...popular history, with enough cliff-hanging episodes to fill a dozen novels."

Which tells us, again, very little, but something.

In my callow and naive youth (which must have been more callow than actually youthful, as I was about thirty at the time), I believed I could appropriate some of those above-mentioned cliff-hanging episodes and write one of the dozen novels to be mined out of *The Fall of Rome.* I was intrigued by Lafferty's characterization of the "goblin child," Galla Placidia, whom Lafferty describes at the end of Chapter 17 as both saint and devil. I thought I would use the firm basis of Lafferty's history and spin off a strange and imaginative tale of my own. What if Galla Placidia were actually, in her youth, a witch...?

As frequently happens to vast edifices built by junior writers going off half-cocked (if I may mix metaphors as such a writer would), this one soon proved to have a foundation of quicksand.

The first step to enlightenment is understanding that *The Fall of Rome* is not history in the modern sense, but history in the *ancient* sense. It does not fit into any conventional publishing category, which is why we should be grateful to the folks at Doubleday who faked out the system in 1971 and caused the book to be published at all.

Presently, we think of history as a kind of scholarly journalism, a matter of research and presenting the facts, and of careful analysis. It is difficult (or just plain confusing) to speak of aesthetics in this context, of history being beautiful in the sense that a poem is beautiful. That is not the Twenty-First Century idea of history.

But it *is* the late fourth-century idea. In the *old* days, the period Lafferty is writing about, history was one of the modes of literary discourse along with dialogue, epic poem, the letter, the satire, and, rather at the bottom of the literary heap, the novel, which, by late Classical times, tended to be trashy romances written in low-class Greek. (The great Latin novelists, Petronius and Apuleius, were already well in the past.) The difference between fiction and non-fiction was not as distinct as it is today. Reaching back well before the Fourth Century, we see that Homer was "true" but not necessarily factual. (Though there were Homeric fundamentalists, who insisted that if Homer says the Indian Ocean is landlocked, then, by Zeus, it is landlocked!) Plutarch wrote to be entertaining, moral, and, oh by the way, if it wasn't too much of a bother, factual. Tacitus wrote in a great, thundering symphony of moral outrage.

History was art in those days, not science, and the distinction between art and science hadn't necessarily been made anyway.

If you start to research into the sources of *The Fall of Rome* you are soon on very shifty ground indeed. We have no major, first-rate historian for the period. The best is Zosimus, a pagan with an axe to grind, who wrote at least fifty years later. His work is fragmentary and stops suddenly with a sneak attack of the Gothic renegade Sarus upon Alaric, which messed up negotiations in mid-crisis, and sent Alaric irrevocably on his collision-course with Destiny. From the poetry of Claudius Claudianus, who was at least a contemporary (and Stilicho's spin-doctor) we learn much about the characters in the story, though anyone who has read "Against Eutropius" cannot possibly believe that Claudianus was even trying to be fair. No, he was a propagandist, a hatchet-man. The letters of St. Jerome convey to us some of the shock felt throughout the world by Alaric's desecration of the Eternal City. *The City of God* by St. Augustine was written in response to the event, to remind us that the city of brick and marble, the City of Man, is not eternal after all. (Lafferty seems to be firmly in the Augustinian camp; note his characterization of the saint as the person "who understood why the world must end, and when.") From ancient sources, it becomes a matter of reconstruction of events from Byzantine chroniclers and occasional bits of backfill provided by the sixth-century Procopius in his *The Gothic War*, from incidental references in the lives of the saints, from church history, stray paragraphs of otherwise lost writers such as Olympiodorus of Thebes, and so forth. The sixth-century Gothic writer, Jordanes, can also be used with caution, as he is both extremely partisan and often confusing.

The modern sources are more obvious: Gibbon, Bury, the Cambridge Medieval History. My interest in Galla Placidia led me directly to Stewart Irvin Oost's *Galla Placidia Augusta* (University of Chicago Press, 1968), which, while book-length, is called "a biographical essay," not a biography, because the sources of information are so sketchy.

In all of these sources, you will find the broad outline of the events narrated by Lafferty, but precious few of the incidental details. You certainly will find nothing of Alaric's interview with a ghostly ancestor on the Island of the Dead in the Danube, as related in Chapter 7. It fits perfectly into the story that the ghost describes the only possible union of Goth and Roman as being like the union of fox and hare after the fox has eaten the hare. That sums up the political situation neatly, from the conservative-tribal Gothic point of view, but I at least cannot discover the ghost's words written down anywhere.

Mr. Oost has nothing to say about the adventures of Galla Placidia as described by Lafferty, much less about the ghost.

The one clearly counter-factual statement I can take Lafferty to task for is the odd one at the end of Chapter 5 that the pro-pagan western pretender Eugenius (A.D. 392-94) placed on his coins and medallions the face of Jesus Christ. No, the coins of Eugenius show a conventional late-Roman emperor's profile. It is not an individual's portrait at all, save that this one is bearded, whereas the contemporaneous, legitimate emperors are depicted as clean-shaven. But Julian the Apostate had made of a political point of his beard too, back in the 360s, when he converted from Christianity to paganism and tried to return to the days of Hadrian and Marcus Aurelius (both of whom were memorably bearded). Most likely the partisans of Eugenius wanted to present their man as another Julian.

Yet this too is interpretation. It is easy to imagine a contemporary Christian viewing the image of Eugenius as a mocking caricature of the Savior, even though late fourth-century Christs are usually shown face-on and not necessarily bearded.

What about the description of Alaric praying by his saddle, and what Singerich thinks finding him thus? This is not the sort of thing you get out of a history-book in the modern sense. It comes out of a novel or out of epic poetry.

Indeed, the ancients thought of history as a form of prose epic. It was perfectly acceptable to insert set-piece speeches into the mouths of the characters, if that was what that person might have said, or even *should* have said. The idea of ancient historiography, as I understand it nearly two thousand years later, was to shape and reconstruct the *meaning* of what happened. It is not mere reportage, but something closer to the codification of myth.

And that's what *The Fall of Rome* is. It is an imaginative reconstruction of some of the most terrible and exciting times the world has ever known. The age of Alaric and Stilicho and Honorius was not one of simple decay, of a dry-rotted edifice given the final shove which made it collapse into a cloud of dust. It was a time of enormous ferment, in which, indeed, everything which had been taken for granted since the beginning of human memory (such as, for instance, Homeric fundamentalism) was being picked up, re-examined, and either cast into the flames or put back on the shelf to be reclassified. It was the age of the Church Fathers, the beginning of the Middle Ages (though of course no one knew it at the time, not seeing themselves in the "middle" of anything), the time in which the political actuality of the Roman Empire was transmogrified into an enormously powerful myth, which is the most enduring of all Roman creations.

Lafferty's *The Fall of Rome* is a history of this time, but a history as Thucydides or Tacitus or Ammianus Marcellinus or even grumbly old Zosimus would have understood the term: a beautifully imagined, epic prose narrative of a time in which the meaning of everything changed. It is also, incidentally, much of the time, factually verifiable.

XVII.

OF ROBERT NATHAN, *JENNIE*, LOST TIME-TRAVEL LITERATURE, AND THE FLEETINGNESS OF FAME

It was one of those sudden dislocations that make you wonder if you've been living on the same planet with everybody else. At a recent Philadelphia Science Fiction Society book discussion of Audrey Niffenegger's elephantine *The Time Traveler's Wife*, I made the rather glib comment, "This is just *Portrait of Jennie* with the genders changed, and ten times as long."

I got back a roomful of blank stares. This was, mind you, a fairly well-read group of people whose average age clustered around fifty. But *nobody* had ever heard of Robert Nathan, a prolific fantasy author, once a huge bestseller, whose career extended from 1919 to 1975. Even John Ashmead, who makes a hobby of the science and literature of time-travel, frequently lectures on the subject, and has complied a bibliography of such literature, knew nothing of what at least used to be the *most famous* romantic time-slip novel of them all.

One person finally remembered that there had been a movie by that name long ago, but had never known it was based on a book.

I must have some persuasive powers, because before the afternoon was out we'd voted in *Portrait of Jennie* as a future discussion topic. It was, after all, in print from Jacob Weissman's Tachyon Press. A copy still resided in a pile of "recent" books I had intended to get around to reviewing. (Tachyon Press, 1998, trade paperback, 118 p.)

Then the weirdness began. Amazon.com lists an edition of *Portrait of Jennie* as a children's book, ages 4-8. Clearly nonsense, but it was the right book. Various members went searching for used copies. (I turned up two paperbacks from 1977.) But few of the used-book dealers in the Philadelphia area were familiar with the book or its author. I found two who were, both over-sixty women, one of whom opined that Joseph Cotten was "too creepy" in the movie of *Jennie* to play the artist protagonist effectively.

In my thirty-some years of book-hunting I've always had the impression that Robert Nathan books are common as dirt. Any used-book store with a large stock is likely to have a shelf of them, gathering dust. Over the years I have accumulated a shelf of them myself, as something picked up for pennies as "of fantasy interest," as fans express it.

It seems those bookstore shelves have been cleaned off lately. Robert Nathan seems to be at the darkest point of his eclipse. Once he was a best-seller. Then he filled up a lot of used-book shelves. Then he became an author whose used titles notoriously failed to sell, so that book dealers threw them out and refused to take more. After that, he became a rarity...and here's the good news. First editions of *Portrait of Jennie* demand high prices on Abebooks.com. A fine one might cost you $250.

Why is this relevant? Let me suggest that the used-book market can be, if not a tool of criticism, at least useful for gauging literary history. That $250 price means that there is still demand for, at least, *Jennie.* The book is remembered in some way as a "classic." There are any number of titles by other authors you won't find listed at all, not because they're fabulously scarce, but because no one wants them. So, while Nathan's fire may have burned low, there are still a few embers left to be stirred.

An expository paragraph or two: Surely the lesson for me was not to take for granted that everyone had heard of a writer or a book merely because I had. What can I say? I'm a bibliographic sponge. I soak up everything. Possibly you *don't* know that Robert Nathan, 1894-1985, wrote thirty-seven novels, several volumes of poetry, a couple plays (including a "what-if?" sequel to *Romeo and Juliet* called *Juliet in Mantua*, about how Mr. & Mrs. Montague got on ten years later), and even a book of "archeology," *The Weans* (1960), which is, to my mind, the very best "archeology of the present" books ever done, part of a tradition that goes at least as far back as J. A. Mitchell's *The Last American* (1889)—one of those books in which people of the remote future dig up traces of our civilization and make muddled guesses about it. Nathan's, which was published in *Harper's Magazine* originally, is more than a gag on the order of *Motel of the Mysteries*. Its effective satire, describing the lost nation of "US" or "WE" (whose capital was called either "Washing Ton" or "Pound Laundry"—but what if anything was ever washed there remains the subject of scholarly debate), and ending on a somber note:

> But as to the history of these unknown ancestors of ours, no more is known than is known of the Romans and, later, the Brythons: they established themselves in the land by killing off the native tribes already there, and built their empire by the sword; when the sword rusted, they perished.

Nathan's novels are frequently comic, whimsical, slightly sentimental, but not without a sense of tragedy, and often quite moving. They belong to a discernable tradition of American fantasy, which extends from Washington Irving through Mark Twain, up through Stephen Vincent Benét and Peter Beagle. *The Bishop's Wife* (1928) is about a woman who falls in love with an angel. *There Is Another Heaven* (1929) is about a Jew who finds himself in Gentile Heaven. Nathan's last book, *Heaven and Hell and the Megas Factor* (1975) is about emissaries from Heaven and Hell coming to Earth to prevent atomic holocaust. *The Innocent Eve* (1951) shares similar concerns. *The Fair* (1964) is Arthurian. Horrifically overtaken by events was *The Road of Ages* (1935), which describes how the Jews were driven out of Europe and exiled to Mongolia; it is simultaneously as valid and as obsolete as Charlie Chaplin's *The Great Dictator*. Other titles "of fantasy interest," as we say, include *Jonah* (1925), *Sir Henry* (1955), *The Wilderness-Stone* (1961), *The Devil With Love* (1963), *The Mallot Diaries* (1965), *Mia* (1970) and *The Elixir* (1971), all of them published by one of the most prestigious of American publishers, Alfred A. Knopf.

Then there was *Portrait of Jennie* (1939), which was Nathan's BIG book (although in size, it is very small). For the rest of his days, he was known as "The author of *Portrait of Jennie*," even has Robert Bloch was followed around by *Psycho* to the end of his career. Nathan told Peter Beagle, for whom Nathan was something of a mentor, when the younger author sent him *The Last Unicorn*, "This thing is going to be your *Portrait of Jennie*. You're stuck with it—it will haunt you for the rest of your life."

When I got the PSFS book discussion group to read this unknown, forgotten work, the response was one of delighted amazement. The group doesn't quite trust me, ever since I introduced them to Mervyn Peake and permanently scared off nearly half the membership ("Separating the wheat from the chaff," I say unapologetically) but *this* was a hit.

We appreciated that *Portrait of Jennie* is concisely and exquisitely written. *The Time Traveler's Wife,* by contrast, is at a middling best-seller level. It might have been a good book if severely edited, and cut to about half its present (more than 700 page) length. But Niffenegger isn't very good at narrative voice. When her male and female characters relate different parts of the story, they sound alike.

Nathan, on the other hand, never misses a note. His prose is lucid and direct in a way that only the best American literary prose of the late 1930s could be, in the era when Hemingway was king. Nathan is true to life and emotion, instantly. The predicament of the artist hero, Eben Adams, gets right to the point. Adams, starving during the Great Depression, cannot find his muse. He struggles to get something across in his painting, but all is conventional rubbish. Sean Stewart, who contributes an introduction to the Tachyon edition, has experienced this, as have most artists in any medium. "Imagine my shock," he writes, "to open a book with a sort of condescending good humor, only to be nailed between the eyes with one of the central dilemmas of my life."

But of course Eben Adams does find his muse, in the person of Jennie, who seems to be about eight when he first meets her playing hopscotch in Central Park. She sings an eerie little song which prefigures the entire plot of the novel:

> Where I come from
> Nobody knows;
> And where I'm going,
> Everything goes.
> The wind blows,
> The sea flows—
> And nobody knows. (p. 6)

One of the other characters suspects so, but Jennie is not a phantom, or a figment of Eben's imagination, but a real girl. Yet we immediately notice something odd about her. Eben is living in 1938. Jennie, whose dress seems a little old-fashioned, makes a reference to "the Kaiser" as if he were a contemporary, and "the war" as if it's going on. Each time Eben meets her thereafter, over the space of several months, she is a bit older, until, by the end of the book she is an adult and falls deeply in love with him, only to drown before his eyes in the great New England hurricane of 1938. But in the meantime Eben has painted a *magnificent* portrait of Jennie, which has

115

made him famous and hangs in the Metropolitan Museum of Art.

Yes, it's a tear-jerker, and if there is any objection to be made, it is that Jennie's death seems a bit rushed, even contrived, but Nathan (and the hero, Eben) would doubtless argue that this is the whole point. It is destiny. Jennie has been moving at a different rate of time, intersecting with Eben's life at intervals which are, to him, a few weeks, but to her, several years. The two are drawn together because they are destined to love one another, despite their having been born, chronologically, apart. We don't see it from Jennie's point of view, but it seems that every few years (as she experiences time) she is somehow compelled to go into the future, to be with Eben, and ultimately to join him at the moment of her death.

One of the things the PSFS book discussion touched on was how this would have been treated if published as science fiction at the late '30s. Of course a story which depended that much on emotion and character wouldn't have been allowed in the SF pulps. There would have been long and elaborate explanations of how the time-slippage occurs. The prose would have been lousy and the characters cardboard. Certainly the *Astounding Science Fiction* version would not have become a mainstream bestseller and remained continuously in print until the 1980s.

Nathan offers no scientific explanation for anything. The events of the novel are a miracle, of love if not of God. The time-slip is no more fantastic to Eben than the fact that, through Jennie, he has found himself as an artist and painted a great painting, even as Robert Nathan created the book which would define his career. *Portrait of Jennie* is, indeed, Nathan's "portrait of Jennie."

Nevertheless the book does belong to a sub-genre of quasi-science-fictional works influenced by J. W. Dunne's *An Experiment With Time* (1927). Edward Wagenknecht discourses interestingly on this in his introduction to *Jennie* in *Six Novels of the Supernatural* (Viking Portable Library, 1944), tracing a lineage from H.G. Wells and *The Time Machine* to Dunne, to John Balderston's *Berkeley Square* (play, 1928, film, 1933), and then cites a whole series of books probably unknown to modern SF readers, or even time-travel connoisseurs: *Uncle Stephen* by Forrest Reid, *Time's Door* by Esther Meynell, *The Gap in the Curtain* by John Buchan, *The Star Wagon* by Maxwell Anderson, *Ember Lane* by Sheila Kaye-Smith, *We Have Been There Before* by J. B. Priestley, *The Middle Window* by Elizabeth Goudge, *A Traveler in Time* by Alison Uttley, *An Old Captivity* by Nevil Shute, *Lovers' Meeting* by Lady Eleanor Smith, and *The Man Who Went Back* by Warwick Deeping. He even cites a non-fiction survey of the subject, "Space-Time in Literary Form" by Margaret Curtis Walters (*Tomorrow*, June 1942). Of course he makes no mention of anything from the pulps. Pulp SF had not yet matured to the point that it could have any impact on general literature.

Yet if we consider why it is that you, the reader of NYRSF have most likely heard of Jack Williamson's *The Legion of Time* (published in *Astounding*, 1938) or Manly Wade Wellman's *Twice in Time* (*Startling Stories*, 1940), and not most of the titles above, we can approach the question of how a book as lovely and as universally appealing as *Portrait of Jennie* dropped into such obscurity. Admittedly *Jennie* lasted a long time. Everybody at the book discussion had a different edition. As far as I can tell, there were multiple printings, in paperback and hardcover, until about 1980. Then the book fell off radar. Now, almost a generation later, it is rescued by a small, SF-genre specialty press.

Genre, I think, the key to it. Nathan's problem in the long run is that he wasn't adopted into the SF/fantasy genre. He isn't protected by our umbrella. A book can be published either as a brand-name product (when the author is famous) or as a genre title (appealing to readers on the basis of subject matter). That thread of mainstream-based, romantic time-travel stories that Wagenknecht wrote about played itself out, only to reappear very sporadically in such works as Matheson's *Bid Time Return* and Finney's *Time and Again.* Of the books Wagenknecht cited, only *The Man Who Went Back* by Warwick Deeping got a second lease on life because it was reprinted in *Famous Fantastic Mysteries* in 1947. Nathan, lacking any clear genre identity, faded away.

Genre-publishing can be limiting, but it can also be a lifesaver. Indeed, Tachyon Press is trying to toss a flotation device to *Portrait of Jennie* by publishing it as a category book. It says quite explicitly on the back cover, "a masterpiece of modern fantasy."

This has worked before. A book like *Lud-in-the-Mist* by Hope Mirrlees had no chance of revival, let alone a mass audience, before Lin Carter identified it as a fantasy and included it in his genre-defining Ballantine Adult Fantasy series in the early '70s.

It's time to do the same thing with Robert Nathan. He spent his whole lifetime writing wonderful fantasies, but he was never quite identified to the fantasy audience as a fantasy writer, which is why I got that whole roomful of blank stares when I mentioned his name. The limitation of genre is that its readers often fail to look beyond the labeled category for more books of similar interest. That was what I urged my fellow PSFS members to do at the conclusion of that book discussion. There are many fantasy writers buried in the mainstream who need to be identified and rescued.

Now, for all he was once Peter Beagle's mentor, the irony is that if you want to sell Nathan, the best way to pitch him might be to Beagle's audience: If you like the work of Peter Beagle, you will like Nathan. Beagle's *A Fine and Private Place* is in many ways a Robert Nathan novel, written by somebody else.

You'll appreciate Nathan's style at once. He writes great openings. Far more elegantly than any pulp writer, he was the master of the narrative hook. Consider this:

> The Jews were going into exile. Eastward across Europe the great columns moved slowly and with difficulty toward the deserts of Asia, where these unhappy people, driven from all the countries of the world, and for the last time in retreat, had been offered a haven by the Mongols. At night their fires burned along the Danube, or lighted the dark Bakony forests; while the wooded reaches of the Tisza echoed with the tramp of feet, the creak of carts, the purring of motors, and conversation in all the languages of the world.
>
> Their columns spread across the desolate Hungarian plains, and crossed the frontiers of Czecho-Slovakia. Whole villages marched together, led by their rabbis; and with them rode or walked the remnant of the race, men and women who had once been citizens of all the nations of earth. They went slowly, for many of them were on foot, and almost all of them had lost their possessions. They carried with them a few sheep, a few goats, the treasures of the synagogues, and a little household furniture.—*The Road of Ages*

Or this:

> On the thirty-first of October, which is to say on All Hallows' Eve, in the year 1949, Lucifer checked into the Hotel Pierre, in New York. The great archangel, who was also known by such names as Typhon, Set, the Serpent, and the Morning Star, was accompanied by his secretary and familiar, a young female

whom he called Samantha. Since the U.N. was in session at the time, no particular notice was taken of him; he was thought to be a Syrian official, or a delegate from one of the Arab states.

The secretary, on the other hand, made an immediate and favorable impression. "That," said the bell captain under his breath, to one of his assistants in the lobby, "is a dish."—*The Innocent Eve*

Hopefully, you'll want to read more.

XVIII.

FANTASTIC PHILADELPHIA: THE QUAKER CITY IN SCIENCE FICTION AND FANTASY

It's easy enough to find a few science-fictional (or fantasy) images of Philadelphia. A lot of movies have been filmed here. Most of us have seen Terry Gilliam's fine SF film, *Twelve Monkeys*, in which we are treated to a scene of Bruce Willis escaping a bear outside City Hall, in a devastated future in which most of mankind has been wiped out by a virus. M. Night Shyamalan's *The Sixth Sense* was also shot in the city, as was *Unbreakable*.

Philadelphia in the written literature is perhaps a more interesting story.

Probably the best-known recent science fiction novel about Philadelphia is Michael Swanwick's *In the Drift*. This was one of the new Ace Specials edited by Terry Carr in 1985, and is the first novel of a local writer who has gone on to considerable prominence. Parts of the book appeared previously as "Mummer Kiss" in Carr's *Universe 11* in 1981 and as "Marrow Death," in *Asimov's* for Mid-December 1984.

"Mummer Kiss," one of the stories that made Swanwick's reputation, puts a particularly sinister spin on the venerable institution of the Mummers. In the book's post-Holocaust society the Mummers are no longer clubs of people who dress up in funny costumes every New Year's and parade through the city—although that element remains. In the chaos of a Balkanized former United States, the Mummers have become the basis for local society, almost feudal gangs.

The nature of the catastrophe which brought all this about makes us realize that *In the Drift* is not a conventionally "realistic" science fiction novel. It takes place in an alternate universe in which the infamous, errant reactor at Three Mile Island actually melted down and exploded. This did not produce something like the disaster

120

at Chernobyl, with dozens of immediate deaths, a long-term increase in cancer rates, a very expensive cleanup, and the need to abandon the surrounding real estate. Instead, all of western civilization, if not the world economy seems to have collapsed. The "Drift" of the title is a forbidden, radioactive area west of Philadelphia. At one point Swanwick's characters drive out to King of Prussia—a mere dozen or so miles beyond the city limits—and view the baleful blue glow of the Drift on the horizon.

Whether this is exaggerated—and Swanwick argues that it is not—is rather beside the point. By the time we get to "Marrow Death," the fallout from Three Mile Island is producing monsters, albeit scientifically rationalized ones, including a variety of "vampires." If you read *In the Drift* as a horror story drawn from modern, anti-technological fears—after all, most of us don't *really* believe in ghosts or black magic, but we *do* believe in radiation poisoning and big, half-comprehensible gizmos run amok—then it makes, at least, artistic sense. It is a dark techno-myth, vividly and carefully written as are all Swanwick's books, and it does ring some very interesting changes on the author's home city.

I have set a few stories in Philadelphia myself. My "Transients," in which others have professed to discover merit (it was reprinted in one of the DAW *Year's Best Fantasy* volumes and was the title story to my World Fantasy Award-nominated collection, *Transients and Other Disquieting Stories*), is about a West Philadelphia resident who gradually slips into an alternate time-stream. (There is something about Philadelphia and alternate universes. More on this later.) He lives in George Scithers' old neighborhood, about 45th and Larchwood, and, at one point, as he is traveling east on the subway-surface line (probably the #34, which runs along Baltimore Ave.), he knows he is becoming unstuck from reality when he goes underground at 40th Street and starts passing stops that shouldn't be there...and ultimately spends the night in 30th St. Station, which changes mysteriously, so that in the morning the World War II memorial of a winged victory lifting up a fallen soldier has become a statue of a charging doughboy (of the World War I, not Pillsbury variety).

My "Short and Nasty" (in the same collection) has a hapless protagonist chased on the same subway line by the physical manifestation of his own death, east to west this time, with his dire doom overtaking him near 69th St. In "Seeing Them," I reveal that flying saucers originate in a small shop in the Frankford section of Northeast Philly. But by and large I tend to set urban fantasy and horror stories in New York, because everybody knows that's where the really *weird* stuff goes on...right? I admit I did manage some decidedly weird goings on in "Pennies from Hell," which describes an imaginary underground comic-book publishing scene in Philadelphia and makes the South Street area circa 1970 sound more like Greenwich Village or even Haight-Ashbury than it ever was. The story also contains a description of the quite real, if short-lived, ultra-tacky neo-'50s restaurant-bar, the Heart-Throb Cafe, which once existed in the Bourse, at 5th and Market St.

Certainly Philadelphia has had a long association with the fantastic. Any number of writers have passed through. H. P. Lovecraft and Sonia spent their honeymoon here, though much of the time was taken up desperately retyping "Imprisoned with the Pharaohs" (a.k.a. "Under the Pyramids," which was HPL's original title), since he had lost the manuscript right before his deadline at the train station in Providence. Lovecraft visited several times. His letters contain a description of the Art Museum just newly opened, circa 1924. He once spent a night sitting on a bench in Fairmount Park because he couldn't afford a hotel room and wanted to see some of the colonial houses in the Strawberry Mansions section.

The city has many associations with Edgar Allan Poe, who lived here between 1938 and 1844. (The Poe House is preserved, though presently there isn't much to be seen there.) Poe's first important publisher was located in Philadelphia, the firm of Lee and Blanchard, who brought out *Tales of the Grotesque and Arabesque* in two volumes in late 1839.

While here, Poe worked as an editor for two magazines, first *Burton's Gentleman's Magazine*, then *Graham's Magazine.* (Arguably these two are one and the same. Poe parted company with Mr. Burton, who then sold his magazine to Mr. Graham, who combined it with his own periodical, *The Casket* to form *Graham's Magazine*. Graham hired Poe back again.) While in Philadelphia Poe wrote many of his most famous and important works, including "The Masque of the Red Death," "The Tell-Tale Heart," "The Gold-Bug," "The Black Cat" and "The Murders in the Rue Morgue." (So it may also be claimed that the mystery story was invented in Philadelphia.)

A. Merritt grew up in Philadelphia, his family having moved there in 1894. He studied law at the University of Pennsylvania, then went on to become a reporter for the *Philadelphia Inquirer*. While covering hospitals he made the acquaintance of the famous author-physician S. Weir Mitchell (who also wrote the occasional science-fiction story). Merritt was living in New York by the time he published "The Moon Pool" but one other Philadelphia connection can be drawn to his famous fantasies. It seems that in his reporter days, young Merritt inadvertently witnessed something terribly embarrassing to a major political candidate, which, if verified by reliable testimony (of, say, a reporter) would have ruined that man's career. Rather than have Merritt rubbed out, all parties agreed to send him on a year-long, all-expenses-paid trip out of the country. He spent the time exploring Central America and the Yucatan, where he picked up much of the background for *Dwellers in the Mirage, et al.*

Other SF writers have lived here or passed through. Nelson Bond, author of *Mr. Mergenthwirker's Lobblies* and other comic fantasies of the 1930s and later, grew up in Northeast Philadelphia, although he had moved away before he started writing. Theodore Sturgeon went to high school here, although not all of his memories of his Philadelphia youth were happy ones. His upbringing was an ongoing battle with a stern (by today's standards, abusive) stepfather, who, among other things, wanted to cure him of the SF-reading habit early. One day Ted came home from school and was told there was a mess in his room to be cleaned up. It was his precious stash of science-fiction pulps, which his stepfather had discovered and torn into tiny pieces! Sturgeon got out of that household as soon as possible.

And of course much has been made (including yet another "alternate Philadelphia" round-robin story in *Asimov's SF* for April 2000, "Green Fire" by Michael Swanwick, Andy Duncan, Eileen Gunn, and Pat Murphy) of the fact that Isaac Asimov, Robert Heinlein, and L. Sprague de Camp worked at the Philadelphia Naval Yard during World War II. Heinlein and de Camp did little or no writing during that period, although Asimov continued to publish Foundation stories in *Astounding* in 1944 and 1945.

In passing, I mention the infamous *Philadelphia Experiment* hoax, whereby a destroyer is alleged to have been teleported from Philadelphia to Virginia, to the considerable distress of the crew. As de Camp assured us, if anything that fantastic was being worked on at the Naval Yard at the time, surely the three SF writers in residence would have known something about it....

The Philadelphia Experiment (book and film) is yet another alternate-Philadelphia fantasy. The truth is a lot more prosaic. De Camp's work at the Naval Yard involved endless experiments in wind tunnels to discover methods of preventing aircraft windshields from icing up at high altitudes. The others did similarly mundane research.

L. Sprague de Camp, although he was more inclined to set stories on the planet Krishna or in the remote past, was a long-time resident of the area and a member of the Philadelphia Science Fiction Society. Other area notables include George Scithers, Millennium Philcon's fan guest of honor, who was also the founding editor of *Asimov's SF* and subsequently editor of *Amazing*; Gardner Dozois, author of *Strangers, The Visible Man,* etc., and subsequent editor of *Asimov's SF*, for which he has won so many Hugos that one begins to lose count; Tom Purdom, who has been publishing since the 1950s and has recently has a series of highly-acclaimed stories in *Asimov's SF*; and Rebecca Ore, author of many notable novels, including *Becoming Alien, Becoming Human, Slow Funeral, The Illegal Rebirth of Billy the Kid,* and the recent *Outlaw School* (Eos, 2000). Alexander M. Phillips, the father of PSFS member Margaret Phillips Trebing, wrote for *Unknown* and *Astounding* before World War II. His one novel, "The Mislaid Charm," published in *Unknown* in 1941, was reprinted in book form in 1947 by the local specialty firm of Prime Press.

But to return to the subject of science fiction *about* Philadelphia, let me bring up one of the very best and most interesting examples of Philadelphian SF, but a writer not many people know anymore.

How many of you have heard of Francis Stevens? Show of hands. A couple? Maybe you have seen paperback reprints of her (indeed Stevens was a woman, despite the spelling of the first name) Merrittesque fantasy *Citadel of Fear*. Some of her other stories are available not too expensively in old issues of the pulp magazines *Famous Fantastic Mysteries* and *Fantastic Novels*. Her story "Friend Island" (arguably an early example of feminist SF) has been anthologized several times.

But I want to talk about *The Heads of Cerberus*, an alternate time-track novel, much of which takes places in a Philadelphia of 2118 which is fully as sinister as anything in Swanwick's "Mummer Kiss."

The author's actual name was Gertrude Barrows Bennett. She was born in 1884 and lived most of her life in Philadelphia. She turned to fiction writing out of financial necessity after her husband drowned and she found herself the sole support for her daughter and invalid mother. She wrote, in all, eleven stories, and there is no indication that she ever regarded her writings as more than make-work. This is a shame because several were of exceptional quality. The first was as novella, "The Nightmare," in *All-Story Weekly* for April 14, 1917. Her serials in *All-Story* and later *Argosy* were *Citadel of*

Fear, Claimed, Serapion, The Labyrinth, and *Avalon.* (The last two are non-fantastic.) Her short stories were the aforementioned "Friend Island," "The Elf-Trap," and "Behind the Curtain." One last serial, *Sunfire,* appeared in *Weird Tales* in 1923. Then she stopped writing. Her daughter grew up, her mother died, and she got work outside of the house. She lived in Philadelphia for most of the rest of her life, then moved to California where she vanished mysteriously and has never been traced. This seems a little melodramatic, if in keeping for someone who wrote about people slipping into other dimensions and time-lines, but all we really know is that, according to the daughter, Gertrude Bennett wrote a short note to her daughter in late 1939, promising a long letter soon. The daughter wrote back, but her letter bounced. Presumably Gertrude Bennett died then or sometime in the '40s, probably unaware that her work would live on.

The Heads of Cerberus is a major piece of alternate-Philadelphia fiction. It appeared serially in 1919, in *Thrill Book,* a magazine which, because of its extreme scarcity, has a reputation for being an early fantasy or science fiction magazine. The truth of the matter is that the magazine was *supposed* to be the world's first magazine of fantastic fiction, but the publisher chickened out at the last minute and made it a general pulp like *Argosy.* Forget about finding copies. A collector who has a complete run has died and gone to heaven. The easiest available text of *The Heads of Cerberus* is the first book edition, from Lloyd Eshbach's Polaris Press in 1952, published in nearby Reading PA. The book was reprinted for libraries by Arno Press in 1978, but probably the Polaris edition is still easier to find.

The story opens in the Philadelphia of 1918 and concerns an unjustly debarred lawyer, Robert Drayton, his friend Terence Trenmore, a stage-Irishman (a giant of a man, quick with his fists and temper, given to odd turns of speech and "Celtic" mysticism, but chivalrous and true; an ideal sidekick), and Trenmore's sister Viola, with whom Drayton is in love. Trenmore is in possession of an odd glass vial with a metal top fashioned into the heads of the three-headed dog Cerberus, allegedly the work of Benvenuto Cellini, and containing dust from the stones of Purgatory collected by Dante during his visit there. Nobody believes the cover story, but the dust turns out to be very special indeed, as it propels the trio (and later a fourth person, a comic burglar) into a supernatural realm where a female personage called the Weaver of Years seems to create parallel time-streams. There are odd temporal effects reminiscent of *The Time Machine.* Then the Moon rises in the west and becomes a gate.

Our brave trio step through—and find themselves back in Philadelphia!

At first they think they're home, as they emerge from a doorway underneath the trolley tracks, which, in 1918, curved down to meet the ferry terminal at the end of Market Street.

But they're not home. They're immediately arrested for not wearing number-badges, and are astonished to discover that no one has names here, only numbers. It is the Philadelphia of 2118, which is isolated from the rest of the world, ignorant of its own past, and run by an alleged meritocracy, but actually a corrupt and despotic elite, the Penn Service. (In many ways, it's all an eerie echo of Swanwick's *In the Drift*.)

For the slightest infractions against the social code, offenders are heaved into the Pit of the Past in the basement of City Hall to be impaled on the spikes of the idol of the war god. Our heroes get into no end of trouble. Among their numerous capital offenses are reading books and trying to send out for a newspaper.

Although, through isolation and rigid conservatism, the place still looks like the Philadelphia of 1918, there have been a lot of changes. William Penn has become a god. His statue atop City Hall is now seen as a fearsome image, which keeps everybody in line by the Threat of Penn. The new symbol of the city is the Liberty Bell crossed by a sword, for good reason too, as the Liberty Bell has been recast into a larger, red bell, which, if struck by the equally enormous Sword of Penn, will disintegrate the city by means of malign vibrations.

The book is full of curious descriptions of this alternate-Philadelphia, as imagined from the perspective of 1918. City Hall, it seems, is pretty much the same, but for a golden dome installed over the inner courtyard, the omnipresent bell-and-sword emblems, and the palatial chambers many of the elite have fashioned for themselves inside. And of course there is the dreaded Pit of the Past, to which the characters from 1918 are sentenced to more than once. They delay their executions by playing off one faction against another, by "running" for office (of Superlative: the Cleverest, the Strongest, the Most Beautiful, or even, much less desirably for Viola, Most Domestic) though the contests are rigged and death awaits the losers. Finally Trenmore strikes the Red Bell with the Sword of Penn, and everybody finds themselves back in 1918, including a woman of the future, who has fallen in love with the comic burglar. (She, however, disappears as soon as she hands over the dog-headed vial, which apparently linked her to "our" world.)

Various explanations follow. We learn that the Philadelphia of 2118 got that way because of the social chaos after world war and a Communist takeover in Europe. The United States broke up, each city isolating itself from all the rest. Grafters, calling themselves "Servants of Penn," took over in Philadelphia, ending education, but giving the populace a fine, decadent time with plenty of bars and pool halls, in exchange for rigid obedience.

But is this the "future" at all? One possibility is that it is a dream, its nasty features caused by the moral imperfections of the dreamers. Another is that it is an alternate time-stream, and, in a manner not much followed up in subsequent alternate-universe stories, it seems that time moves at a different rate in various time-streams. So, when the characters from our world step "sidewise" from 1918, they find themselves 200 years in the future, but not necessarily in *their* (or our) future.

The dust, we learn, was not from Purgatory at all, but invented in modern times by a scientist who hoped to demonstrate the physical basis for mystical experiences. In the end, the scientist's colleague, who was chasing Terence Trenmore from the beginning of the story and hired the comic burglar, makes off with the sole remaining sample.

This mix of mysticism and "science" is typical of the popular fiction of time. Recall that but a few years earlier, John Carter had wished himself to Mars. 1918's idea of a "fantastic" story did not require any clear distinction between science fiction and fantasy. The stereotyped character of Trenmore should be taken in stride, also of the period. In any case, the book reads quite well. Bennett was a good stylist, with an excellent sense of pacing and an eye for detail. One of the great ironies of her career was that, though she was an admirer of A. Merritt, and to some extent influenced by him (and her work was in turn admired by Merritt, who praised it in letters), she was at one point paid the ultimate compliment by the readers of being taken for a *pseudonym* of Merritt! (Remember that Merritt sold millions of copies, and was probably the most popular writer of fantasy in English between H. Rider Haggard and J. R. R. Tolkien. So this was no slight comparison.)

Actually, Bennett was a better writer, less given to gushing, purple prose, and very much an individual artist, who deserves to be rediscovered. She remains one of the great pioneers of the Philadelphian science fiction scene.

XIX.

FUNERAL GAMES

I remember it as a sunny, late winter morning, about two years ago now, as time and chance and the press of other things prevented me from writing this essay when the impressions were immediate. But they are still vivid enough: late winter, when the snows have melted and car tires leave great, muddy gouges in unpaved driveways.

I was standing with about twenty other people on the porch of a sprawling Victorian house, one of those hodge-podges of stone and wood with peaked gables, a turret or two, an enormous porch, and a "barn" in the back yard (actually a large garage-and-shed) which, I deduce from their proximity to one another (*i.e.*, with less-than-an-acre yards) must have passed for middle-class development houses circa 1890.

Wayne Pennsylvania, where I grew up, has sections of such housing. I may well have stood on this porch as a kid, trick-or-treating, but now I was there for something all book-people have experienced. I was in line, early in the morning, in the company of strangers, near-strangers, and a few familiar faces, waiting for a book sale to start.

This was the house of the late Ms. X, a lady whose name was apparently well-known in the mail-order and internet business. She also sold books by appointment. She had a large invitational clientele. I had not known her, and had in fact had passed by this house many times without ever knowing what wonders were hoarded within. After her (recent) death, her family held a series of sales, first for her invitational clientele, at which everything was offered for 50% off. But today was different. It was the everything-for-a-dollar blow-out, not advertised, but more or less open to anyone. I had been tipped off by a bookseller friend. I simply showed up, acted like I belonged there, and I more-or-less did.

But as I listened to the conversation around me, as people reminisced about what great bookseller the dead woman was, what excellent things they had bought from her, what a shame it was to see her magnificent collection picked over like this (even as the speakers, like a school of piranhas, were prepared to wipe it out completely), I realized that I was intruding on a funeral. All the sad-and-weepy personal stuff aside, this was the send-off that mattered in the bookselling world. A bookseller's funeral.

I take my title from a book, of course. *Funeral Games* is a novel by Mary Renault, in which she extends the metaphor of "funeral games"—the various athletic contests and such which the ancient Greeks held in honor of a dead king—to describe the scramble for power as Alexander the Great's generals carved up his empire among themselves after his death. The Greek version was much more polite than the Etruscan and (later) Roman versions, where the "games" turned bloody, one flattered the dead by adding to their number, and the undertakers invented gladiatorialism.

Bookseller funerals are always polite.

Now the doors were opened. We filed inside, ever so politely, nobody pushing, no elbows making contact (despite all the jokes you hear at more ordinary book sales, where the "usual suspects" make comments like, "We're all here! That's the end of this sale!" and "I think I'll get a pair of spikes for my elbows next time!"). Some people said a few words to the family members and helpers who admitted us.

Then the race was on. Even here there was a unspoken code, an etiquette. You may not shove. The younger and more agile persons may twist and weave a little, and slip by. But you never grab something out of someone's hand, or even right under their nose (in the latter case, unless you say "Excuse me," first).

I was at a disadvantage at this point, because most of these people (who were of the invitational clientele) had been to the earlier half-price sales, not so much to buy (since Ms. X's prices, even reduced by 50%, tended to be quite high) as to case the joint. They knew exactly where everything was. All I could do was follow the crowd, while a little alarm was going off in my head: *Emergency! Emergency! Where is the science fiction section? Where are her Arkham House books?*

Sometimes, half a second before I reached a given shelf, someone swept the entire contents into a box with their arm. (I think they'd done more than case the joint. They'd very likely sneakily arranged the desired books just *so* during a previous visit, ready for the quick grab on the dollar-day.)

This was a piranha-frenzy, but, yes, a very, very genteel one, with voices in low tones, everyone making quick, purposeful motions. Before long piles of books began to assemble themselves, in the middle of the floor, under coats and drop cloths. Another part of the book sale code—you never, never take a book someone else has selected. That is tantamount to stealing (and in a place like this would get you kicked out). If there is any doubt, you hold up the book and ask aloud, "Does this belong to anybody?" and if it *does*, you can be certain the owner will be upon you in an instant, even if he's on the other end of a long gallery. Book people have special senses. They can feel someone else's fingers on their books from great distances. Then you politely give it back, and everyone goes about their polite ravening.

What you do is bring a cloth or use your coat to drape over your goodies once they have become too heavy to carry. In the summer, bring a light jacket, not so much to wear as to mark territory with. Another technique, which doesn't work so well in a crowded room, is to acquire the nearest cardboard box, fill it with your stuff, and push this long the floor with your foot.

The purposeful crowd spread throughout the house. I felt the inevitable anxiety: *the Heinlein first editions and the run of* Weird Tales *are in the OTHER room which I haven't discovered yet.*

All this overwhelming politeness reminded me of the etiquette of trash-pickers. *No*, I don't mean bums going through trashcans—although if someone drops *books* into a trashcan he is by definition a barbarian, whose opinion and contempt do not matter. (In the wealthy neighborhood where I grew up, I once discovered an entire such can full of hardcover books. I pawed through them while a passerby saw me, and didn't pause. Nothing special, but the books didn't belong *there*. I later resold the first edition of *Lizzie Borden, the Untold Story* I rescued.)

I am instead referring to *high-class* scavengers like the ones you meet at major outdoor computer fairs. Toward the end of the day, the large companies represented in the "flea market" section start disposing of their unsold inventory. So you climb into these huge dumpsters the size of railroad cars, often deep enough (if the accumulation is insufficiently high) that nobody's head sticks up over the edge. Safety necessitates speaking *loudly* and maybe even stationing someone on guard at the dumpster's edge, to make sure that incoming projectiles don't come crashing down on somebody's head. Everybody helps everybody else find whatever they're looking for: free televisions, spare parts, sacks of diskettes, or whatever. They lend screwdrivers and wrenches back and forth.

Trash-picking, I like to explain, is a gentlemanly occupation, closely related to archeology. Complete strangers cooperate with one another, following an unspoken code. ("You, Sir, are a gentleman and a scholar," a techno-scavenger said to me once, "but don't worry. Your secret is safe with me.")

There was no danger of incoming books landing on someone's head at Ms. X's place, but it felt very much like truly elegant dumpster-driving. It was part of the same cultural experience.

I realized, ultimately, that this wasn't an ancient Greek funeral (with foot-races and discus-hurling) that I'd barged in on here. It was *Ferengi* funeral. Watchers of *Star Trek: Deep Space 9* will remember those comic, rascally, cheapskate interstellar traders with the big ears who live by a sacred scripture called *The Rules of Acquisition*. There was a wonderful episode in which Quark the Ferengi has been tricked into thinking he is dying. Therefore he does what any sensible member of his species would do under such circumstances. He endeavors to make a *profit*, so that he will be honorably remembered, which is all-important to a Ferengi. (Indeed, a dream-sequence affords us a glimpse of Ferengi Heaven, a gaudy, gold-plated shopping mall, where you present your account books to the equivalent of St. Peter, to show you made a profit in life, before they let you in.)

So Quark offers pieces of his own body for sale on interstellar eBay. It seems that Ferengi corpses are freeze-dried, chopped up into little bits, encased in plastic disks, and sold as coasters. Relics of famous Ferengi become expensive collector's items.

Quark makes a "killing," if you will pardon the expression, a bigger profit than all his lifetime of sales put together. Later when he discovers that, as part of a complicated conspiracy, his medical records have been switched, he is *not* dying after all, and an enemy has maliciously run the bidding up to incredible levels, Quark is terribly torn. He would almost rather die than give up that profit.

So here we were scrambling for the bits and pieces of the late Ms. X's life and career, thus increasing her profit and her honor, since bookseller-Ferengi are ultimately remembered for greatness of their hoard and the quality of their final, going-out-of-business sale. She was doing well, it seemed, from the praise I was overhearing from all around me. What great stuff she always had. What a shame to see her place taken apart like this—even as it was being taken apart.

But what about the *loot*? You want to hear about the *loot*? A tale of acquisition must include descriptions of the haul. I understand, having, as Quark would say, "the lobes" for these things.

The Rare First Editions shelf (in what must have been the dining room) was almost bare by the time I got to it, 2.3 seconds into the sale. One of the few volumes left was a book called *The Corrector of Destinies* by Melville Davidson Post from 1908 ("being the tales of Randolph Mason, as related by his private secretary, Courtlandt parks"), a beautiful, almost new copy with a Mylar protector over the boards. *What is this? I've vaguely heard of Melville Post. Some kind of Sherlockian mystery?* I drop it in my tote bag (which grew to a box, which grew to a pile on the floor under my coat) to buy and sort out later.

If there was an Arkham House shelf or a pile of *Weird Tales*, I did not find them. I don't think so. One of the things I always do (and I am sure most of you do too) when visiting an unfamiliar house is to glance at the books on the shelves. They tell so much about the person who lives there.

Ms. X was a conventional literary person, although one of considerable refinement. She sold what she knew and liked, which was very sensible of her. You will never succeed in bookselling unless you can think like your customer, and appreciate what they appreciate. Her stock included a lot of poetry and art books, and a lot of odd little items from the nineteenth century with interesting bindings. There was no science-fiction section, though I found a couple of late Heinlein first editions (*To Sail Beyond the Sunset*, and *The Cat Who Walked Through Walls*) along with a British first of Arthur C. Clarke's *The Ghost from the Grand Banks* in the mainstream literature/modern first editions section. (Not that they're particularly worth anything. Not that I have since been able to resell them, but when something like that is a buck, you take it now and ask questions later.) The one old science fiction book was Ralph Milne Farley's *The Radio Man* in hardcover, published by FPCI, 1948. I suspect I was the only person there who knew what that was. It had been left behind on that nearly swept-clean Rare First Editions shelf.

It was interesting to note that no one showed much interest in the mainstream/modern first editions area. *Those* shelves were packed solid, hours into the sale. I could go through them at leisure, after the initial frenzy had long abated, pick out the above-mentioned Heinleins and the Clarke, and also find a Salman Rushdie book I didn't have, *The Jaguar Smile: A Nicaraguan Journey*.

Upstairs, in a little side room which had gotten messy—debris on the floor, papers, envelopes, even a few boards from a few crumbling leather-bound volumes on a nearby shelf—I found a first edition of Kipling's *With the Night Mail* in the midst of that same pile of debris. A nice copy, with one plate loose. I shall have to carefully examine another copy to see precisely where that plate goes before I glue it back in. Then the book will be worth about $100.

In that same room was an entire shelf of Christopher Morley first editions which had apparently interested no one. Poor Christopher Morley. His star has fallen.

After a while, as the crowd thinned out a bit (politely, politely...) it was time to really *pick* over the remains. Now (as long-time customers, my fellow Ferengi who had actually known Ms. X lamented) the house was beginning to look a bit shabby, many of the shelves (save for mainstream modern first editions) almost bare, books fallen onto the floor. It was time to grab the expensive literary reference books in what must have once been an office—books which had not been for sale when Ms. X was alive. Wow. *The Penguin Companion to World Literature*, a boxed, four-volume set, in immaculate condition. It counted as one item. I got it for a buck. I found an odd little book called *The Poet, the Fool, and the Fairies* by Madison Cawein (Boston: Small, Maynard and Company, 1912), a volume of verse, with nicely gilt-decorated boards. Immaculate condition. The title item seems to be a play of sorts ("A Lyrical Eclogue"). Is this worth reading/owning/selling? Buy now, research later.

Two hours into the sale, as I had assembled my first couple of crates of books, and was milling around the check-out table, I noticed Peter Ruber's *The Last Bookman* (a coffee-table-sized volume of tributes to Vincent Starrett, a great member of our tribe, Candlelight Press, 1968) among the cookbooks by the kitchen. After the feeding-frenzy, you have to look for odd misshelvings like that.

I'd gone through everything, in every room of the house that was open to the public. How did I feel picking through the books in the shelf over Ms. X's bed, the ones which were her obvious favorites, which she read through before she went to sleep each night. Did I feel like a ghoul, a scavenger, a tomb-raider...? Hell, no. She was *one of us*. She would have *understood*. We were helping her orphaned books find good homes. Even though I had never known her, I honored her, by making her last book sale all the more memorable (at least to me). While I can remember what books I bought from her stock, she lives on through them. It's all part of the Code. Quark the Ferengi would understand too, and salute her.

So there I was at checkout, maybe two and a half hours after this all started. I had just scarfed the copy of *The Last Bookman* (which ultimately turns out to be only worth about $50, according to ABEBooks.com listings, but was still a pleasant find) when I learned, again from overheard conversation that the "barn" out back *was also full of books!*

Oh, my God....

The sellers had made a major strategic error, which worked to my advantage. I deserved some advantage after everybody else got the jump on me in the first minutes of the sale. They should have put up a huge sign saying, MORE BOOKS IN BARN, but possibly, since even this sale was not, theoretically, open to the public, perhaps they didn't want to get mobbed. Or else they just didn't think of it. In any case, few of my fellow book-vultures (some of whom were elderly) had braved the ankle-deep mud in the unpaved driveway and the puddles in the back yard to go out to the barn. It was almost untouched. *That* was where I found the early William Morris book, the Dunsany first edition, the Rider Haggards, the history, photography, and old periodicals section.

It went on and on. Most of this material was tangential to my own interests, but stuff I could easily resell. I made, of course, a huge profit that day. My car was full when I left. I resold much of the loot to my friend the bookseller who had tipped me off about this sale in the first place. We both understood exactly what was going on. She had been unable to get away from her shop to attend. The service I had performed for her, for which I was rewarded by mark-ups on the books I resold to her, is called, in the trade, "scouting." If you buy for a dealer, you are a book-scout.

Some of the remainder I resold elsewhere. Some went into my own collection. It was not the very best book sale I had ever been to, but it was a very good one. A year or so later I got myself onto eBay, thus greatly expanding my capacity to resell things that I might not, myself, particularly want to keep. So of course I think back and wonder: *what should I have taken, that I left behind?* At the end of such a day, as your car fills up, you begin to feel a sense of "restraint." Maybe I have enough. Maybe I should leave a little for somebody else. What am I going to *do* with all this stuff? In retrospect you always come to appreciate a further Law of Acquisition which Quark the Ferengi has not yet explicitly revealed to humans: *restraint is for losers.*

Hail and farewell to the valiant Ms. X, whom I never knew. Thus do I praise and remember her. Thus did we all praise and remember her. By the time the sale was over, I was no longer an interloper, but one more of her "mourners." I could have addressed anybody there by their first name, if I knew their first name.

This kind of "funeral" sure beats having yourself chopped up into little bits and sold as coasters.

And a profit, of course, is not without honor.

XX.

GOING TO HELL WITH SLIDE RULE IN HAND: HARD SCIENCE THEOLOGY: SOME THOUGHTS ON LARRY NIVEN & JERRY POURNELLE'S *INFERNO*

I.

Two statements, one so obvious as to be cliché, the other perhaps eyebrow-raising:

- There is an essential difference between narratives intended as science fiction and those intended as fantasy.
- Virtually all science fiction is religious to some degree, whether the author likes it or not.

Allow me to explain, perhaps demonstrate.

Science fiction, we are often told, is a literature, not merely of ideas, but of *rational* ideas. The way we tell science fiction from fantasy is by the presence or absence of the *attempt to understand* whatever strangeness the narrative may present. This is a yes/no, on/off switch. It is the difference between the *unknown* and the *unknowable*. Science fiction rejects the latter, as a matter of policy.

Sure, *any* fantasy or supernatural motif can be grafted onto science fiction if the author makes a pretense of explaining it. Richard Matheson's *I Am Legend* is about genuine, bloodsucking, only-out-at-night, must-be-staked-through-the-heart vampires, but they are science fiction vampires, because their condition is caused by a disease, as the hero somewhat implausibly discovers while squinting at vampire blood through a microscope. This is of course gobbledygook, but no more or less so than most time machines, faster-than-

136

light drives, or immortality pills. The important thing is that Matheson's vampires are placed within the realm of human understanding. They are part of the natural world. This inevitably makes them less frightening, because they can be overcome if someone studies them and learns their weaknesses. It is a tribute to Matheson's narrative intensity that they still remain very frightening indeed.

But Stoker's *Dracula* remains frightening, even if Van Helsing makes noises about "occult science," because the Count represents a supernatural evil, which perverts and transcends natural law, and can never fully be comprehended. *Unknowable*. Lovecraft's cosmic menaces are at their best when they approach this quality, but less impressive when displayed and labeled like something in a museum exhibit.

For this reason, fantasy horror is easier to do. It is much easier to make the *unknowable* and possibly limitless frightening. Science fiction horror, though possible, is far more difficult, because you have to scare within a set of rules the readers (and the characters) know that somebody, somewhere is capable of understanding.

Of course most science fiction, and a good deal of fantasy, is not concerned with horror. It is concerned with awe, what we call the Sense of Wonder.

The difference, then, is not so much the subject matter, but the narrative attitude toward the subject matter.

Terror and religious awe are very closely related. According to all available reports, persons visited by gods or other supernatural beings tend to show symptoms of abject fright. Some even drop dead if they don't shield their eyes from a direct view of the Presence. Saith the Prophet (Isaiah): *Woe is me, for I am undone. For I come from a people of unclean lips, and mine eyes have seen the King.*

What is the basic subject matter of religion, any religion? It is the place of mankind in the universe. How did we get here? Where are we going? Who and what are we in the first place? *Eschatology* is the consideration of mankind's ultimate fate. Until the last couple of centuries, it was the exclusive domain of religion. But nowadays, as SF critic John J. Pierce used to tell us at great length, it is the subject matter of science fiction. "Eschatological romanticism" was his avowed creed back in the days of the Second Foundation, when he was out to save SF from the menace of the New Wave.

Religious texts such as the Bible purport provide answers to the above questions. When those answers are taken as absolute, when everything you need to know is revealed in the Sacred Writing, there is no room for speculation. There is no science fiction in a theocracy. *In the beginning, God created the heaven and the earth.* Period. A frivolous story of some years back, in which our universe proves to be the effluent of an extra-cosmic flush toilet, would have earned its author an *auto da fé* in the sixteenth century.

More seriously, Olaf Stapledon in such works as *The Last and First Men* and *The Star Maker* offers a hypothetical alternative to the standard version of our destiny. He has influenced any number of writers since, most notably Arthur C. Clarke. No winged, hosanna-singing heavenly hosts at the science-fictional End of Days, unless, perhaps, they are battery-powered. Of course the difference between science fiction and a religious text is that the science-fiction writer doesn't claim to have then *truth.* He is writing fiction, not divine revelation. As long as the prevailing religious orthodoxy doesn't rule so firmly as to preclude speculation, science fiction can rush in and grab a chunk of Sacred Territory.

It does so in a science-fictional way, which means through the mode of rational materialism. The characters in the story may not comprehend all the mysteries placed before them—any more than the hero of Lem's *Solaris* ever does—but there is at least the implication that somebody, with sufficient effort and maybe a bit of brain enhancement if necessary, *could.* We can even have a science fiction story about God Himself, as long as there is that knowing wink from the author to the effect that, yes, even the Almighty is bound by the laws of the universe, however yet-undiscovered some of those laws might be.

Now it becomes possible to have genuine science friction on subject once monopolized by theologians.

II.

Larry Niven's novel, *Inferno*, first serialized in *Galaxy* in 1975 and published as a book in 1976, is still, a quarter of a century later, one of the most interesting attempts by science fiction to take up the subject matter of religion and probe it in the manner of a mineralogist examining a strange rock.

The story starts fannishly. A hard-science type science-fiction writer, Allen Carpentier, gets drunk at a science-fiction convention, falls out a window to his death, and wakes up in the vestibule of Dante's Hell, just across the River Acheron from the First Circle. This is the not-too-uncomfortable domain of virtuous pagans, who kept the commandments but never knew God. But, as Carpentier learns, the only way out is down, through the center of the Inferno.

Our hero is led on his journey by a poor man's Vergil, a bulldog-faced Italian named Benito, a.k.a. Benny...you know who, though Carpentier doesn't figure it out until halfway through the book.

The prospect is immediately disconcerting to the agnostic Carpentier:

> Scary. It would mean that there was a real God, and maybe Jonah was swallowed by a whale in the Mediterranean Sea, and Joshua ben Nun stopped the Earth's rotation for trivial purposes. (p. 24-25)

It gets even scarier when Allen and Benny meet a five-hundred-pound woman, so condemned forever because she helped ban cyclamates and doomed thousands to fat, who explains, "We're in the hands of infinite power and infinite sadism."

But our hero refuses to believe this is the genuine Hell and keeps trying to think in science-fictional terms: it's really an artifact, perhaps an alien amusement park for creatures who get their kicks torturing humans. Throughout the first few circles, there is some evidence to support this, including a super planetarium in the territory of the virtuous pagans (and scientists?), but nothing is conclusive.

The result is that as *Inferno* progresses, the ideas and attitudes of science—and science fiction—collide head-on with those of traditional fantasy, and with theology. The situation is either rational, and therefore science fiction, or it is not. The book's growing ambiguity irritated a lot of critics when *Inferno* first came out. They, like Allen Carpentier, wanted a comfortable science-fiction novel.

Because he tries to rationalize everything, Carpentier sees a different Inferno than did Dante. Consider the following description of red lights flashing on the tower before the City of Dis. This is from John Ciardi's translation of the *Inferno,* which was used by Niven and Pournelle:

> Returning to my theme, I saw we came
> to the foot of a great Tower; but long before
> we reached it through the marsh, two horns of flame
> flared from the summit, one from either side,
> and then, far off, so far we could scarce see it
> across the mist, another flame replied.
> (Canto VIII)

When Carpentier reaches the same point, he remarks:

> Red? Ruby? A laser! Not magic, just a laser sig-
> nal from an old stone tower. Far out in the murk there
> was a flash of light, blinking, the same color as the
> signal. (p. 66)

This sort of thing goes on for half the book, as long as Carpentier remains convinced that the Hell he travels through is the product of natural, finite beings who can be dealt with. His efforts come to a glorious (or perhaps inglorious) climax when he builds a glider, launches it off a cliff in the vicinity of the Sixth Circle, catches a thermal updraft over the City of Dis, then reaches the winds of the Second Circle (where Dante observed the doomed lovers, Paulo and Francesca), with the ultimate intent of flying clear of the enormous funnel of Hell.

It docsn't work. The glider collides with too many souls amid the winds, picks up a passenger (a former space shuttle pilot) and eventually crashes just beyond the wall of Dis. Benito had told Carpentier that the glider wouldn't work, but he insisted on trying it anyway.

From this point on, Carpentier's rationalism is on the defensive. Eventually it collapses altogether.

III.

Niven and Pournelle did their homework well. Of course, as would obviously suit their purpose, they borrowed selectively from the *Comedia*. They didn't retell everything. They begin where Dante was in the middle of Canto III, already inside Hell, so we never see the famous inscription: ABANDON ALL HOPE YE WHO ENTER HERE. Abandoning all hope is precisely what Allen Carpentier never does.

The first recognizable set-piece from Dante, in Niven and Pournelle, is the crowd of the unthinking, those who never concerned themselves with questions of good and evil. They run after banners which they will never catch. This may keep them fit, but it's certainly a frustratingly dull way to spend eternity.

Then Carpentier moves across the Acheron, past the virtuous pagans, to the place of judgment, where Minos assigns the damned their stations. Dante's Minos told you what circle you were bound for by wrapping his tail around his body that many times. But in Niven and Pournelle he picks the damned up with the aforesaid appendage and puts them where they belong. The tail can apparently stretch, Plastic Man style, to infinite length, without considerations of mass and gravity. Carpentier, who is still thinking like a science-fiction writer at this point, is certain it's done through hyperspace.

After that, the main similarities between the version of 1300 that of 1975 one are in the geography. Niven and Pournelle follow Dante closely most of the time. They even manage to make the layout of the Inferno easier to comprehend than it is in the original. They go into great detail in the Eighth Circle with its many subdivisions. The most immediately obvious differences are in the modernizations: self-driven automobiles raging across the plain of fire, soldiers with machine guns replacing the centaur archers who prevent the wrathful from escaping the lake of boiling blood, and so on.

Very few of Dante's actual characters show up. Carpentier asks his guide why they don't meet all the medieval Italians Dante did, and Benito's only explanation is that one tends to notice one's own contemporaries and countrymen. Thus Allen keeps seeing twentieth-century Americans.

The Divine Comedy was a scandalous book when it was written. Dante put his enemies, political opponents, literary rivals, and even some of his friends in Hell, not to mention several popes of recent memory. He devoted much space to satirical comments. To get the same effect, Niven and Pournelle had to select people their readers would recognize without a barrage of footnotes, though of course in time, their book will date as Dante's did and (if it is still read centuries hence) require just as much explanation.

Some examples: A Hell's Angel motorcycle gang member among the sodomites. Aimee Semple MacPherson (the radio evangelist of the 1920s whose career collapsed in scandal; the inspiration for Sinclair Lewis's *Elmer Gantry*) among the religious hypocrites. American senators who put party line in ahead of their country's welfare in the frozen lake at the center of Hell, among the traitors.

Even as Dante made jabs at the poets and poetry of his time, Niven and Pournelle talk about science fiction. In a section decidedly *not* in the original, Allen and Benny come to a place outside the city of Dis where the proud are locked in their gaudy tombs and discover that of none other than Kurt Vonnegut, Jr.

Carpentier is furious to see Vonnegut so well memorialized:

> "*Him*. Why him? A science fiction writer who
> lied about being a science fiction writer because he
> got more money that way. He wrote novels in baby
> talk, with sixth-grade drawings in them, and third

grade science, and he *knew* better. How does he rate a monument that size?" (p. 115)

There's even a neon sign overhead, blinking on and off: SO IT GOES.

L. Ron Hubbard turns up in Pit 6, Circle 8, among the religious hypocrites, as a human face mounted on a body of "flopping fist-torsos and forelegs and hands, a tremendous unmatched centipede." Of him we are told:

> "He founded a religion that masks as a form of lay psychiatry. Members try to recall previous lives in their presumed ancestry. They also recall their own past lives...and that adds an interesting blackmail angle, because those who hear confession are often more dedicated than honorable." (p. 206)

And among the grafters we find someone already well on his way to being forgotten:

> "He hardly counts anyway. He stole a few hundred bucks from a friend who needed an eye operation." (p. 172)

This refers to a certain fan and sometime magazine editor who became agent for a British science-fiction writer in the early '70s, but started dipping into his client's funds. When the affair went public, he confessed all in the pages of *Science Fiction Review.*

How unfair. He was actually a good editor. But as the fat lady said, whoever runs this place has no sense of proportion. And probably doesn't read science-fiction magazines.

Finally, the ultimate in-joke: is Allen Carpentier supposed to be Philip José Farmer, who is most famous for his Riverworld series, in which all of humanity is raised from the dead along an enormous river? There is one specific clue. We are told that Allen Carpent*i*er added the "I" in his name to make his byline more exotic, even as Farmer added the "José" for the same reason.

There are undoubtedly more in-references, some perhaps only comprehensible to members of Los Angeles fandom. Remember, this was the same Niven who starred a good bit of the Los Angeles Science Fiction Society in "Or What About Chocolate Covered Manhole Covers?"

IV.

On a more serious, thematic level, Niven and Pournelle's *Inferno* differs greatly from its namesake. The first half uses the techniques of science fiction, trying to render Hell comprehensible. But after the glider crash, Carpentier's skepticism gradually erodes into belief, and the *supernatural,* as opposed to the super-scientific, takes over. Past this point the book is unabashedly religious fantasy, on the order of C. S. Lewis or Charles Williams.

On the order of Lewis, certainly. When I interviewed Niven in 1979, he said that you have to read Lewis's *The Great Divorce* in order to fully understand *Inferno.* (He also added that those who wanted this to be a proper science fiction novel will have to be disappointed.) Pournelle also mentioned Lewis in an interview in *Science Fiction Review* #16. He and Niven wanted to soften Dante's theology a bit and make it more like Lewis. So they did, and their *Inferno* doesn't work like Dante's at all.

The main idea they have taken from Lewis is that Hell is *not permanent*. It is more of an extended, elaborate, and painful Purgatory, in which sinners enmesh themselves. In *The Great Divorce* they recede deeper and deeper into Hell out of sheer orneriness. If they could just let go of the sins that landed them there in the first place. Thus, in a sense, all mortal sins are sins of pride: the delusion that a mere human being *could* commit a sin meriting the attention and wrath of the creator of the universe for all eternity.

Dante's Hell, on the other hand, is a place of divine and justified retribution. It is quite straightforward and has no other purpose.

Carpentier, halfway removed from his rationalist stance, toys with the idea that Hell is a counterbalance to Heaven in accordance to some cosmic moral law. Maybe so, but Dante's sinners get out only under the most extraordinary circumstances. The Roman Emperor Trajan (as is told in Dante's *Paradiso*) was redeemed by the prayers of later Christians, who admired him. Christ himself spent much of Easter weekend rescuing Old Testament figures in what the Middle Ages called the Harrowing of Hell. But certainly, in Dante's view, it was not possible to escape under one's own power.

In Niven and Pournelle, damned souls slip from one niche to another. Devils aren't very bright and sometimes they don't notice. Benito (Mussolini) really belongs in the lake of fire in the Eighth Circle, along with the evil counselors, but he got loose, not once, but *twice*, the second time when he is pushed back into the lake by the self-righteous Carpentier when he *finally* figures out who his traveling companion is. Allen is briefly caught among the men-lizards of the pit of thieves, but escapes.

By the end of the book, we discover that this does not happen because of diabolical (or divine) sloppiness. There is a reason. Once Allen has accepted Hell on its own terms, he concludes that the place is a violent ward for the theologically insane, the equivalent of painful shock treatment. A psychiatrist gives him the paradigm he needs: a catatonic, placed in a hotbox, yelled for help, the first words he had uttered in thirteen years, and thus was no longer catatonic.

That's one theory, anyway. Satan, when we finally meet him embedded in the frozen lake at the center of Hell, agrees with the fat lady. As Allen and Benito climb down his leg on the way out, the Devil has a request and a message for God:

> "Will you tell Him that He could learn morality
> from Vlad the Impaler?" (p. 233)

In any case, this is certainly *not* the infinitely just and merciful God of traditional Christianity. Our intrepid authors grapple with problems which have vexed theologians for centuries. If God is infinitely just, how can he be merciful? If he is infinitely merciful, then how can he damn *anyone*? The fat lady would say that eternal damnation proves her "infinite sadism" theory, since no human crime goes on forever. The idea that it is only *presumption* on the part of the sinner that makes damnation possible comes from both Lewis and from *Jurgen* by James Branch Cabell (a favorite of Niven), which has a comic sequence in which the hero, arriving in Hell, relieves the overworked devils by telling them that, no, he doesn't require them to torture him at all, thank you very much.

The ultimate solutions offered in Niven and Pournelle's *Inferno* are clever, and about as good as writers can do when reaching toward what may be (in the theological or fantasy sense) unknowable. One works one's way out of this Hell. Benito, having conducted Allen Carpentier and several others through Hell, now is able to leave, climbing up a long tunnel into the unknown, possibly toward Dante's Mount of Purgatory. Carpentier, who, as Norman Spinrad suggests in the introduction to the Gregg Press edition, may be in Hell for the same reason Mussolini was, for moral indifference, now finds a purpose. He takes over Benny's job.

So maybe God isn't infinitely sadistic after all, but is benevolently trying to straighten sinners out by painful but necessary methods. We never know. Answers aren't provided. This isn't a science-fiction novel, for all it speaks the language of science fiction much of the time.

It never *was* a science-fiction novel either, not even in the opening chapters. It just sounded like one. One could *not* fairly describe *Inferno* as something that began as honest science fiction, then copped out into fuzzy-minded fantasy, though some of Niven and Pournelle's disappointed readers might say that. The authors' purpose was there from the start. It is rather startling, considering their rest of their output. *Inferno* is nothing less than a deconstruction of the science-fiction method, an examination of its limitations. By the time Benito Mussolini is climbing past the Devil's backside, up a long tunnel through the core of the Earth, nobody worries about how such a structure could hold up under the gravitational pressures involved.

The result is their most profound and least popular work.

V.

But just how serious are Niven and Pournelle about all this? There is certainly an element of play in *Inferno*, the sort we see in Niven's fiction often enough. But this is more than an elaborate game. One gets the impression that it may have begun that way, but that the authors, as honest writers, began to seriously grapple with the implications of their material.

Niven mentioned in the interview I did with him that the idea for the book has been with him for years before he was able to write it. Finally he managed to get it out of his system. I asked him why it had such a grip on him. "It's a neat fantasy," he replied. He'd read Dante (the Ciardi version) in college, and it struck him as "neat." Then he started "daydreaming in class…. I started wondering what I would do in Dante's *Inferno* if I couldn't call on any angels. There was nothing but *deus ex machina* every step of the way in *Inferno.* Suppose I didn't have a guide at all? How would I get out? That was fairly exciting daydreaming."

But he never managed to write the novel until he began to collaborate with Pournelle, "who had the theological background I needed. So I talked him into it, and it grabbed him the way it grabbed me, very rapidly. When we actually started writing, we spat it out in about four months, and in some ways these were the strangest four months in my life. I had more fun in terms of imaginary experiences, and went through more pain, again in terms of the imaginary, and Jerry couldn't stop writing any more than I could. We had to get *out* of that place."

When Niven started writing, he didn't realize that there was any difference between science fiction and fantasy approaches. That took a while, and when he did, he knew he didn't "have a head for fantasy." It took "several years to develop one."

Inferno shows him (and Pournelle) in an advanced state of development along those lines. As the tone of the book shifts in the latter half and the façade of rationalism breaks down, I think we can see it all becoming more than just "a neat fantasy." Spinrad argues in his introduction to the Gregg Press edition that this very seriousness saves the novel from being "a hideous pornography of pain." His contention is that the story's meaning hinges on the redemption of Mussolini, the change from the morally indifferent to the responsible. Certainly as we get deeper and deeper into the infernal depths, the book takes on an increasing degree of meaning. It deals with mysteries, in the religious sense. Is the creator of the Inferno exactly what the fat lady said he was? Even the "extended purgatory" explanation is never made wholly convincing.

When Niven and Pournelle's *Inferno* is telling us is that when we get down to the really serious questions, to eschatology, then all the platitudes, glib answers, and shallow shortcuts of the sort that produced Allen Carpentier's glider won't work. They fail was quickly as the glider did, because there are shortcuts. Mussolini tells Allen that the only way out of Hell is through its depths, and slowly he becomes to accept that.

Had the book stayed a science-fiction gimmick story all the way through, it *would* have been a cop-out. This may tell us something about the limitations of science fiction, at least in the specific area of eschatology. Certainly it tells us something about why *Inferno* had to become something else in order to become more than a cheap trick.

I remember how someone described *The Great Divorce* to me once. "It's true," she said. "It touches reality."

All joking aside, so does *Inferno*, at least fleetingly, as do the blind men in the Hindu fable touch the elephant.

Stay away from windows at convention parties.

WORKS CITED

Dante Alighieri, *The Divine Comedy*. Translated by John Ciardi. New York: W. W. Norton & Co, 1977.

Larry Niven and Jerry Pournelle, *Inferno.* Boston, MA: Gregg Press, 1979. A facsimile reprint of the 1976 Pocket Books first edition, with a new introduction by Norman Spinrad.

Darrell Schweitzer, "An Interview with Larry Niven." *Thrust* #21, Fall 1984/Winter 1985.

XX.

TALES BY H. P. LOVECRAFT

New York: Library of America, 2004, 838 p.

Let's get the triumphalism out of the way first:

Wow! Lovecraft in Library of America! Hooray for our side! Take *that*, Edmund Wilson!

Sometimes, it seems, the truly great writers are the ones the critics *cannot stop.*

Any serious Lovecraft fan or student of fantastic literature probably already has the three, definitive Arkham House volumes of Lovecraft's fiction, and so little in the Library of America collection will be new except for the notes, but a lot of such fans, at least, are going to want this book anyway, as a *trophy*, evidence that One of Our Own has now reached the highest level of literary acceptance that the United States has to offer. The Old Gent of Providence is also in Penguin Classics and is reportedly forthcoming in Modern Library. He is now canonical, right up there with his own idols, Poe and Hawthorne, beating out all those writers you had to read in school, like, say, Ernest Hemingway.

Certainly no other contributor to the Gernsback *Amazing Stories* or the Tremaine *Astounding Stories* or even (let's admit it) *Weird Tales* has achieved such status, and with the possible exception of *Weird Tales* alumnus Ray Bradbury, it is unlikely that any other ever will.

Once result has been increased notice in the mainstream press, and reviews of this volume which have ranged from the obvious to the grudgingly appreciative to the downright clueless. "The Most important US horror writer since Poe," wrote *Publishers Weekly.* Yes, but *we* knew that decades before *PW* did. T. O. Mabbot (a leading Poe scholar) and Fritz Leiber were saying as much in the mid-

1940s, even before Edmund Wilson's infamous blast in *The New Yorker*, which, as such things inevitably do, failed utterly to stop Lovecraft in his tracks, though it did becloud the halls of academe for nearly a half-century.

"If Lovecraft had been a film director, he might have come up with a movie much like *The Blair Witch Project*, only scarier," wrote *The Wall Street Journal*. What precisely is *that* supposed to mean? That Lovecraft would not have passed off amateurish, shabby work as the real thing and relied on promotional hype to hide the difference? No, he would not have. As any reader of the Lovecraftian letters know, HPL was an artist of unflinching integrity.

Yes, hooray for our side. A Library of America edition is intended to be definitive. It has a pleasant, distinctive heft. It is compact, but well designed, extremely legible, printed and bound with the most durable materials. Its texts are subjected to rigorous scholarly standards. Library of America books are as close to definitive as such editions can be.

Reportedly, Lovecraft's *Tales* has sold better than any other volume in Library of America's history, going through four printings in a matter of months, doubtless fueling suspicions by some mainstream diehards the Library has gone commercial after all, and sold out to the mass taste of the moment. But if anything, the persistence of Lovecraft over what is now the better part of a century and the continued fascination with him (he is perhaps the single most documented literary person of the twentieth century) demonstrate that he is not of the moment.

Yet those sales can be explained without more congratulations on the part of genre insiders. The simple truth is that in the real world, where people acquire books by walking into bookstores in shopping malls, not by ordering from specialist catalogues or picking them up at the World Fantasy Convention, there has been no convenient edition of Lovecraft in hardcover since *The Best Supernatural Stories of H. P. Lovecraft,* published by a cheesy outfit called World Editions, came out in 1945. It too was a smashing success.

The rest, in the United States at least, has been paperbacks. While Arkham House has done admirable work keeping Lovecraft in print in hardcover, in handsome and affordable editions, Arkham House books do not get into many stores. The general public, at least prior to the age of the Internet, had little reason to suspect their existence, much less any chance of actually encountering them. The more important function of Arkham House over the years was as a broker of rights and permissions, so that Lancer Books or Ballantine or even movie studios would know where to get their contracts signed. As a contribution to Lovecraft's rise to fame, this cannot be underestimated. Yes, genius is required, but nothing consigns a writer, even a genius, to oblivion faster than a badly managed or disputed estate. Unless it is clearly in the public domain (not the case with Lovecraft for most of that time), work will not be re-printed unless it is possible to buy the rights in a clearly legal manner.

It was in paperback, then, that Lovecraft reached a mass, then world audience, which also helped delay critical recognition because critics don't take paperbacks seriously. But the strictly commercial point, and the reason that the Library of America Lovecraft did so well, is that while many readers may have already owned adequate editions of Poe, Hawthorne, Irving, or Melville, they did not have a decent hardcover of Lovecraft. *Tales* has no competition. Hence, a relative best-seller. Hardly any revelation there.

In effect, *Tales* is an introductory volume, reaching an even larger and very likely more sophisticated readership than ever before. It is edited by Peter Straub, with assistance from the two most eminent Lovecraft scholars, S. T. Joshi and David E. Schultz. It is hard to fault the textual methodology. One might, however, question some of the selections. Straub has stated elsewhere that his intent was to concentrate on the most purely *Lovecraftian* of Lovecraft's stories, avoiding those that were either collaboration (like the splendid "Through the Gates of the Silver Key," with E. Hoffmann Price) or the whole cycle of stories derivative of Lord Dunsany, such as "The Dream Quest of Unknown Kadath."

Of course this standard cannot be applied consistently. Lovecraft himself remarked that in "The Outsider" his imitation of Poe had reached something of a frenzied climax—but it would be unthinkable not to include that story, one of Lovecraft's most famous and intriguing, and Straub has included it. What is a little more dubious is the presence of "Herbert West—Reanimator" and "The Lurking Fear," two serials written to order for a sub-pulp effusion called *Home Brew*, the first fiction for which Lovecraft was ever paid, and which caused him to announce to a correspondent, "I have become a Grub-Street hack." Both of these will quite understandably puzzle the mainstream critic, or even the uninitiated reader who is left wondering how exactly this sort of thing got to be canonical Literature with a capital L. The artificiality of these stories, their formulaic lurching toward ghastly and thrilling pseudo-climaxes at the end of each installment, was much bemoaned by Lovecraft at the time, even as, quite obviously, he was writing with tongue in cheek. The least he could do, if he had to indulge in such things, was make fun of them.

"The Horror At Red Hook" isn't very good either, and is one of Lovecraft's most xenophobic stories. "He" begins with a wonderfully evocative description of New York, then devolves into some nonsense about the ghosts of murdered Indians who seem to move about as an amorphous, shoggothian blob.

Beyond that, the contents make up the solid core of Lovecraft's greatness: "The Statement of Randolph Carter," "The Outsider," "The Music of Erich Zann," "The Rats in the Walls"—which must have come like a blast of lightning out of a clear blue sky in the dreary pages of the early, pre-Farnsworth Wright *Weird Tales*; the most brilliant American horror story since Poe—and all the rest: "The Call of Cthulhu," "Pickman's Model," "The Dunwich Horror," "The Case of Charles Dexter Ward," "The Whisperer in Darkness," "The Thing on the Doorstep," and so many more classics, including the really, *really* definitive text of "The Shadow Out of Time," based on the latest research (and the discovery, at last, of an original holograph manuscript and now in mass-circulation for the first time).

What ultimately commands our attention, and the reason this Library of America edition exists, is the continued vitality of Lovecraft's work, which puts him well ahead of all other writers of fantastic fiction of his generation. When he was actually penning these tales (not a figure of speech; we know that he loathed typewriters and could not compose at one) the leading lights of the pulp field, as far as fantasy and science fiction went, were Edgar Rice Burroughs, Ray Cummings, Otis Adelbert Kline, and perhaps Ralph Milne Farley, *Argosy* stalwarts all, claiming top pulp rates (which, if adjusted for inflation, work out to thirty or forty cents a word, *for novels*) and (with the exception of Farley), regularly published in book form. Burroughs is still read, and even studied, but as "popular culture," never "literature." The others, to put it mildly, have not done as well.

In his collection of memoirs, *Book of the Dead* (Arkham House, 2001), old-time pulp writer E. Hoffmann Price explained Lovecraft's posthumous success this way:

> ...August Derleth ballyhooed Lovecraft from HPL's death until his own death. Arkham began as HPL promotion, and was financed for years by Derleth's earnings as a big-time writer of non-fantasy. If ever a

labor of love, this was it. Fans finally bought the fanatic over-rating, and lo! (p. 42)

Price was saying this to the widow of Otis Adelbert Kline, implying that with similar efforts, a "Kline boom" could be made to
happen. Was he just trying to comfort an old lady, or did he really
not get it? The rest of his book, and statements he made elsewhere,
suggest the latter. Lovecraft once bemoaned the decline in Price's
own work after he became a full-time writer during the Depression:
"...he caters painfully to the pulp standard. I fear we shan't see anything more of the quality of 'The Stranger from Kurdistan'" (*Selected Letters* IV, p. 87), again remarking on the effects of commer-
cialism on his colleagues, "The literary ruin of brilliant figures like
Long, Quinn, Price, Merritt, & Wandrei speaks for itself" (*Letters* V,
327).

E. Hoffmann Price became the perfect pulp-generalist, a worthy
colleague of H. Bedford-Jones and Frank Gruber and other very
successful, often wealthy professionals whose careers died when the
pulps did. Price will be remembered, if at all, for his association
with Lovecraft, as will August Derleth. Never mind Derleth's high-
paying, non-fantastic novels. It is his *taste* which may just barely
save his name from oblivion.

Price surely didn't understand that more than fan-hype has
caused a good deal of twentieth-century fantastic literature go into
orbit around Lovecraft, rather the way the entire Elizabethan-
Jacobean theatre scene went into orbit around Shakespeare. It is because of Shakespeare that we know there was a Globe Theatre. Who
were Beaumont and Fletcher? Contemporaries of Shakespeare, of
course. Because of Shakespeare we even know the name of the theatre manager, Mr. Henslowe, whose famous diary is pored over by
Shakespeare scholars. Likewise, because of Lovecraft, *Weird Tales*
is a famous name, and other *Weird Tales* writers are remembered
and read, including, to a limited degree, Price. No one cares about
what he wrote for *Argosy* or *Adventure*, the top-paying pulps he
"graduated" to when he got out of *Weird Tales.* Only his *Weird
Tales* material matters. Because of Lovecraft the future will also
know the name of that magazine's editor, Farnsworth Wright (with
whom Lovecraft had a sometimes difficult relationship), and the
publisher of Arkham House, August Derleth.

Coming out ahead of a pack of pulp writers might not seem
much of an accomplishment. It is worth noting that the leading "literary" masters of the ghostly and ghastly sort were exactly who

Lovecraft said they were in his monumental *Supernatural Horror in Literature*. He named Arthur Machen, M. R. James, Lord Dunsany, and Algernon Blackwood as the "Modern Masters." He has long since overtaken all of them. James has a certain independence, but most readers nowadays encounter the other three through Lovecraft, usually from references in introductions to his books. So, Lovecraftian wrote "Dunsanian" stories? Who? It happens that Dunsany is in Penguin Classics too these days, in a volume edited by the Lovecraft scholar, S. T. Joshi. Being Anglo-Irish, Dunsany is ineligible for Library of America. He has always had a tenuous connection to the Canon through his association with the Irish Renaissance. (Another famous theatre: the Abbey. Who was Dunsany? Another playwright whose work was performed there alongside Yeats and Synge. His fantasy fiction has, by and large, fallen out of mainstream critical awareness. His Penguin volume resulted in reviews nearly as befuddled as some of those of Lovecraft's.)

In popularity, and very likely in influence, Lovecraft has also overtaken Poe. He is a world figure. Why is this? What exactly did E. Hoffmann Price (and for that matter, Edmund Wilson) completely fail to comprehend?

It is simply this: Lovecraft's career and posthumous success represent the absolute triumph of the literary artist over the tradesman (Dunsany's term). Lovecraft might dash off "Herbert West—Reanimator" as a favor for a friend (one of his amateur press colleagues was editing *Home Brew*), make the task bearable by inserting a large dollop of parody, then laughingly disown the result, but when it came to the *real stuff*, his serious work, when he was writing "The Colour Out of Space" or "At the Mountains of Madness," he completely refused to compromise his personal vision, which was as compelling and unique as that of Kafka or Borges or Samuel Beckett or J. R. R. Tolkien or any other of the twentieth century's true originals.

Otis Adelbert Kline, as Price would never have been able to tell Mrs. Kline, simply didn't have any personal vision in his fiction. He produced what was popular at the moment, and crafted it about as well as lots of other pulp writers did, which meant, of course, that he could easily be replaced by someone else as soon as he stopped writing. But for his Edgar Rice Burroughs imitations, which enjoyed some shadowy success in the wake of ERB, that's exactly what happened. Price himself showed real artistic tendencies early on, but, as a prim Victorian might have phrased it, "he overcame them."

Lovecraft simply did not adhere to the rules imposed by pulp editors or anybody else. He did not write what was expected, what fit convenient categories and formulas. Sometimes even Farnsworth Wright, the great editor of *Weird Tales*, hesitated over the results. To give credit where it is due, Wright was the only editor of the day who would or even *could* publish most of what is now gathered in the Library of America *Tales*. But he once turned down "The Call of Cthulhu," not because he did not personally admire it, but because he was afraid his readers would not understand it. Too weird for *Weird Tales,* in other words. Wright was *the* cutting-edge fantasy editor of the time, but sometimes he lacked the courage of his convictions. Fortunately he later reconsidered, published the story, and found that his fears were entirely unfounded. In terms of influence, everything from derivative stories (the entire Cthulhu Mythos) to role-playing games to the existence of Lovecraftian plush-toys manufactured in China (*what* must Chinese factory workers make of an Elvis Cthulhu doll that the crazy Americans order by the caseload...?) this was surely the most significant American short story published in the later 1920s, at least.

Lovecraft wrote what he had to write, often with no serious expectation of publication, with little hope of financial success, although he was not indifferent to such things, as the despairing tone of some of his letters makes clear. Yet he did not waver, he did not relent or compromise, and he has triumphed. Admittedly he has also given rise to an unfortunate myth, that all you have to do is be uncompromising as Lovecraft and you will be as great as Lovecraft. *No,* it doesn't work that way. This idea has probably been as pernicious for would-be horror writers as the myth of Thomas Wolfe and Maxwell Perkins once was for mainstream novelists. (Remember that one? All the writer has to do is gush out words of ineffable brilliance, enough to fill a piano-case, and the perceptive editor will read down to the keyboard, recognize genius, and put it all into publishable shape for you. *No....)*

It isn't enough to be uncompromising. You have to have something worth being uncompromising *about.* The genius has to be there. Then it must not collapse under commercial pressure or fade away from the writer's lack of drive. Lovecraft held on desperately to the very end and it was enough.

What about that special vision? What was it? "The indefatigable" S. T. Joshi has written whole tomes with such portentous titles as *H. P. Lovecraft: The Decline of the West* (1990) to describe Lovecraft's philosophical outlook and why it is so compelling.

Fritz Leiber, who was many years ahead of the rest of us, wrote the following in "A Literary Copernicus" (in *The Acolyte,* 1944; revised for *Something About Cats,* 1949):

> Howard Phillips Lovecraft was the Copernicus
> of the horror story. He shifted the focus of supernatu-
> ral dread from man and his little world and his gods,
> to the stars and black and unplumbed gulfs of interga-
> lactic space. To do this effectively, he created a new
> kind of horror story and new methods of telling it....
> The universe of modern science engendered a pro-
> founder horror in Lovecraft's writings than that
> stemming solely from its tremendous distances and
> its highly probable alien and powerful non-human in-
> habitants. For the chief reason that man fears the uni-
> verse revealed by materialistic science is that it is a
> purposeless, soulless place. To quote Lovecraft's
> "The Silver Key," man can hardly bear the realization
> "the blind cosmos grinds aimlessly on from nothing
> to something back to nothing again, neither heeding
> or knowing the wishes or existence of the minds that
> flicker for a second now and then in the darkness."
> (*Discovering H. P. Lovecraft,* Schweitzer ed., p. 7-9.)

Nietzsche, who much influenced Lovecraft's thinking, called this "confronting the abyss." What Lovecraft did, far more effec-tively than any number of pulp ghost-mongers, or more than charm-ing, literary, mystical writers like Machen or Blackwood, is find something *genuinely scary* and compellingly real, and focus on it absolutely. Even as, for instance, all of Philip K. Dick's work is about the plastic nature of reality, all of Lovecraft's is about con-fronting the endless, mindless, godless, and *dead* universe which will ultimately devour us all. Nothing matters in the long-run, not even art. In a billion years, the works of William Shakespeare will be one with those of William McGonagall, and Lovecraft will be one with Otis Adelbert Kline.

But in the meantime, HPL is the creepiest writer going, pre-cisely because is work is not just a bunch of theatrical fright-effects, but genuinely about something.

Left out of the Library of America *Tales* are several lesser but still quite interesting stories, such as "The Unnamable," "The Tomb," "Dagon," "The Festival," "The Nameless City," and others, including the entire "Dunsanian" cycle. There is enough left over for a second volume, which should also include some of his essays, in-cluding "Supernatural Horror in Literature" (which is itself so influential that the reputations of many writers are kept alive merely because of what Lovecraft said about them) and others, plus a substantial selection of his brilliant letters (he was one of literature's great epistolarians), and a very judicious sampling of his poetry. To keep things in perspective, with all this talk of Shakespeare and analogies to the Globe Theatre, we need to remember that Lovecraft was only a sporadically interesting poet, nowhere near as good as Shakespeare, or Poe, or even his contemporaries, Clark Ashton Smith and Robert E. Howard.

But he is our genre's most famous son.

XXI.

THE GERNSBACK DAYS

The Gernsback Days by Mike Ashley and Robert A.W. Lowndes. Holicong, PA: Wildside Press, 2004, 499 p.

"It is easy to argue," Brian Aldiss is quoted (from *Billion Year Spree)* as saying in the introduction,

> that Hugo Gernsback was one of the worst disasters ever to hit the science fiction field. Not only did the segregation of science fiction into magazines designed especially for it, ghetto-fashion, guarantee that various orthodoxies would be established inimical to a thriving literature, but Gernsback himself was utterly without literary understanding. He created dangerous precedents which many later editors in the field followed.

Indeed, it was sufficiently easy to argue thus that I did so myself, with a "vitriolic attack" on Gernsback, originally written as "Was Hugo Gernsback Really the Father of Science Fiction?" and published in *Algol* in 1977 as "Keeper of the Flame." (Not my title.) Ashley also quotes my resounding conclusion, "I doubt anyone else could have been a *worse* influence on the field."

The Gernsback Days was written to refute that sort of thing, more aimed at Aldiss than Schweitzer without any doubt. Of my own youthful effusion, I would say from the perspective of twenty-eight years, that it contains perhaps more passion than strict adherence to the facts, and in any case, with the publication of the present excellently researched and detailed volume, more facts are available than before. The case against Gernsback becomes, like most historical indictments, somewhat ambiguous.

But I do not back down entirely from my original thesis, which was based on a reading of, ironically, such Sam Moskowitz anthologies as *Science Fiction by Gaslight* and *Under the Moons of Mars*. The "Father of Science Fiction" certainly did not invent science fiction. It was published routinely in a variety of places, and by most book publishers, in the nineteenth and early twentieth centuries. Yet by the end of the 1920s, this had ceased. If we turn to the early Science Fiction magazines, particularly the Gernsback *Amazing Stories* and *Science Wonder Stories*, we find material of such markedly inferior quality labeled "Science Fiction" that this (one can certainly argue) surely lowered the standards of the whole field (and public expectations of same). The "Great Retarded Period" ensued, in which Science Fiction was not only cut off from general literature (as it had not been in H. G. Wells's heyday) but it was even *sub-pulp*. It took nearly ten years for most SF writers to learn enough basic narrative skills to reach the level of average pulp western, detective, or adventure fiction. This happened, according to Aldiss, because Gernsback had no literary understanding at all. Anybody else then, particularly an editor with a real appreciation of good storytelling, could have done a better job founding the first all-Science Fiction magazine.

Today I would say that literary alternate-history is a futile exercise. It was *Gernsback* who actually did it. Others may have contemplated such a thing (including Farnsworth Wright, the great *Weird Tales* editor), but Gernsback did it, so the genre's history enters its phase of self-awareness with him.

I would suggest further, and I think Brian Aldiss would agree upon reflection, that if you examine the SF of the period, *outside of the Gernsback magazines*, there seems to be plenty of blame to go around.

Something happened to science fiction between the 1890s, when Wells could publish *The War of the Worlds* or *The First Men in the Moon* in *Cosmopolitan* or E. M. Forster could publish an overtly science-fictional reply to Wells with "The Machine Stops" (1909) with complete literary respectability, and the middle 1920s. Science Fiction crashed and burned. Part of this was a cultural shift, particularly in the United States, away from the "scientific romance" and toward detective stories and westerns in the pulps and realism in the mainstream, but also it must be admitted that the thrilling sagas of Ray Cummings or Otis Adelbert Kline in *Argosy* were hardly going to propel the form into the forefront of modern literature. The science fiction in the early *Weird Tales*, ranging from A. G. Birch's

"The Moon Terror" (1923) to Edmond Hamilton's "Crashing Suns" (1928), was not exactly on the level of Wells or of Huxley's *Brave New World* (1932) either. From the perspective of the literary mainstream, ignoring the pulps entirely, science fiction was something which, but for the occasional volume like Huxley's, had *died out* about the time Gernsback came onto the scene. I own an edition Conan Doyle's Professor Challenger stories with a curiously myopic introduction by John Dickson Carr expressing the regret, circa 1950, that no one seems to write that sort of imaginative, scientifically speculative story anymore.

This is the fundamental problem the historian of our genre has to wrestle with. It is our Fall of Rome. What happened? Why? Could Gernsback have mitigated the catastrophe or did he, because of his unique limitations, only make things worse?

The first half of *The Gernsback Days*, by Mike Ashley, is an examination of the life and career of Hugo Gernsback. The Lowndes portion is a nostalgic survey of all the pulp science fiction of the period, in Gernsback's magazines and outside of them (ignoring isolated literary works like *Brave New World* or John Collier's 1933 post-holocaust novel, *Tom's A-Cold*). It is perhaps the last time we will be able to see this material re-examined by one of its original readers. That is charming, and certainly interesting, but the Ashley half is what matters, drawn from Gernsback's papers, correspondence, the testimony of people who worked with him, and particularly a great deal of information obtained from Gernsback's longtime friend and advocate, Sam Moskowitz.

Also of interest is an appendix by Charles Hornig, a memoir of his time working as managing editor for Gernsback's *Wonder Stories* between the ages of seventeen and twenty.

Ashley presents Gernsback first and foremost as a science tinkerer and visionary, a salesman of science and technology, sort of a cross between Thomas Edison and Carl Sagan. He was a boy genius, who experimented with electricity, then wired his own house and a local convent by the time he was thirteen. Once when he was trapped in a shed in sub-freezing temperatures with only a crude electrical light handy, his knowledge of practical science saved his life. He shorted out the battery, started a fire, and burned the door down. Gernsback was also a relatively wealthy person with an easy-come, easy-go attitude toward money. When he emigrated to the United States from Luxembourg in 1903, he was so confident of his success that he spent $20 of the $100 he had with him on a new silk hat.

And succeed he did, setting himself up in business almost at once, founding the Electro Importing Company in 1905, beginning to publish his first magazine, *Modern Electrics*, in 1908. At this point he was zealous to convert the public to the wonders of new technology, particularly electricity. In 1906 he had perfected a portable home radio transmitter, which he offered for sale for $7.50, when a regular transmitter would cost about $50,000 to build. (Multiply all of these amounts by twenty to get some idea of what they mean in 2005 dollars.) The police were called. Gernsback was accused of fraud. He was able to demonstrate that his device worked, but the policeman went away grumbling, "I still think yez are fakers. Your ad here sez it is a wire*less* set, so what are all dem wires for?" That rankled, even years later. Gernsback's mission was to overcome precisely that sort of ignorance.

His science writing became increasingly speculative. He described television (though he only popularized the term and did not coin it, as is sometimes reported) in 1909. In 1911 he serialized his own novel *Ralph 124C41+* in *Modern Electrics.* In many ways Ralph typified what we have since come to think of as Gernsbackian SF, stilted, ridiculously plotted, completely rotten as literature or even pulp entertainment, but filled with a parade of brilliant inventions, including a complete description (with diagrams) of radar.

Modern Electrics was succeeded by *The Electrical Experimenter,* and later by *Science and Invention.* All of these featured increasing numbers of speculative articles, and then fiction of a sort, scientific skits, often humorous, but occasionally a genuinely good short story. He serialized two Ray Cummings novels. The June 1923 *Science and Invention* was a special "Scientific Fiction Number," which contained four stories and part of a serial. The fiction only made up about 20% of the issue, but one of the stories was "The Man from the Atom" by a teenaged G. Peyton Wertenbacker, Gernsback's first important discovery.

Both Ashley and Lowndes praise Wertenbacker's work. Born in 1907, Wertenbacker lived until 1968. He wrote a few more stories for Gernsback, and that was it. One of the surprising perspectives that comes out of *The Gernsback Days* is an appreciation of how long the survivors of the Gernsback Era remained out of touch with the subsequent development of Science Fiction, ignored by historians and fans as if they were just names from a long-vanished past. How startling to realize that Claire Winger Harris, the first woman to sell a story to a science fiction magazine, was still alive in 1969. Ed Earl Repp survived until 1979, Benson Herbert until 1991, J. Harvey Haggard until 2001. What was it about Gernsback writers which caused so many of them to give up so early and be forgotten?

Part of the answer comes from my theory of the Great Retarded Period. Once Gernsback had started *Amazing Stories* in 1926, as an outgrowth of his experiments with SF in his other magazines, he began to have difficulty getting material its pages. Ashley admits as much, that the writers were amateurs (p. 43), that they did not write nearly as well as the pulp generalists (p. 56) and that Gernsback had a bad habit of treating the payment for stories as being more akin to contest winnings, rather than professional work.

While Ashley is clearly a partisan of Gernsback, and occasionally waxes Moskowitzian when he says of Gernsback's 1911 activities, "the dawn of science fiction was about to unfold" (p. 21) anyone afraid this book is going to be another club history of Science Fiction need not be. Ashley achieves an admirably broad context in chapter 6, "The Dawn of Scientific Fiction," which is all about Wells, Verne, Conan Doyle, Edgar Rice Burroughs, the various contributors to *Argosy* and *All-Story*, and the like. He is perfectly aware that Gernsback was trying to draw on and shape an already existing tradition of literature, what Wells had called "scientific romance," and what the editors of *Argosy* called the "fantastic" (an adjective used as a noun, analogous to the "western").

As soon as the subject of money raises its ugly head, Gernsback's limitations begin to show. He was, even in prosperous times, we must reluctantly admit, both greedy and stingy. He paid himself an annual salary of $50,000 (and his brother Sidney got $39,000) in an era when the average worker was lucky to get $20 a week and a new car might cost $500. Despite this, he paid writers as little as a fifth of a cent a word. He dickered with H. G. Wells, who charged for reprints, £20 for short stories and £100 for novels. As a pound was worth about five dollars in those days, that worked out to about $1000 per novel, a (US) penny a word, not an unreasonable rate. But Gernsback chose to interpret Wells's figures as *dollars*. He stiffed Wells and managed to keep it up (somehow) for several years before Wells refused to sell him anything more.

This pattern, alas, continued. By sheer stinginess, Gernsback managed to alienate H. P. Lovecraft (and coined for him the long-lasting epithet of "Hugo the Rat") and keep away the top purveyors of original pulp SF, Murray Leinster, Ray Cummings, and Ralph Milne Farley. Cummings had written for Gernsback in the *Science and Invention* days, but not now. Leinster was reprinted in Gernsback's *Amazing* but never had an original story there. At the same time, all three of these worthies were the star contributors of science fiction to *Argosy*, which paid two cents a word. When Gernsback began to face real, professional competition, in the form of *Astounding Stories of Super-Science* in 1930, which also paid two cents a word, *on acceptance*, Leinster, Cummings, and as many Gernsback regulars as could write well enough to get in flocked there.

One way to look at Gernsback's career is as a sad decline from the optimistic young gadgeteer in the $20 silk hat into shifty Hugo the Rat. When Gernsback's company went into receivership in 1929 (largely because the profits from the magazines were being poured into inventions and Gernsback's radio station), the first thing the bank that took charge did was fire both Gernsback brothers. But Hugo bounced back, with *Science Wonder Stories, Air Wonder Stories,* and *Wonder Quarterly.* Unfortunately his managerial skills and very possibly his honesty got no better. He was sued many times. There really *was*, as has often been reported, a New York lawyer who specialized in Gernsback debts. (Her name was Ione Weber.) Probably the saddest cut of all came in 1937, after Gernsback had been forced to sell *Wonder Stories,* when he was finally sued by his most loyal contributor, David H. Keller M.D., whose "The Revolt of the Pedestrians" had made SF history in *Amazing* in 1928. Keller stayed with Gernsback to the end, and was also editing and writing much of the contents of two medical/science magazines, *The Facts of Life* and *Your Body*. Gernsback didn't pay. Keller felt used. He sued. Gernsback paid then, but never hired Keller again and had to shut down both magazines.

In the appendix Charles Hornig reveals the astonishing fact that Gernsback never paid Stanley G. Weinbaum for "A Martian Odyssey" *at all.* Needless to say, Weinbaum, the hottest new writer of the day, placed his major work in non-Gernsback magazines as soon as he could. That he had anything at all in *Wonder Stories*, even as a last resort, suggests that either he still held out hope that he would be paid eventually, or that he felt a certain gratitude to Gernsback for publishing his first story, despite everything. Maybe a combination of the two.

There is a cautionary tale here, as relevant to publishing in 2005 as it was in 1935. *Reliable* payment is more important than high payment. *Fast* payment is more important than high payment. Donald A. Wollheim, one of the many writers who once sued Gernsback, seems to have taken this to heart throughout his career. Ace Books paid less than anybody else in the early days, but if you signed, I have heard it said, Wollheim would cut you a check before you got out of the building.

If Gernsback had even been able to offer even half a cent a

word, *on acceptance* rather than on threat of lawsuit, he might have been able to maintain some sort of steady presence. Instead he lost his contributors as quickly as any alternative markets appeared, and in 1934 was completely blown away by the early Orlin Tremaine *Astounding*. In a field that basically consisted of three magazines, *Astounding, Amazing* (edited by the increasingly doddering T. O'Conor Sloane, who thought space travel was nonsense), and *Wonder*, Gernsback's *Wonder* could not even hold an honorable third place. By 1935, *Wonder* was limping. After two issues in 1936, it was gone.

A bit more of that perspective *The Gernsback Days* is so strong on: Gernsback's writers, circa 1928, were amateurs. Their narrative and stylistic skills were not, on the whole, good enough for them to sell any other sort of fiction. You can see this in a work like *The Skylark of Space* by E. E. Smith, published by Gernsback in 1928. It has *only* science fiction virtues. It is imaginative. It opens up vast new perspectives. But, sure enough, when Doc Smith tried to write detective stories, they were not good enough to sell. A pro writer like Will F. Jenkins (Murray Leinster) could write anything he wanted, SF, western, detective, or adventure. But he expected to be treated like a pro. Pros stayed away from Gernsback.

In 1930 the pulp publisher William Clayton started *Astounding Stories of Super Science*, not because he had any particular interest in SF, but (so the story goes) because the expensive covers for pulp magazines were printed in huge sheets of sixteen covers. Clayton had only fifteen titles, so the sixteen space would go to waste. Since the cover was more expensive to print than the interior pages, he could start a new magazine almost for free. Clayton was contemptuous of the contents of Gernsback's publications, which he described as "Awful stuff! Packed with puerilities. Written by unimaginables" (p. 161). He concluded, though, that the "pseudo-science" field had commercial potential, and decided to bring out the first real, professional magazine of Science Fiction.

It is important to understand that the Gernsback magazines to this point, *Amazing,* and the early *Science Wonder Stories* were larger sized, printed on a very different sort of paper (stiff and thick, almost like cardboard) and had trimmed edges. They tried very hard to position themselves next to the science-hobbyist magazines of the *Science and Invention* sort. They were not pulps. Pulps, as everybody knew, were lurid trash for the masses.

The long-time fan Robert Madle, who was a reader in those days, once told me that his reaction to the news of the advent of *Astounding* was: "Oh, *no!* They're going to do a *pulp magazine* of Science Fiction!" "It was as if your sister had just become a prostitute," he explained. Eventually fans warmed to *Astounding* and Clayton (and his editor, Harry Bates, later remembered as the author of one classic story, "Farewell to the Master," the basis for *The Day the Earth Stood Still*) warmed to science fiction. While I would hold that the Clayton *Astounding* was a lot better than Mike Ashley says it was (he cites only *one* good story in the entire three-year run), it is fair to say that much of the content was so formulaic and action-driven that *nothing happened* in many of the stories. You know: hero lands on planet, fights monsters, gets chased by aliens, trips over a cliché, is captured, escapes, confronts villain...and in terms of the development of theme or idea, there is, indeed, no content at all. Even his readers took Bates to task for this.

However, *Astounding* brought professional writing into Science Fiction in a consistent way. In terms of plotting, characterization, and general narrative skills, the *Astounding* writers were exactly as good as the folks who wrote for cowboy, detective, and air-war pulps. The stars of *Argosy*, particularly Leinster and Cummings, moved right in.

More importantly, when *Astounding* was sold to Street and Smith, another thoroughly professional, well-heeled pulp publisher, and the new editor, Tremaine, began to put a much stronger emphasis on genuinely imaginative content, what he called "thought variant" stories, this combination of strong ideation and competent writing blew Gernsback's *Wonder Stories* out of the water. *Amazing* didn't last much longer, selling out in 1938. Both it, now edited by Ray Palmer, and *Wonder*, retitled *Thrilling Wonder Stories* and edited by Mort Weisinger, avoided direct competition with *Astounding* (which was about to go on to John Campbell's Golden Age in a couple years) and emphasized the more juvenile sort of bang-bang story that Harry Bates had published. They were virtually reincarnations of the Clayton *Astounding.* One of the ironies was that both Palmer and Weisinger were early fans, involved in the fandom that Gernsback more or less started with his Science Fiction League in *Wonder Stories.* Both of them went on to completely repudiate everything Gernsback stood for. (Palmer had even sold fiction to Gernsback and been stiffed by him.) Pulp science fiction was, henceforth, to be entertainment first, second, and third, and educational, as Gernsback wanted it to be, only incidentally.

That is one way to look at it: Gernsback, enthusiastic in his mission, limited in perspective, shoddy in his business practices, crippled his own dream by too much penny-pinching. His vision of Science Fiction was superseded as fast as possible. As soon as *any* alternative existed, readers and writers flocked to it.

But there is more. Hugo Gernsback was a joy to work with, says Charles Hornig. Yes, money was a problem, but otherwise Gernsback encouraged innovation and new ideas. He never stopped trying.

Hornig was one of two managing or sub-editors hired by Gernsback to run *Wonder Stories.* The most interesting and important parts of *The Gernsback Days* are a discussion of how these two, and Gernsback himself, were engaged in a kind of tug-of-war with Science Fiction itself, trying to shape the evolution of the form.

And evolution *did* take place. An important point made by Ashley, which somewhat refutes Brian Aldiss, is that, prior to the institution of specialized Science Fiction magazines, the evolution of SF was slow and diffuse. The *Argosy* SF story of 1914 was not a whole lot different from one of ten or fifteen years later, but in the pressure-cooker environment of the SF pulps, radical changes came very fast. The difference between 1932, doldrums, and 1934, when the *Astounding* "thought variant" era was in full swing, is quite remarkable.

Gernsback started with gadget stories, humorous science skits, and fiction that was overwhelmingly didactic and educational. He had never quite gotten over that cop who refused to believe a wireless radio could have wires in it. He was out to *teach* and to inspire young men to become scientists. But readers wanted *stories.* They wanted the sensation of exotic adventure, strange vistas, new perspectives. Inasmuch as Aldiss is correct and Gernsback lacked any literary understanding at all, Gernsback's failure was his inability to recognize that any fiction, even a fiction of ideas, works through shared, vicarious experience. It is not about the mere *concept* of going to another planet. It is about what it *feels like* to do so. Wells was well aware of this when he was the first writer to describe the physical sensations of time-travel in "The Time Machine." Any story is ultimately emotional rather than intellectual—vivid scenes, atmosphere, characters the reader cares about. For all a story may have a generative idea at its core, like the grain of sand at the heart of a pearl, the idea sticks in the reader's mind by association with sensations and textures—more like a leaf to the surface of a tar-pit. It is far more than a matter of just "sugar-coating" the message with a few exciting action scenes.

Even in the earliest *Amazing*, which was mostly a reprint magazine, the most popular items were those which offered the strongest stories, not the niftiest ideas. A. Merritt's "The Moon Pool" and Edgar Rice Burroughs's *The Land That Time Forgot* (both published in

1927) were what the readers wanted, not more of *Ralph 124C41+* or "The Scientific Adventures of Mr. Fosdick." Merritt and Burroughs set the precedent for what was to follow, in *Astounding* and elsewhere. Science Fiction refused to remain what Gernsback originally intended it to be. It mutated, and slithered from his grasp.

One way of describing it is to say that the *Argosy* model of Science Fiction, as typified by *A Princess of Mars* (1911), supplanted Gernsback's own vision of SF, in his own magazine and in all of its successors.

Ashley, however, describes something more complex. Gernsback had to compromise on the question of story values, realizing the need for considerably more story, and fewer footnotes and schematic diagrams. By his own admission, "The Moon Pool" lurched dangerously close to what he dismissed as the "fairy tale," *i.e.* sheer fantasy. But, intriguingly, Gernsback's sub-editors, particularly David Lasser (Managing Editor, 1930-33) sought something more sophisticated, with better writing, better characterization, more developed ideas. Lasser may have been the first genuinely talented science-fiction editor. Charles Hornig (1933-36), probably because of his youth, proved inferior, rejecting big names for bumptious reasons and sending them straight to the competition. Yet he too thought he was striving for higher standards.

But by then the lawsuits were coming thick and fast. *Wonder* never had a chance to evolve. It couldn't hold its contributors. Hugo the Rat ultimately starved to death the creation of the optimistic young man in the silk hat. It is to Ashley's credit that he does not whitewash any of this. It is not enough to say this was the Great Depression and times were hard. The Depression was a prosperous time for pulps. Gernsback's own business practices did him in.

After the sale of *Wonder Stories,* Gernsback experimented with *Superworld Comics* in 1940. It tried to be as educational as the earliest *Amazing* and lasted three issues. In 1953 he launched a large-sized, *slick* magazine called *Science Fiction Plus,* but the contents showed no growth at all since the '30s. It didn't make it into 1954. Late in life, he was complaining that most science fiction, including those stories given the award named after him—the Hugo winners—were just "fairy tales," not what he recognized as science fiction at all.

Speaking of awards, let me first say that *The Gernsback Days* is an important book, a major work of scholarship. It is worth nominating for Best Non-Fiction Book for the 2005 Hugos.

Then let me suggest that maybe I was unfair in 1977. Maybe

Hugo Gernsback *was* the father of Science Fiction as a self-aware genre after all. He got a lot of things *started*, as Ashley convincingly demonstrates.

But if Gernsback was the father of Science Fiction, it was necessary for his offspring to run away from home as soon as possible, and seek its fortune in the big, wide world where Papa, because of his limitations, could not follow.

XXII.

ROMA ETERNA

Roma Eterna by Robert Silverberg. New York: Eos, 2003, cloth, 396 p.

So now Silverberg's done it too. Everybody is writing Alternate Histories these days. As Judith Berman has suggested in the pages of *NYRSF*, in her celebrated essay, "Science Fiction Without a Future" this may be because SF writers have given up on the future. Maybe Ballard had it right all along. The Space Age has faded away within a single lifetime. It's a matter of crumbling launch pads and elderly astronauts trying to convince anyone who will listen that they really did go to the Moon once. That's one take on it. The bright vision of 1940s and 1950's SF, of a space-faring, galactic future has died, and so the last SF writers are idling their time away with impossible speculations about things that didn't happen.

Robert Silverberg is unlikely to agree. He has certainly written just about every kind of SF there is, and so why shouldn't he explore this form too? Certainly the Alternate History has been around for a long time, since well before modern SF allegedly lost its sense of vision and purpose. It grew from two discernable roots, one being the political warning story, such as Saki's *When William Came* (1914). The other is the time-travel story. What if someone goes back and changes history...then what? There are hints of alternate history (used satirically) in Nat Schachner's "Ancestral Voices" (1933), and Murray Leinster's "Sidewise in Time" (1934) opens all the possibilities, for all the story itself does not venture very far into them. Ward Moore's *Bring the Jubilee* (1953) revolutionized the form by starting in the alternate world, and only halfway through the book bringing in the element of time-travel and the possibility of setting history "right." That *Bring the Jubilee* follows many of the tropes of the 1950s post-holocaust novel only adds to its meaning and continuing interest.

Actually one of the very best alternate history stories comes from outside the genre proper. Stephen Vincent Benét's "The Curfew Tolls" (published in *The Saturday Evening Post* in 1935) is about Napoleon Bonaparte born a generation too soon, in frustrated retirement right as the French Revolution might be about to break out. It is a meditation on history itself: the Great Man theory versus the idea of the Times Must Be Right.

This is the key to what might be called the aesthetic usefulness of the alternate history story. At its worst, alternate history is an extension of wargaming, a working out of clever scenarios of how this or that battle might have gone differently if so-and-so had fallen off his horse at the right moment. Such stories often lose sight of human detail. Most of them are about war, but they often ignore the drama and suffering of war. Dying under a bush far from home with a spear in your guts is probably the same experience whether the war is recorded in our timeline or not.

The key question is simply this: does the author's alteration of the historical facts mean anything? It's a matter, not of clever scenarios and overlooked details, but of thematic content. Benét's story was clearly about something. So was Moore's.

How about Silverberg's? That a new Robert Silverberg book is deftly constructed and elegantly written almost goes without saying. He is a master of craft. His prose is smooth, lucid, his story-telling easy to follow without ever being unintelligent. The present volume is not a novel, but a collection of linked stories, forming a cycle, like Keith Roberts's *Pavane*. There are undeniably fine stories here. But does the overall structure succeed?

Silverberg has avoided the Big Two cliché subjects of alternate histories (at least as written by Americans)—Hitler Wins and The Civil War Turns Out Differently—but certainly The Roman Empire Never Fell is hardly a new idea either. It was even done on *Star Trek* thirty-plus years ago.

It can even be argued that Silverberg has broken one of the cardinal "rules" of the alternate-history game, which is that you change *one* thing and let all else develop from that. To begin with, he has changed two things. First, the Pharaoh's army overtook the Israelites and the Exodus was a total failure. Moses drowned in the Red Sea. The few survivors of the Jewish people returned to slavery in Egypt. There was no land of Israel, no Bible as we know it, and no heretical offshoot called Christianity. The Roman Empire remained solidly pagan.

But the Roman Empire also ran into an extraordinary series of lucky breaks. After the death of tyrant Caracalla (A.D. 217 in our timeline), there came, not the mediocre Macrinus, followed by the insane volumptuary Elagabalus, followed by another mediocrity (Severus Alexander), followed by military anarchy, but instead a Great Man, one Titus Gallius, a reformer on the order of Augustus or Diocletian, who set things on a firm footing for centuries to come. The stronger and more capable later emperors still seem to have occurred in the resultant alternate history—Diocletian himself, Constantine (a great warlord, though of no religious significance), and Theodosius the Great, who manages to outlive his inept son Honorius. (In our timeline, he did not—Honorius is the one who mistook Rome for a chicken, on whose watch the capital was sacked by the Goths while the emperor did nothing). Then come a whole series of invented figures, great men, who save the Empire again and again. One of them allegedly wipes out the Vandal and Goth menace forever. (How did he do that? By total genocide? Otherwise, as real Roman emperors discovered to their grief, no matter how many barbarians you killed, somewhere there were barbarian children who would grow up with a grudge and it would start all over again.) If there is any single premise to this book, it is that history was jiggered as many times as necessary to allow the Roman Empire to survive well beyond its allotted time. So there are no Dark Ages. Conveniently, Islam is nipped in the bud. (One might ask if it would ever have developed, without the examples of Judaism and Christianity before it.) So the Empire goes on and on, discovering Mexico in what would be, in our timeline, the twelfth century.

In fact, this is a book you should read with a calculator at hand. Silverberg does interesting tricks with the dates, using the Roman calendar, Ab Urbe Condita (Year of the City—*i.e.*, a calculation from the legendary founding of Rome in 753 B.C.), but if you deduct 753 from everything, interesting results pop out. "With Caesar in the Underworld" (the story of a Roman Falstaff, and a Prince Hal who turns out to be one of those saviors of the Empire) takes place in A.D. 529, early in the reign of Justinian. That fits. "A Hero of the Empire," about the elimination of Mohammed, takes place in 612, ten years before the Hegira. Now that the Dark Ages have been prevented, and, rather implausibly, the new Pax Romana extends for five hundred years, "The Second Wave" takes place in 1108, the Crusader Era in our timeline. Here the Romans make a futile and ultimately destructive attempt to conquer Mexico. This takes us to "Waiting for the End" in 1198, the year (in our timeline) in which the Fourth Crusade was preached, resulting in the sack of Constantinople in 1204. Here the Eastern Empire takes Rome, which is a nice, ironic reversal. But it is not the end. In "An Outpost of the Realm" in 1453 (the year we know for the Fall of Constantinople to the Turks) a resurgent West conquers the East. Silverberg's Rome goes on to become a truly global state, until finally overthrown by a revolutionary reign of terror in 1815, when the emperor is replaced by an equally despotic First Consul, echoing Napoleon all the way. And finally, in a coda to it all, "To the Promised Land," in what would be A.D. 1970 the last remnants of the Jews, led by a second Moses, launch a spaceship in the Egyptian desert, hoping to start a new Exodus to the stars. It is a completely mad scheme. It's not as if they've been sending out probes for years and know where they're going. What are they going to do? Cram everybody into a spaceship and then pick a star at random? But nobody has to think it through that far. The spaceship explodes. The second Moses perishes. But in a moment of fanatical rationalization, the chief surviving disciple declares the dead man to have been the Son of God, who was called home to Heaven. What should have been a disaster is instead, at last, the beginning of a messianic, monotheistic religion which will sweep away the carcass of the Roman Empire (which now pretends to be a Republic under the First Consuls) and create a new world.

It's all a very grand scheme, but, one suspects, too conservative, reminiscent of Silverberg's Majipoor (particularly *Valentine Pontifex*), where, amid unparalleled splendor, dynasties and kingdoms go on in a stately procession for thousands of years, as if there are no social developments and nobody has a new idea more than once in a half-millennium. Real history, our history, has been more vigorous than that. The still waters of the Silverbergian monarchies don't seem to get stirred very often.

Does it mean anything? If that is the standard one applies to alternate histories, is this one about anything?

Yes, it is. It is not about dates or the number of extra emperors the author can invent. It is about the *myth* of Rome, which in our own timeline has been a very potent force and a lively political ghost indeed. Our whole concept of a Dark Age, of a post-holocaust society looking back on a better time, derives from the memory of Rome. The entire medieval period may be defined as a period in which somebody, somewhere, still claimed to be the Roman emperor, although it must be admitted that the imperial ghost did not lie still even after that. The Holy Roman Empire was abolished in 1806 precisely to prevent Napoleon Bonaparte from making himself Caesar and Augustus, which is what he was up to when, echoing Charlemagne (crowned Emperor of the Romans in 800), Bonaparte crowned himself in the presence of the pope in 1804. Roman imperial imagery is evident in the art and coinage of the Napoleonic period. Napoleon appears crowned in laurel, like a Caesar.

Even after Waterloo (1815, the year of Silverberg's anti-imperial Terror), the myth of the Pax Romana, when all the known world was allegedly ruled with serene grace by wise and benevolent emperors persisted. There were Tsars and Kaisers into the twentieth century. Historians have long puzzled over the Fall of Rome as *the* problem of history. Possibly the idea of re-establishing the Empire finally died a shabby death with Mussolini, but even so it remains almost hard-wired into our collective psyche that the End of the Empire was an awful catastrophe from which profound truths may be learned about the nature of civilization and perhaps of the historical process itself.

We see this in science fiction, in Poul Anderson's future history, where the Long Night follows Dominic Flandry's time, for all that worthy servant of the Empire might stave it off for a while. In Isaac Asimov's *Foundation* series, the great work of the genius Hari Seldon is a new science for charting the inevitable decline of the Roman Empire of the Galaxy, which encompasses all of mankind. Historical determinism versus human free will is expressed by Asimov (and by many writers before him) in terms of the echo of Rome's fall.

As a work of myth, Silverberg's *Roma Eterna* overcomes its own contrivances. There is something to be said for all that glacial grandeur, and the myth itself is deftly reversed by the epilogue, in which the narrator, a Jewish historian who is to write the new Gospel, observes:

> By its shrewd acceptance and absorption of the alien gods and the alien ways of the peoples it had conquered, the Empire had flattened everything into shapelessness...so that we had nothing left to venerate except the status quo itself, the holy stability of the world government. I had felt for years that the time was long overdue for some great revolution, in which all fixed, fast-frozen relationships, with their train of ancient and venerable prejudices and opinions, would be swept away.... for the Empire was defunct and didn't know it. Like some immense dead beast it lay upon the soul of humanity, smothering it beneath it-

self: a beast so huge that its limbs hadn't yet heard the news of its own death. (p. 387)

And yet Silverberg presents the last emperors sympathetically, and their passing, and that of the Empire continues to stir a sense of tragedy.

XXIII.

THE PLEASURES OF A FUTUROSCOPE

The Pleasures of a Futuroscope by Lord Dunsany. New York: Hippocampus Press, 2003, cloth, 200 p.

There's something to be said for reading in context. Never mind those critics who insist that a literary work must stand entirely on its own, just words on a page, in the pure white void of historical and biographical nothingness. Here's a book that would be worth reading even if it *were* floating in a void, but which offers quite a bit more to the reader with some understanding of when it was written and by whom.

First of all, it comes as a surprise: not merely unpublished, but a previously unknown science fiction novel by Lord Dunsany, the author of *The Gods of Pegāna* and *The King of Elfland's Daughter,* written in 1955. He doesn't seem to have told anyone about it. All the books about Dunsany, such as Mark Amory's *Lord Dunsany: a Biography* (1972) fail to mention it. This gives a completely false view of the final phase of Dunsany's career. He continued writing until the end (late 1957), and apparently even took a manuscript with him to work on when sent to a nursing home for what he didn't expect to be his last illness, but the conventional view has always been of a slow winding down: the last novel, *His Fellow Men* (1952), an interesting but rather labored parable about a "modern saint" who tries to be tolerant of all religions and gets into no end of trouble for it, followed by putterings-about with the short stories, some pretty good, but nothing epoch-making. It's like trying to evaluate late Hemingway without *The Old Man and the Sea.* Much of the problem seems to have been that Dunsany's son, the Nineteenth Baron Dunsany, took little interest in his father's literary properties. The Dunsany Estate has only been really active in the past few years, under the auspices of the Twentieth Baron, and the resultant discoveries have been significant, including a whole sixth volume of Jorkens stories all ready to go to the publisher but apparently never sent out (soon to be published by Night Shade Books), some long-lost, unpublished plays (*The Murderers* and *The Ginger Cat*, to be included in a Wildside Press volume), and now this.

The Pleasures of a Futuroscope might be described as a novel by a seventy-seven-year-old man suffering, not so much from future shock as present shock. Like many people of his generation, Lord Dunsany had some difficulty coming to terms with technological progress. In a 1946 booklet, *A Glimpse from the Watchtower,* he remarks on the (to him) completely startling news of the atomic bomb, he remarks, "The picture I have long seen in the dark of the future, growing rapidly less dim as our strange age goes by, is the picture of Man grown cleverer than he was intended to be, but not clever enough, and destroying himself by his own skill."

Science was never Dunsany's strong point. In the book of his correspondence with Arthur C. Clarke (*Arthur C. Clarke & Lord Dunsany: a Correspondence* ed. Keith Allen Daniels, Anamnesis Press, 1998) we find the young RAF officer and science-fiction fan Clarke, circa 1944, trying to explain the basics of rocketry and astronomy to Dunsany (then in his sixties), who, rather touchingly, is having some difficulty keeping up, but is open-minded enough to want to try. Throughout his entire literary corpus, there are "warnings" that maybe technological progress was not a good idea, even a play called "The Evil Kettle" (1925) in which James Watt's discovery of steam power is the work of the Devil. A devoted ruralist (also world-traveler, adventurer, and big-game hunter), Dunsany railed against the ugliness of the industrial cities, the impurity of processed foods, and the evils of unsightly billboards. Technophobic reactionary or visionary environmentalist? A key passage occurs in his autobiography, *Patches of Sunlight* (1938), in which he recalls a discussion with a lady on the subject:

> I argued against machinery and the Black Country, and argued that such things were spoiling England. She won the discussion with an argument that was so new to me that her words remain clear in my memory. "If it were not for machinery," she said, "four-fifths of the people in England would not be living today. For a fifth of our present population is all that England could support a hundred and fifty years ago."

I saw no answer to that. Alas that I see an answer now. I fear that the answer is that what machines can support for a while in peace machines may one day tear to pieces in war. Machines were our slaves in 1911. May they not turn against us? And looking at a house they are building today in London I get a feeling that man is no longer the master; for instead of shaping metal into the dreams of man, still bronze blossoms with leaves and figures, we are building houses like packing cases. (p. 205)

Here we see the genesis of Dunsany's first science fiction novel, *The Last Revolution* (1951), which is about a revolt of the machines, and *The Pleasures of a Futuroscope,* in which a retired journalist borrows a device which enables him to observe the future. The "futuroscope" sounds rather like an old-fashioned camera (one puts a cloth over one's head and peers into a glass viewer) but the narrator is able to explain it to the curious as being rather like a new kind of television, with much of the same entertainment potential. (Remember that television was still new in 1955.) In fact, the narrator goes on repeatedly about how he is merely amusing himself, not engaging in serious scientific or historical research, and is writing so that the public may want to buy futuroscopes when they come on the market at reasonable prices. Alas that the inventor seems to be an unworldly sort, unaware of his invention's commercial potential.

Coming from Dunsany, this is clearly the product of a (no doubt quill) pen dripping with irony. What the narrator sees, peering into the future, is urban blight spreading over the rural landscape. (The view from his window is that from Dunsany's, at Dunstall Priory in Shoreham, Kent.) He observes a future civilization increasingly out of harmony with nature. Then there is a bright, blinding flash, after which the narrator goes to the doctor to get his eyes checked and is told his tears are radioactive. But he recovers. He dares not look at that particular point in the future again, but settles down to follow the adventures of a neo-Neolithic family five or six hundred years hence. The novel becomes a book of the sort that goes all the way back to such works as Richard Jeffries's *After London* (1884). (In Dunsany's version, London has become a crater lake, filled in by the Thames.) The scenario bears much resemblance to that of Stephen Vincent Benét's "By the Waters of Babylon" (1937), particularly with the idea that post-holocaust savages would regard metal with superstitious dread. It also echoes some of the earliest Dunsany stories. The works of man are transitory, he told us from the start. Civilization may pass away as if it had never existed. One thinks of the story "In Zaccarath" in *A Dreamer's Tales* (1910), which extols the eternal grandeur of a fabulous city until the author's voice breaks in at the end:

> And only the other day I found a stone that had undoubtedly been a part of Zaccarath, it was three inches long and an inch broad; I saw the edge of it uncovered by the sand. I believe that only three other pieces have been found like it. (p. 174)

Apologizing over and over for the triviality of what he is doing, and babbling on about the entertainment value of the futuroscope, the narrator follows his family of stone-age farmers in real time, not skipping ahead to see what they're doing in their tomorrow, but viewing events as they experience them. To some extent, their world seems Edenic, a comparison Dunsany makes, remarking that it is as if the angel with the flaming sword had gone away. But there are dangers, from wolves, and from a naked, decidedly Paleolithic "Wild Man," who resembles the figures ancient Britons scratched on the chalk hills. One of the women of the household is kidnapped by the Wild Man (but she ends up marrying him and tidying up his cave—an old railway tunnel). The sweetheart of another is carried off by the Gypsies, who, alone of pre-holocaust peoples, seem to have survived as they always were (a notion that Jeffries explores at length in Chapter 3 of *After London*), though they are still tainted by their occasional use of metal. There isn't a very much plot, just a good deal of running about, which, in the hands of, say, Edgar Rice Burroughs would have been just that, running about, as Tarzan rescues Jane one more time to pad out a few more chapters.

But Dunsany's narrative has an odd effect. The gentleman with the futuroscope pay observe but not intervene. Only once is he able to get the attention of a dog and make it bark to give away the Gypsies' position. (Dogs are more sensitive than humans, who remain completely unaware of their eavesdropper from the past.) Present-day life intrudes. The narrator's concentration on the future is broken again and again, as he looks out his window to see the landscape as it appears in 1955, then compares it to that of half a millennium hence. Still claiming to be writing, in effect, a commercial for futuroscopes as entertainment, he is actually meditating on the nature of civilization, for all he protests that he us too superficial a fellow to do anything of the sort.

Dunsany was a master of the framed-story, the kind that tells how someone else told a story, usually in a club or bar, about adventures the frame-character cannot verify. There were ultimately six volumes of Jorkens, working every possible variation of this device. But usually frame narrators and storytellers are themselves devices, static cartoons who serve to set up the core narrative. In *The Pleasures of a Futuroscope* the frame-narrator is something more. He is an actual character. The *story* is not so much how the flint-wielding farmers of the future rescued a girl from the Gypsies, as how an elderly gentleman in Kent in 1955 gained a view of the future, which turned into a kind of obsession and changed his understanding of things.

There's no indication that Dunsany regarded this book as a philosophical summing-up, but it is a major rallying of his talent late in life. At seventy-seven, he could still write, not merely well, but beautifully. He could describe the traces of ancient urbanization: "...though Nature has overcome it and hidden it with her greenery, something of its outlines still disturbs the smooth faces of the hills, like a mark in a human face left by a troubled dream." (p. 68). The narrator, looking at the same landscape in 1955 and circa 2500, remarks that he recognized its features, "as one may recognize the outlines of bones in a face much altered by age." (p. 87). He speaks of the Gypsies wandering away, "lost in the sounds and silence that haunted the grey of the hills." (p. 91). The prose is far removed from that of *The Gods of Pegāna* or *A Dreamer's Tales*, but it is rolling and musical, more poetic than that of *The Last Revolution* or *His Fellow Men,* perhaps because in his descriptions of Nature, Dunsany was rhapsodizing about something he knew intimately and loved very much.

Mankind, of course, merely passes across landscapes and ultimately leaves little trace on them.

XXIV.

ARTHUR C. CLARKE & LORD DUNSANY

Arthur C. Clarke & Lord Dunsany: A Correspondence, edited by Keith Allen Daniels. Anamnesis Press, 1998, trade paperback, 84 p.

To the uninformed, this may seem an unlikely pairing.

Lord Dunsany, the author of *The Gods of Pegāna* and *The King of Elfland's Daughter* was a paragon of High Fantasy, one of the inventors of the form, associated in (at least) the fannish mind with the Ballantine Adult Fantasy Series and H. P. Lovecraft. Indeed, the most recent Dunsany reprint, *The Complete Pegāna*, was published by Chaosium as "Call of Cthulhu Fiction." It may well be that Dunsany, along with most of his other weird/fantasy contemporaries, Machen, Blackwood, Clark Ashton Smith, etc., are becoming satellites of Lovecraft in precisely the same way Christopher Marlowe or Beaumont & Fletcher are satellites of Shakespeare.

Clarke's only obvious connection to Lovecraft is that he wrote a fanzine parody, "At the Mountains of Murkiness," in the late '30s. He is otherwise, of course, one of the century's top science fiction writers and was an extremely eloquent prophet of the on-coming Space Age.

But wait, there's more. For one thing, it was Clarke who introduced Dunsany to Lovecraft, sending him a copy of *The Arkham Sampler* in 1948, an issue containing an installment of *The Dream-Quest of Unknown Kadath*. (Writes Dunsany graciously, "I see Lovecraft borrowed my style, & I don't grudge it to him.") More importantly, Clarke initiated the correspondence in 1944 because of his admiration for Dunsany's poetry of outer space.

Now it must be admitted that Dunsany's poetry has drawn little praise, even from his admirers. While the newspapers of the '40s and '50s heralded Dunsany as "the great Irish poet," *etc.*, the bureaucracy that guards the Literary Canon has afforded him no place at all for his poetry. Most of Dunsany's verse *is* rather bland, conventionally rhymed and metered, conventional in imagery and sentiment, and frankly not as "poetic" as his best prose. Clarke (who wrote extensively about Dunsany's poetry in *1984: Spring—a Choice of Futures*) has been one of the few to find any real merit in it. He was drawn to the occasionally visionary quality of such lines as:

Beautiful when the world lies dreaming
Are the lights from the Evening Star's
Oceans of pale blue wate gleaming,
And the tawny deserts of Mars.

That was quite enough to excite the young Clarke, space enthusiast, particularly coming from an established literary figure. Lest I seem to contradict myself, I hasten to explain that Dunsany's reputation, at times considerable and decidedly non-generic—he was never part of the pulp magazine scene, but wrote for *Punch* and *The Atlantic Monthly*—was based on his plays and his prose fiction, particularly his short stories. He was, at the time Clarke was writing to him, regarded as a great imaginative writer, maybe a little passé yet someone who could still hold his own even after the Mainstream had been completely conquered by realists. But he wasn't a great poet.

Nevertheless, he was able to make the imaginative leap to at least dream of space-travel. (Even if the voyager to Mars in his famous story "Our Distant Cousins" gets there by airplane.) Clarke quickly, if politely points out that even then it seemed unlikely that there could be oceans on Venus.

More remarkably, Dunsany, for all he was a literary and social conservative ("You read Dunsany for his prose," another Dunsany admirer, Ursula Le Guin, once remarked, "because he was such a dreadful reactionary."), was open-minded enough even as he approached his 70s to respect and learn from Clarke, who was at that time an unknown science fiction fan and RAF radar officer. This was in an era when the astronomer royal notoriously dismissed space-travel as "bunk."

It's clear from the letters that Dunsany's grasp of science is not the best. Clarke explains how a spacesuit works, and some basic astronomy. He even has to explain how rocket works. Dunsany, like most people, thinks it needs air to push against. Clarke sets him straight, with the same lucidity which would later characterize his bestseller *The Conquest of Space*. He makes it quite clear that space travel is coming soon, comparing the 1940s to the 1890s, when heavier-than-air flight was a certainty, but not yet achieved. He predicts a moon landing within a generation, even as Dunsany was always telling people that children then alive would one day see a photo of the far side of the Moon. ("No more interesting than the near side!" quipped a considerably less visionary Peer.) Then Clarke, after casually predicting spaceflight by about 1980, hits one of those amazing bull's eyes which all hard SF writers can only hope for:

> ...I believe most young people today will see the actual landing [on the Moon]—probably literally, through their television sets! (p. 79)

Too bad he didn't write that into a story. Nobody else did either, as far as I can tell.

There's more to these letters than Clarke educating Dunsany. A friendship develops. Clarke is less shy than many new writers about sending his first published stories to the older man. (In perhaps the first SF magazines Dunsany saw.) Their conversation begins to shift to such topics as the implications of atomic energy. Clarke sees atomic rockets, reducing interplanetary distances from months to days. But he also sees the possibility of human extinction and at one point comes to the melancholy conclusion that if we're to have a nuclear war, it would be best to get it over by 1960, before the bombs get so big they sterilize the planet.

Dunsany had also written in his *A Glimpse from the Watch Tower* (1946) of the new responsibility not to destroy the future. There's some literary back-and-forth as Dunsany uses some of Clarke's ideas in an essay, and then, perhaps, in his first science-fiction novel (the disappointingly archaic *The Last Revolution*, 1951). The influence goes both ways. Clarke's stately, poetic prose in such stories as "The Wall of Darkness" and *Against the Fall of Night* owe as much to Dunsany as to Wells, and of course Clarke greatly admired and imitated Dunsany's Jorkens series in his *Tales from the White Hart*. (Indeed, Dunsany was hugely prolific, the father of the fantastic tale-told-in-a-bar story. In five volumes of Jorkens and several uncollected stories, Dunsany probably produced more examples of this genre than all subsequent practitioners put together.)

Clarke finally met Dunsany in 1948. They remained in friendly contact thereafter. They're an appealing pair. Clarke was the bright visionary on his way to the top. Dunsany, an elder statesman, had his most famous work behind him, but was by no means burned out, and would write often excellent stories (and a couple of interesting novels) until his death in 1957. He even wrote his best poetry late. (*To Awaken Pegasus*, 1949, won't exactly rate him alongside T. S. Eliot—a writer Dunsany despised, by the way—but it does contain several decent poems.) Most importantly, he was *not* stuck in the Edwardian world of his youth, and could appreciate, and to some extent, follow Clarke's lead.

Keith Allen Daniels deserves only praise for bringing out this volume. As an added feature, he's reproduced several of Dunsany's letters in facsimile. (Dunsany wrote with a quill and blotted the ink with sand.) One might argue that $19.95 is a bit steep for an eight-four-page paperback, though, alas, it is not by the standards of many specialized non-fiction volumes aimed at libraries. Hardcore Dunsany or Clarke fans are going to have to have this, and there are enough of them. The only quibble one might have is that bracketed asides from the editor, within the texts of the letters, are intrusive. Footnotes would have been preferable.

XXV.

THE KING OF ELFLAND'S DAUGHTER

The King of Elfland's Daughter by Lord Dunsany. New York: Del Rey/Impact, 1999, trade paperback, 368 p.

What does this book mean?

Suffice it to say that the latest Del Rey edition, with its new introduction by Neil Gaiman, marks the return of an old friend; more than that, of one of the great and beloved classics of fantasy, a book wholly worthy to share a shelf with *The Lord of the Rings*, *The Gormenghast Trilogy*, *The Worm Ouroboros*, *Jurgen*, *Little Big*, and a very few others.

Its return just now is particularly welcome, as it has been gone from American bookstores for a generation, and its music (to use one of the many metaphors in a metaphor-rich book) should come as a shock and revelation to readers (and writers) raised on clone trilogies or generic novels set in trademarked, and otherwise prefabricated settings. Here's a fantasy which is the real thing, exquisitely beautiful, and suggesting possibilities of content and language which may indeed seem a miracle for such readers as can hear (to borrow another metaphor, which Dunsany got from Tennyson) the horns of Elfland blowing, and haven't heard them in a long time, if ever.

But what precisely does it *mean*?

For much of Dunsany's work, that would be a useless question. What does "The Fortress Unvanquishable, Save for Sacnoth," *mean*? It merely is. But *The King of Elfland's Daughter* is a subtly gleaming, lacquered puzzle box, full of secrets. It invites interpretation.

The *plot* is one of the many surface-facets, and may be summarized thus: the folk of Erl, a placid, hamlet which seems to lie outside of maps and history, but still within (to use the phrase which is the key to the book, and one perhaps repeated a few times too often)

183

The Fields We Know, go before their Lord, desiring a little variety in their dull but idyllic lives. They want to be ruled by "a magic lord." So the Old Lord sends his son, Alveric, into Elfland to steal away the lady of the book's title, which he does with the aid of a sword given him by a witch, who forged it out of thunderbolts she swept up "in a high land, near the thunder."

But mortal Prince and fairy Princess don't live happily ever after. Lirazel, the princess, cannot adjust to life on Earth. She does unseemly things, like pray to stars and stones. Yet she loves Alveric and has a son by him. But Elfland beckons, and one day she drifts back away on the wind. Alveric can't fetch her again, because the King of Elfland has withdrawn his kingdom across "a space that to cross would weary the comet." He spends the rest of the book trying, accompanied by a diminishing band of increasingly mad attendants. The couple's son, Orion, grows up and spends most of the book hunting unicorns. The folk of Erl become increasingly nervous about the amount of magic that is seeping over the border from Elfland, and at one point behold a unicorn, then hold a parliamentary vote and decide no unicorn was seen after all. At last Lirazel beseeches of her father the last, greatest Rune of Elfland, whereby Elfland flows over Erl, enclosing it forever beyond the ravages of Time.

But what does it actually mean?

For Dunsany himself, the book meant a triumphant and slightly labored return to his earlier mode. He had written his gem-like fantasy, *The Gods of Pegāna*, *etc.* in the salad days of the Edwardian era, which was a good time to be rich, young, and politically out of touch. But even then, as Lovecraft ruefully noted some years later, a whiff of sophistication had come into Dunsany's fantasies. *The Book of Wonder* (1912) began to parody itself. Of the stories in *The Last Book of Wonder*, the best by far are those set in Our Fields. The ones set in never-never land seem a bit anemic. *The Last Book of Wonder*, of course, was published in 1916, after World War I had ruined everything. It became very hard to write of ideal and beautiful things when so many friends were dying in Flanders' mud. (Dunsany himself did time in the trenches, but was actually wounded in Dublin, during the Easter Rebellion as he raced into town to offer his services to the British.) The melancholy preface to *The Last Book of Wonder* compares that book to a beautiful thing thrown in desperation from the window of a burning house. By about 1917, Dunsany was in a profound depression, and wrote little but war propaganda: *Tales of War* and *Unhappy Far-Off Things.*

Afterwards, it took him a while to get back into form.

He began to experiment for the first time with novels. *Don Rodriguez: The Chronicles of Shadow Valley* came first (1922) came first. It is a picaresque, rambling thing, full of clever moments and jolly humor, which doesn't, as a whole, seem to mean anything.

The King of Elfland's Daughter is another matter entirely. One envisions Dunsany, like the King of Elfland in Chapter 25, deliberately mustering all his strength to call up all the miracles of Elfland. The King is trying to impress Lirazel so she won't pine for things of Earth. ("But she sighed: it was not enough.")

Dunsany, like the King, was perhaps trying just a little too hard. The book is arguably too long. Some of the language is a little too flowery in a way that *The Gods of Pegāna* never was, and the reader has to stop and parse out a sentence to find the verb or puzzle through the often eccentric punctuation. It may seem odd that a man who proclaimed in *If I Were Dictator* (1934) that all marks of punctuation are property of the state and their deletion should be severely punished would allow two or even three modifiers to go without commas between them. But the secret is to read the "difficult" or "slow" passages aloud. They need to be intoned. Then they flow. Commas are used, not in their conventional manner, but merely to mark the flow of the word-rhythms. They make us pause, draw breath, or keep time.

I confess that I possess a recourse available to no more than 250 people on the planet, which is to say I own a copy of the limited, large-paper first edition of the novel published by Putnam in 1924. Its velum binding and slightly rippled, off-white paper give it the feel of a *tome*, the very sort of thing the King of Elfland would open while sitting in eternal twilight in his palace "which may be told of only in song," from which he would read to summon forth the Potencies of his realm. I often found that I preferred to put aside the more ordinary Del Rey trade paperback and open up the magical tome, and the experience of the book was somehow subtly different, and, indeed, more "magical." One can only wish that *The King of Elfland's Daughter* will one day be reissued in a beautiful, coffee-table edition illustrated by, perhaps, Brian Froud.

But back to the text. What flows out is the *perfect fantasy sentence,* which deserves recognition alongside such perfect science-fictional phrases as Heinlein's "the door dilated." It occurs on page 120:

But when Alveric with his sword was far to the North the Elf King loosened his grip with which he

had withdrawn Elfland, as the Moon that withdraws
the tide lets it flow back again, and Elfland came racing back as the tide over flat sands.

That is a sentence with which people who hate fantasy cannot
cope; for Dunsany's fantasy is not mere, undisciplined imagination,
the equivalent of tennis with the net down. This is not sloppy science fiction, which could be "fixed," as innumerable pulp novels
were, by calling Elfland a "dimension" and the Elf King an alien.

It is the nature and meaning of Elfland which is the core and
meaning of this book, and of Dunsany's art. Elfland represents, first,
ideal beauty. It is outside of Time, and exists Beyond the Fields We
Know, on the other side of the Frontier of Twilight, which may be
glimpsed sometimes in the gloaming, across Earthly fields. It is,
perhaps, the place which cast its shadows on the wall of Plato's
cave, the realm of Nature which is beyond human comprehension.

Very few humans may hear the horns of Elfland blowing, and
few dare to glance upon the Elfin Mountains aglow beyond the twilight. Indeed, most people turn fearfully away. All of the houses
near to the border face west. No one ever talks of what lies eastward.
This is most especially discouraged by the clergy, about whom,
more in a moment.

When Alveric searches after Lirazel, and the Elf King draws his
boundary far away, what remains is a wasteland of stone, stretching,
perhaps, to infinity.

But among the boulders, left behind like fish flopping when a
tide goes out too suddenly, are fragments of faded memories. One
hears a line of an old song, beloved from childhood, and finds things
long lost:

> Next Alveric saw lying there on the flat dry
> ground a toy that he yet remembered...which had
> been a childish joy to him...and one unlucky day it
> had been broken, and one unhappy day it had been
> thrown away. And now he saw it lying there not
> merely new and unbroken, but with a wonder about
> it, a splendour and a romance, a radiant transfigured
> thing that his young fancy had known. (p. 68)

Like Lovecraft's Silver Key to Dreams, Elfland represents
childhood dreams, nostalgia, all the things we lose with the perspective of age.

186

The King of Elfland's Daughter is about the loss and recovery of Elfland, which is far more than merely finding one's way back to a physical place, in the same sense that the Holy Grail was more than a cup somebody lost. The Grail could only be glimpsed as the questing knight approached spiritual perfection. Alveric, who seems to have learned little, still hopes to retake Lirazel by force and achieves nothing. Only after his sword is disenchanted can he approach the border of Elfland, but by then the last followers on his years-long quest are madmen and they haul him away, as unwilling as are the sane and respectable folk of Erl to gaze upon Elfland, which is beyond the scope of their mundane ravings.

Another of Alveric's companions, now a shepherd, dismisses Elfland as a folly of his youth. Elfland represents, too, imaginings, and also emotional release, a lack of restraint. Deep down, one could argue, it represents sexual release, because it is a pagan place, quite apart from salvation, roundly condemned by the "Freer of Christom." (Who is treated with extreme deference, for all he seems a most intolerant chap. Indeed, clergymen are always so treated in Dunsany, for all that Dunsany himself was not conventionally religious.)

The loss of Elfland was to become a major theme of Dunsany's subsequent work. In his next, *The Charwoman's Shadow* (1926) set more in the "real" world, it is the magical realm which must retreat at the end. In *The Blessing of Pan* another of Dunsany's sympathetic clergymen must cope with an outbreak of paganism in his parish, for people are able to hear the music of Pan, which is the same as the horns of Elfland, and this leads them to impropriety. The clergyman himself succumbs, but the magic is all offstage and at a distance.

After that, Elfland recedes rapidly, through *The Curse of the Wise Woman* (1933), where magic is probably just superstition and the Celtic paradise of Tir-nan-Og a pretty illusion; through *Up in the Hills* (1936) in which curses frighten only ignorant peasants; on to *Rory and Bran* (1937) with its simpleton hero who alone believes in Romance; all the way down to *The Story of Mona Sheehy* (1939) which is about a girl who believed to be a child of the fairies. But it is, explicitly, a delusion.

"I never saw a more mortal child," someone says in the opening line. In the same book someone else says, "Let's chase no more rainbows." By the time *The Story of Mona Sheehy* came out, Dunsany was sixty-one, World War II was about to begin, and Dunsany had, as surely as Alveric's ex-companion who had become a shepherd, lost the vision of Elfland. In 1949 he published an essay in *The Atlantic Monthly* called "The Fantastic Dreams," in which he seems to renounce the Elflandish sort of fantasy, not voluntarily, but because he can no longer write of such things. World events themselves, the World Wars and the atomic bomb, have become too fantastic, he explains.

So, one more definition: Elfland is inspiration itself, which fades over time, or is murdered by trauma.

Actually, Dunsany did write fantasy in his old age, but it was firmly set in The Fields We Know, and most of it comic, the adventures of the Munchausen-like clubman Jorkens predominating. But he never returned to Elfland, or even glimpsed it from afar.

Elfland, the loss of which Dunsany so touchingly chronicled, is his greatest metaphor, and he was a master of metaphors. (He could describe a desert as, "...all yellow it is, and spotted with shadows of stones, and Death is in it, like a leopard lying in the sun.") It is not just childhood, nostalgia, sweetness, Gee-I-wish and Wouldn't-it-be-lovely-if-only? Reconsider the way that the respectable and responsible folk of Erl *feared* the Elfin border. After all, in Elfland, there is supernal beauty, but no passage of time, no growth, no life, other than that of the curiously energetic, jolly, childlike trolls. To be in Elfland is to be frozen, as in a block of ice, perfectly preserved, but not alive. (Indeed, when Lirazel comes to our fields for the first time, her crown of ice has melted away.)

Elfland represents all indescribable longings. Its palace, after all, "may only be told of in song." But there is a profound ambiguity here. It isn't just the dullards and the fusty parliamentarians of Erl who fear Elfland. Elfland also represents shadows, nightmares, the loss of emotional control, the "panic" of Pan. And, paradoxically, its immortality represents death, or at least something other than life. Recall all those heroes who entered the world of Faerie through a mound or hill, or Sir Orfeo in the ballad who "came to a long grey stone" very much resembling a grave.

For Elves have no souls, that they are things of air, not fully alive, and their emotions are of the most are not real and true, for all their forms may be ravishingly beautiful. In Elfland love and desire, beauty, and even life itself, may be utterly unrestrained, but somehow they dissipate into airy nothingness. Lirazel could actually love Alveric precisely *because* she entered the earthly fields and felt the ravages of Time.

What Dunsany seems to be saying is that only in a fairy tale, like *The King of Elfland's Daughter*, can Elfland swallow up earthly fields and habitations and that be a happy ending for anyone. Otherwise, as we live and grow, it must fade away; and the longing for

Elfland is all the more poignant for its inevitability, and it became the great subject of Dunsany's art.

XXVI.

WHAT? AND LEAVE SHOW BUSINESS? A MOVIE REVIEW OF *GLADIATOR*, WITH A NEW ENDING

I was looking over a newsstand in an airport recently, when I noticed some sports magazine or other with a picture on it, of a muscular, beaming athlete, and it occurred to me: if they'd had glossy magazines in the Roman Empire, this could well have been an issue of *Modern Gladiator* with a feature story, "Maximus, Champion Mankiller!" and other splashy cover lines, "Exclusive New Slaughter Pix!" and "One Man's Courage Versus Three Tigers!"

It would work. That, I think, is part of the dark fascination we have with the Roman arena. We already have a stupid, violent sports show on the tube called *American Gladiator.* If executions were televised, they'd have an audience. If that audience got bored, and it became necessary to jazz up the executions with special effects, fake personas, and choreography, the audience would go along, I'm sure of it. The bestial side of mankind forever lurks right under the surface. It's why people go to professional wrestling matches, or attend auto races (or even air shows) with at least the subconscious hope of seeing a wreck.

Certain lusts are universal. Not to get too far off the topic, but it seems to me that the reason Fascism is alive today and Communism really did not work out is that Communism, however distorted and evil it may have become in practice, ultimately stemmed from generous impulses, the desire to set things right, to make everybody equal. It was ultimately too mystical and abstract to command passions for very long. Fascism, in contrast, deliberately lets the Beast out, pandering to that same id-monster that the rest of civilization seeks to suppress. It's okay to hate, the Fascist tells us. It's okay, even salutary, to toss somebody else to the lions, and, while you're doing that, you might as well enjoy it.

The yahoos who become skinheads and Klansmen today would have had a grand time in good old Rome.

For those id-monster is always there, and always will be.

When I first heard that Ridley Scott's *Gladiator* was set in the Second Century, I was encouraged, because at least (as sometimes happens, usually in Jesus movies) we can't have Christians tossed into the Flavian Ampitheatre by Nero some years before it was built. (As it turns out, there are no Christians in *Gladiator*.)

Hollywood can be a bit weak on that sort of detail. Did you notice Elizabeth Taylor in *Cleopatra* making her triumphant entry into the City through the Arch of Titus (several times larger than it really is) a century and more before *it* was built? Or how about, much more subtly, the bust of Hadrian in the background of the (very good) early '50s *Julius Caesar*? That's like having a portrait of Abraham Lincoln on the wall of George Washington's office.

But the American public is almost totally a-historical, and probably doesn't know whether Hadrian comes before Caesar or not, or even whether Washington comes before Lincoln.

You can be certain that *everything* the general public thinks it knows about the Second Century comes from this movie. That's not much. I suppose we should be grateful to Ridley Scott (and to screenwriters David Franzoni, John Logan, and William Nicholson) for what we do get.

Before I go on, let me say that you should see this film. What it does right, it does extraordinarily well; and what it does extraordinarily well is give us a sense of the power of the Games, showing us how both the public *and* the performers, even the ones who lose control of their bladders before going on, could get *drunk* on the frenzy and adulation.

They were an *awesome* institution, these Games, and the whole Empire was intoxicated with them. They started out in Etruscan times, as a religious ritual, a form of human sacrifice to appease the dead. The Romans, great imitators and even greater organizers and engineers, turned them into big business. Gradually the religious aspect declined, though writers continue to speak of "sacred games" well into the Imperial era. In Caesar's day, there was still a sense of sportsmanship. Young aristocrats sometimes leapt into the arena to steal the show and prove themselves. Others, down on their luck, volunteered. But a couple centuries later, *no one* would go into the arena voluntarily. It had become pure, sadistic murder. As the masses felt less and less in control of their lives, the one outlet they

191

had was to enjoy the deaths of others.

For life was a chancy thing. This was an era in which men sacrificed to many deities, including Fortuna, who could be fickle. One day you might be cheering and laughing in the stands. The next it might be *you* down there on the sand, with the people cheering and laughing at you.

And if you were good at what you did, you might even learn to enjoy it.

This is one of the great mysteries of history. An Empire which aspired to (and to some extend achieved) universal peace and a commonwealth in which all nations were ruled fairly and equally under noble laws, where literature and philosophy were fostered, where the standard of living was the best the world had yet seen, a civilization which became the very standard by which civilization was measured for more than a millennium, had this obscenity at its heart, absolutely integral to what it was.

The Games were a drug. They were better than sex. Ovid tells the girls that if you can get a man's attention while he's at the Games, then you've got him. Indeed, people went into orgasms while watching gladiators.

Not even Christians were immune. One recalls the story told by St. Augustine of the young Christian student in the late fourth century who was dragged off to the games by pagan friends. He covered his eyes, but, alas, could not cover his ears. When the crowd roared, the boy looked, and, despite himself, was utterly caught up in the frenzy of it all. The whole nation was addicted. No emperor, be he the decadent but somewhat squeamish Nero (who once proposed that gladiators fights with blunted weapons so no one would actually be killed) or the virtuous Marcus Aurelius could stop it. Julius Caesar gained opprobrium by doing his paperwork while sitting at the games. But he had to sit there.

Gladiators had groupies. They were adulated like rock stars. Rich women paid enormous amounts to have sex with them. Others, men and women, even more perverted, fondled the condemned as they were going to die, fascinated and sexually excited by the proximity of death. (And once, during the reign of Caligula, such persons followed the gladiators all the way into the arena. The gate slammed shut. The perverts protested that they were innocent citizens. The emperor laughed and watched them die.)

It's precisely this sense of universal madness which comes across so splendidly in the film *Gladiator.* If you know what you're looking at, you see those perverts and groupies.

The fight scenes are spectacular, as vivid and convincing as the chariot race in *Ben Hur.* And the Colosseum itself overwhelms. Of course it's computer generated, as are the sweeping aerial views of the City, some more convincing than others. (At one point I recognized the famous model of Rome that you see in all the books, one of the few worthwhile things to come out of Mussolini's archeological efforts.) The computer is the rejuvenator of the spectacle film, when casts of thousands and enormous sets are no longer economical. Stanley Kubrick had to borrow the Spanish army for the battle scenes in *Spartacus.* Nowadays, you only need a couple hundred extras, who can be computer-multiplied to the horizon. Or, in this case, one or two rows of spectators, who are then multiplied all the way up to the top of the Colosseum. (Note spelling. From "Colossus," referring to a colossus of Nero—later the Sun God—which stood nearby. I was in Denver recently, where they have a "Coliseum.")

The middle-range shots, inside the arena, when the action is going, are very convincing indeed. The look is awesome. As our hero comments, even though he may be about to die there very soon, "I didn't know men could build something like this."

Ah, but the plot. That's another matter.

When I heard that *Gladiator* was to be a remake of *The Fall of the Roman Empire* (1964), that galumphing epic which, along with the aforementioned *Cleopatra* finished off the *previous* cycle of spectacle films, I had fewer expectations.

The Fall of the Roman Empire, after all, is one of the stupidest films ever made. "Swirling robes and swirling clichés," as Alec Guinness put it. Remember it this way: Wise, virtuous, stoical Obi Wan Aurelius (Guinness), after what seems like a half an hour of parades and space-filler, tells Moronicus (Stephen Boyd), his degenerate son Commodus's virtuous and lifelong friend, whose political perspicacity he professes to admire, "I've got this problem. My son is a complete loser. So I'm going to make you my successor instead."

Now of course you may ask, if they're so opposite, what is the basis for this friendship? But don't expect an answer.

Then there's the political perspicacity. What does the good guy do upon being told this portentous news, but immediately reveal to the evil prince, *privately,* "Your dad is going to disinherit you and make me emperor. Tough luck, old chum." Which of course translates into, "Stick a knife in me *now,* before the secret gets out."

You don't have to know any history to understand how dumb it all is. *The Fall of the Roman Empire* then lumbers on its way, playing up love interest between Boyd's character and Commodus's sister Lucilla (Sophia Loren). Its only virtues are the sets and costumes, some of the best ever created for a historical film. (The artist Bob Walters, who actually knows more about this stuff than I do, assures me that the uniforms etc. were carefully copied from the Column of Marcus Aurelius, and the only mistake he could spot was infantry in cavalry getup, a huge advance over most Roman movies in which all the soldiers dress like 1st Century Praetorians.)

Gladiator, I am happy to report, improves on the original in just about every way. The costumes and sets look right. Writers, director, and actors all seem to do their best to paper over the gaping holes in the plot. Richard Harris cannily plays the Guinness role, Emperor Marcus Aurelius, as more than a little bit dotty. *This* Aurelius, exhausted from his German wars, taking a page from *I, Claudius,* yearns for the restoration of the Republic. He wants our hero Maximus (Russell Crowe, roughly corresponding to the Stephen Boyd character) to seize power instead of Commodus, then hand it over to the Senate. This, in the second century A.D., would have been sheer lunacy. The monarchy was two hundred years old. The Republic wasn't even a dream, except among wooly-headed senators. The army, in particular, would never have allowed such a thing. It preferred a stable dynasty, which meant stable pay. So Harris is right to depict Marcus was perhaps on the edge of senility. (But the real Marcus died at age fifty-nine. Harris looks twenty years too old for the part.)

Joaquin Phoenix plays Commodus as a lost soul, a sorrowful, angry son who wants his father's approval but can never have it. It's a standout performance, devoid of the usual scenery chewing of Evil Emperors. (Think of Jay Robinson as Caligula in *The Robe.*) Among his assorted depravities, he gets to imply a Caligulan incest with Lucilla (Connie Nielsen).

But he also gets to behave more sensibly than Christopher Plummer did in the same role in *The Fall of the Roman Empire.* When Marcus tells him he is not to succeed, in grief and anger he embraces the old emperor, then smothers him against his chest. Our hero Maximus is a popular general, devoted to the old emperor, but now there is no possibility of his carrying out Marcus's plans. Commodus is emperor. With surprising generosity, he offers Maximus his hand in friendship. ("I only offer it once.") Maximus refuses and stalks out. Commodus, as any emperor would have to do with a disloyal general, has him arrested seconds later.

Maximus escapes his executioners, deserts, and rides all the way to Spain, where he finds that Commodus's men have crucified his wife and son, massacred the servants, and burned down the villa. Maximus, then, exhausted, perhaps dying, with maggot-infested wounds, is found by slavers and carried off to North Africa, where he is sold to a gladiatorial school.

That's something that could happen in those days. It was not safe to be away from town alone. Stray people could be grabbed and sold, and no one asked very many questions.

What follows is another effective performance. Crowe's character is a bit of a softie for a Roman general, a sentimentalist who worships little statues of his wife and son as if they were household gods, but this aspect of him dies. He becomes a killing machine, bent on revenge. He works his way through the provinces, becoming grimly friendly with his owner (Oliver Reed in his final role). They make it to Rome, where he achieves success, fame, and that intoxicating adulation of the mob. Finally Commodus, who fancies himself a bit of a gladiator himself, challenges him in the arena, with suitable cheating beforehand, but still loses and dies. Maximus also dies, but is immediately heralded as a hero of the Roman people.

Up to this point the film had generated considerable suspense of a special kind. They were doing so well. It was all so convincing. *Were* they going to wreck it in the last few minutes?

Yes, alas. Not fatally, but the film is wounded by the ending, in which the evil emperor dies in the arena, senators who plotted against him (led by Derek Jacobi) are instantly released, and there's the upbeat suggestion that because of Maximus's sacrifice old-fashioned virtue and dignity are restored, maybe even the Republic.

It's all very uplifting, and all crap. Even *The Fall of the Roman Empire* did better slightly than that. It skipped over the reign of Pertinax and got right to the infamous auction in which the Praetorians put the Empire up for sale to the highest bidder—and then misled the audience by suggesting that the demise of the imperial system followed swiftly thereafter.

To American audiences, it's all fantasy anyway. What most people don't realize is that even at this point we're only in the *middle* of the imperial era.

You want to know what really happened? Commodus didn't die like that. Increasingly deranged, he reigned until 192. There had never been any question of succession. Marcus had made him co-emperor in 177, three years before his own death, to insure a smooth transition. But Commodus disgraced the principate by appearing in the arena hundreds of times. He was a superb athlete, who delighted the people. He fancied himself the Roman Hercules, sometimes dressed the part. His busts show him with lion skin and club. He issued coins with the same image, on which he is described as HERCULES ROMANUS AUGUSTUS. The one moment of actual historical accuracy in *The Fall of the Roman Empire* (actually about thirty seconds) occurs when Christopher Plummer, in the bath, says, "I'll rename the empire the Empire of Commodus and the city the City of Commodus," *etc.*

Contrary to rumor, this emperor did not invent the commode, but he did, most insultingly, plough ground outside the City, announcing that he had refounded the city as Colonia Commodiana, implying that all history up to this point had been erased, and everything started with him. There hadn't been such an egotist on the throne since Caligula 139 years before.

Commodus, incidentally, put his wife Crispina to death shortly after his accession (she is not in either film) and then killed his sister Lucilla after a plot two years later. The character of Lucilla in these movies is a conflation of the emperor's sister and his mistress, Marcia, who survived him and engineered the conspiracy that finally brought him down. Commodus didn't die in the arena, or at the hand of the Senate. Marcia poisoned him, and when that didn't work she had a wrestler strangle him.

After that, virtue and order (but not the Republic) were restored briefly under Pertinax. But like Galba after the death of Nero, he proved stingy and unpopular. He gave no orgies and few if any games. People longed for the fun times. The Praetorians killed him after three months, and *then* put the Empire up for auction. It was bought by a foolish senator, Didius Julianus, whose accession was essentially the most expensive suicide in history. A three-way civil war broke out, then stability was restored under Septimius Severus (193-211), under whose dynasty the wealth and ease of Roman life (not to mention the gladiatorial spectacles) continued unabated. The murder of Severus Alexander (235) was the end of the Good Old Days. The rest of the third century was rough, a time of invasions and anarchy, and ended with the state restored in strength, but thoroughly totalitarian under Diocletian's Tetrarchy. In the fourth century, the state became Christian. In the fifth, the western half did indeed finally fall, almost exactly three hundred years after the events depicted in *The Fall of the Roman Empire* and *Gladiator*. Gladiatorial combats ended in the early fifth century, but the Colosseum remained in use even after the end of the Empire, with wrestling matches, acrobatics, and beast fights continuing there into the early sixth, during the days of the Ostrogothic kingdom.

What is the importance (or even point) of historical accuracy in such films? They're entertainment, not education. And who was the Hollywood mogul who said, "If the legend is better than the truth, film the legend" or words to that effect?

Let me suggest that sometimes the truth is a pretty good story too. Until its finale, *Gladiator* doesn't violate the truth too violently. I think it could have continued in that mode all the way to the end.

But a truthful ending would have been darker, and this has already been a very dark film about the institutionalization of the very worst aspect of the human psyche. Maybe Scott lost his nerve and could not stay with his vision until the end.

Some sort of payoff is necessary in drama, or else it becomes what George Scithers used to call Futility in the *Isaac Asimov's SF Magazine* rejection slips. If it's all for nothing, if nothing is accomplished, and the hero just gets killed at the end, we are unsatisfied. Having Maximus kill Commodus in the arena before he dies himself, then concluding on a note of uplift *is* an ending, and completes the dramatic structure, but it's too simple, in addition to being dishonest.

Let me suggest a compromise: Commodus, having cheated by dealing Maximus a crippling wound before his (Maximus's) armor is put on, wins the bout. He kills Maximus. But *he too* is drunk on the awful adulation of the crowd. Being emperor is not enough. He craves to be a hero of the arena. He holds up his bloody sword, shouting, "Look! Look! I am victorious!"

But there is dead silence. No applause at all. The look on the emperor's face is one of abject terror. Maximus was a popular favorite. The crowd is angry.

Cut to darkness. We hear Lucilla/Marcia's voice: "Do it now!"

Interior. Night. We see the emperor in his bed chamber, the exact same look of terror on his face as the wrestler strangles him. Lucilla/Marcia looks on.

Cut to credits. As they roll we hear the increasing roar of the crowd in the arena.

That too would complete the dramatic structure. None of this nonsense about the restoration of virtue and the Republic. The Beast wins. Commodus, bestial as he himself is, is consumed by it. Maximus's adventures are *not* wasted in futility, as that quick cutting implies (without doing too much damage to history) that the murder of Maximus set the successful conspiracy against the emperor into motion.

Of course in real life it didn't. The actual final straw was that Commodus planned to appear in the Senate House and appoint the new consuls for the year 193 *while dressed as a gladiator.* This was too great an insult to Roman dignity. Many people, including the emperor's mistress and the prefect of the Praetorian Guards, who had excellent reasons to fear for their lives, took action.

The story needs one more patch. The ending is fully as absurd as the suggestion that Marcus Aurelius, in his right mind, would make someone other than his son his successor and try to restore the long-dead Republic.

As drama, all considerations of history aside, *Gladiator* works very well until the last five minutes. The ending is sappy by any standard. You should see the film for what comes before, the many fine performances, and for the vivid depiction of the Great Beast which was the Arena, which devoured human lives like popcorn, while the onlookers *adored* it obscenely.

XXVII.

A POUND OF PAPER

A Pound of Paper by John Baxter. Bantam Books (UK), 2004, trade paperback, 336 p.

John Baxter is a member of my tribe. That's what I conclude from reading this delightful memoir. Superficially, the book is the autobiography of a man I don't know, whose works I have more heard of than read, and whose interests do not necessarily coincide with my own. It's not really a fan memoir either, though the narrative weaves in and out of science fiction and fandom at times.

Certainly a fan will recognize the Moment of Contact, when the proto-fan first meets another science-fictionist or attends a fan meeting for the first time. (How appropriate that the first SF story Baxter read was Murray Leinster's "First Contact.")

Mine happened a little earlier than Baxter's. I attended a Philadelphia Science Fiction Society meeting for the first time when I was fifteen. The PSFS is a most venerable organization, founded in 1936, one of the two surviving chapters of Hugo Gernsback's Science Fiction League, still engaged in a genial dispute with the Los Angeles chapter over which is the oldest continuous fan group in the country or even the world, the question being whether PSFS can genuinely claim continuity through World War II. I wasn't sure, before I went to that first meeting, whether I was going to a convention such as I had read about in Lin Carter's "Our Man in Fandom" columns in *Worlds of If* magazine, or something smaller. ("Don't buy the place out," my father said to me.) The first fan I ever met, in the stairway on the way to the meeting room, was the PSFS president, J. B. Post, later famous for *The Atlas of Fantasy* and still a good friend after thirty-seven years.

Baxter was seventeen at this point, considerably more mature (out of school and living on his own), but I could readily relate to his description of his first fan meeting in Sydney.

There's another early moment that's happened to all of us, described in Chapter 4. Somewhere in the early teens, the proto-fan has a friend whose father reads science fiction and who will lend out science fiction magazines. Thus I gained access to the *Galaxy*s and *F&SF*s of the 1950's. Baxter's first SF magazine seems to have been the February 1940 *Super Science Stories*, which he borrowed and read sometime in the late '50s. I read that issue about ten years later, but by then I was in fandom and bought that issue from a mail-order dealer.

I am sure that if John Baxter and I ever got together, we could have a long and pleasant convention which wouldn't mention science fiction all that much. If I visited him, he could show me his rarities. If he visited me, I could show him mine. What we truly have in common is that we are both members of the Tribe of Book People. H. P. Lovecraft, who was not, complained to one of his younger correspondents (I think it was Donald Wandrei), "I love literature. You love *books.*"

There is something to be said for the book as *object.* Hopefully the collector does not lose touch with an appreciation for the contents, but the *book* is considerably more. Non-collectors, with whom Baxter has had many colorful encounters, will never grasp this. Baxter tells one ghastly incident in which someone casually ripped the flyleaf out of a Nigel Kneale book to make a note on it, and couldn't understand why he and the bookseller were virtually in a state of shock.

That brought to my mind a scene from *Buffy the Vampire Slayer*, in which a high school bimbo is very obviously chewing gum. "Get rid of the gum," says Giles the librarian. The bimbo tears the flyleaf out of one of those *Necronomicon*-like tomes with which Sunnydale High's library is so mysteriously well equipped. Giles looks like he's been slugged in the gut. "But...that's a six-hundred year old book!" he manages to gasp. "Well at least it wasn't a new one!" the bimbo says cheerfully. Giles is appalled.

Even TV fantasy sometimes touches on real life.

Books are part of real life. An obsession with them is not mere escapism. To quote the late L. Sprague de Camp, a book is as real as a board or a baby.

All through various mundane jobs and career moves, Baxter has been a devoted bookman. Of course he reacted like that to the desecration of a book. Any member of the tribe would. In fact, he has quite a bit to say about flyleaves and endpapers. Inscriptions by authors are one thing, but Baxter resents the sort of nobody who inscribes to another nobody messages of no significance even to the recipient. He tries to avoid having endpapers stamped by the bookseller, even when that allegedly makes the book more collectible. Endpapers, he remarks, are like the silences in a Pinter play, a pause between the cover and the text (p. 79). They are not to be marked on lightly. Condition matters. It is a major concern for book people. The *book* is more than just the words inside it. It is a whole object, a thing in itself.

Any one of us knows what it means to get up in the dimmest hours of the breaking down and travel to some remote, dingy district where other members of the book-tribe drift out of the gloom in search of bibliographic treasures. Most of them are shabbily dressed—there are few dapper book people, particularly when on the hunt—and all of them have soon-to-be-filled bags in hand.

We all have book-stalking stories. Great Buy stories. The One that Got Away stories. The "I bought *one*" story, with the subtext of, "If I'd bought the whole stack I'd be a rich man today." The dust jacket stories. Baxter tells of a find of ex-library Graham Greene books, not worth much for themselves, but a fabulous hoard of dust jackets, which could be put on better copies. I once bought a jacketless first edition of Stephen King's *Carrie* for two dollars back in the late '70s. I got King to sign it at a convention when that was still possible. I found a very ratty ex-library copy of *The Shining* for twenty-five cents, swapped that for an equally ratty ex-library *Carrie*, then extracted the wrinkled but intact jacket from the pasteddown Mylar protector.... We've all done that. In American bookseller idiom, this process is called, suggestively, "mating."

Baxter's has some great bits here, wonderful digressions, one about the various intrigues regarding the authorship of *The Story of O,* another about verified copies of books bound in human skin. What bookman would not be at least curious to see such a thing? Yes, the book world has a dark side. Morbid as it may have sounded at the time, the story of the Poppy Z. Brite books that smelled like burnt human flesh makes more sense in this context.

(Not a story that Baxter tells, but I am sure he could appreciate it: A suicide or would-be vandal incinerated himself in a postal lobby. The smoke penetrated the post boxes, leaving four copies of a signed-limited Brite book smelling of charred human flesh. Rather than discard them as damaged books, bookseller Barry Levin wrapped them in plastic and listed them as unique collector's items for about four thousand dollars each—and got it. Ms. Brite expressed regret that she could not afford one.)

201

Books, for members of the Book Tribe, are a way of life. Baxter describes what we all do. Whenever he settles in a new place, he immediately checks out the local book scene. His cast of characters includes authors, eccentrics, and grotesques. His scenes are great bookshops and obscure ones, sales in alleys, and what the English or Australians call "boot sales"—which were once called "tailgate sales" in America when cars had tailgates. It is precisely the universality of what he describes which makes *A Pound of Paper* so appealing. Even when the details are different, when the scene is in Sydney, London, or Paris, we've all been there. It is almost as if Baxter is bringing shared memories alive on the page.

XXVIII.

THE STORY OF A REVISION

I.

In his 1973 graduation lecture at the U.S. Naval Academy, which is available on tape, Robert Heinlein expresses nostalgia for his own naval days, tells a few jokes, and then gets down to business advising the would-be writers in his audience, reiterating his famous Five Rules, which he originally stated in his 1947 essay, "On the Writing of Speculative Fiction":

1) You must write.
2) You must *finish* what you write.
3) You must refrain from rewriting except to editorial order.
4) You must put it on the market.
5) You must keep it on the market until sold.

All of this would seem to make excellent sense, particularly when coming from the most successful science-fiction writer America has yet produced, but surely most writers, and particularly those of us who also teach writing, find ourselves hemming and hawing a bit on that third rule.

Don't rewrite? Ever?

Heinlein is emphatic. He goes on to add:

> This is very difficult for a great many beginners to believe. A myth has grown up that writing, in order to be publishable, must be rewritten at least twice. Not true. It's utterly false. The way to write efficiently is the way to do any other job whatsoever. *Do it right the first time.* This myth is based on the assumption that you're smarter today than you were

yesterday. But you're not. Oh you may have learned something today that you use the rest of your life, but you're no smarter. Consider a man who makes custom-made furniture. If he thinks of a new design for a chair, he doesn't tear up the chair he made yesterday. He puts that on the display floor and tries to sell it, and he makes a new chair by the new design that he thought of. This is the no-rewriting rule.

Dare I suggest that a lot of professionals find that hard to believe too? Let me go a bit further. Here the Dean of Science Fiction is speaking appalling rubbish. It is hard to imagine worse advice to beginning writers, unless one is to tell them to type everything single-spaced in all capitals on pink paper and take no arguments about it. Hey, that worked for Jacqueline Susann.

The fifth rule is a bit dodgy too. Twenty or thirty rejection slips all of which say the same thing perhaps should be heeded. You and I *can* produce an unpublishable abortion every once in a while, and should be willing to admit it. Maybe Heinlein should have too.

But Heinlein also quipped, in his 1947 essay: "you will somewhere find some editor somewhere, sometime, so unwary or so desperate for copy as to buy the worst old dog you, I, or anybody else can throw at him."

I doubt many slush-pile readers would agree.

In any case, a cautionary tale: During the decline of *Galaxy*, I fobbed off on one of the later editors a dumb short-short I'd written as a joke at Clarion. Years later I met a reader who asked, "Did you ever write anything other than that stupid story in *Galaxy*?"

Remember that everything you publish will be, for some reader, the *first* thing of yours that reader has seen. Try to make sure it's not the last. Maybe some of your "old dogs" should be retired to the kennel, or else put out of their misery.

II.

I want to tell you about a particularly complicated revision I did once. Maybe there does exist that ideal writer of Mozartian genius, to whom everything comes perfectly formed (Lord Dunsany seems to have been one such), but you and I might have to do it the hard way. So did Robert Heinlein, by the way, who despite his bluster seems to have written long, sloppy first drafts and then *revised* them into shape. And he was not above a substantial rewrite of *Methuse-*

lah's Children between serial and book versions, because it needed it.

Do *not* try to sell your first drafts. Writers are *not* furniture makers. Our chairs may lack a few legs the first time out, or they might evolve into a chest of drawers if we let them.

I usually write two drafts, a first and a final, then touch up the final, but I will do more if I'm not getting it right and know it.

Case in point is my novelette, "A Servant of Satan," about which I think I can write with some authority. It was published in *Interzone* for October 1998 and got an honorable mention in the next volume of *The Year's Best Fantasy and Horror* for all that, in my opinion, it's science fiction.

In the writing it proved, if you will pardon the expression, a slippery little devil....

It all began with Richard Dalby's *The Mammoth Book of Victorian and Edwardian Ghost Stories* (Carroll & Graf, 1995) which I read to review for *The New York Review of Science Fiction.* After 573 pages of graveyard mold and (often) prose to match, I thought that, just for a lark, I could write one of these stories.

Okay, then. I began fishing about for a premise, and thinking about all that alleged decadence of the early Romantic era—not inappropriate since Victorian ghost stories were often set before their own period—I came up with the idea of a schoolboy necromancer who is really quite innocent, but wants to desperately to be wicked, so that he may draw Satan to himself, even as a moth is drawn to a bright light. I started with the quote from Shakespeare's *Henry IV* about summoning spirits from the vasty deep. ("And so can I, and so can any man, but will they come when you do call them?")

I chose the structure of what I call the Old School Chum story, which I've written several times. The narrator tells of some remarkable person he met in his youth, who led him on an improbable, frightening adventure...

The narrator, the well-to-do son of a merchant, goes off with his friend Titus, the penniless son of a dissolute lord, to France to complete their education. The time is about 1820, the age of Byron and the Gothic novelists.

The two join a circle of exquisites, decadents, and all-around party types, and are completely enraptured by the amazingly beautiful Countess Sophie-Marie Devereaux, and are drawn to *her* like the proverbial moths. She "tests" them by sending them to steal the skull of a sainted bishop from his tomb. A frightful number of orgies, conjurations, and wannabe wickednesses follow, despite which Titus is still basically a child. He's in over his head. So is the narrator. Then, just as suddenly as she appeared, the alleged Countess vanishes.

The two young men are devastated. They realize that they have utterly compromised themselves for nothing. They part. The narrator tries to exorcise his demons writing trashy Gothic novels which cannot even hint at what he has really been through.

Twenty years go by. (That's the key to the Old School Chum Story.) The second part happens when the narrator, now comfortable and respectable and able to pretend that none of it ever happened, suddenly gets a note from his old friend Titus, now a Lord, albeit as penniless as ever. Titus has continued all this time with his occult activities, convinced that the "Countess" was in fact a demon, sent to damn the two of them. *"She is here!"* the note breathlessly concludes.... And the narrator, for all he doesn't want this intruding into his life just now, can't resist going out to his friend's crumbling country estate....

And at this point the story starts to jump the rails. The first thing I found that I had to do was revise it stylistically, resisting the temptation toward sesquipedalian prose, which is not a characteristic of *good* Victorian writing. So, prune, edit, prune some more. My stylistic models were Sheridan Le Fanu (for narrative) and Conan Doyle (for dialogue, and for the sparseness of his style).

But there were a problem of tone. The story started to get funny. Titus, who had aged rather badly, has a hulking henchman in a turban and a French assistant, Monsieur Delacroix, who seems to exist as an excuse for one line of dialogue: "Monsieur Of-the-Cross, an odd name for a diabolist, don't you think?"

Out with him. Snip, delete.

But still I had to ask myself: what is this story actually about? It seems like a supernatural Gothic, written in a Gothic style, but is there any supernatural element in this at all?

At the climax, Titus lures his friend into to a ruined abbey, which has been converted to unspeakable purposes. Titus tries to sacrifice the narrator to Satan, convinced this will bring the ageless and alluring Countess back to him. The narrator shoots the henchman. But he cannot bring himself to harm his friend. The night passes. With the dawn, nothing happens. Is this because the ceremony failed and the demoness didn't materialize, for all she'd been lurking about of late? Was Titus mad, and serving a "Satan" of his own imagination? The narrator is, again, devastated.

I tried this out on various readers. They liked the exciting graverobbing sequence, but were cold to much of the rest. George Scithers said, "You've certainly done better than this."

Okay, so I tried to spruce up the ending. Suppose the Countess really *did* show up, but in half-human, half-bestial form, offering the pair a dubious immortality, at the end of which, irresistibly, "the flames await"? The ending becomes touching. Titus, never as wicked as he tried to be, cannot bring himself to murder his friend, so they heave the dead henchman (he of the turban, remember?) onto the altar and hope he'll prove acceptable...

Then there's the problem of the metaphorical skeleton of this opus, its core *motif* if you will. The *Henry IV* quote expresses skepticism, saying that anyone can *summon* devils, but there's some question if they'll actually come.

It was no longer a question. The storyline began to resemble a Faustian bargain. Out went the *Henry IV* quote and in came one from Marlowe. The title became "Stand Still, You Ever-Moving Spheres of Heaven," which is the plaintive cry of Dr. Faustus on the last night of his life, as the hour of midnight inexorably nears.

III.

In this form, I sent the story to David Pringle. He wasn't greatly impressed either, though I was flattered that he thought I'd pulled off the nineteenth-century British narrative voice convincingly. What I had *not* pulled off was what I had set out to do: write a supernatural Gothic story in the Victorian mode, within the Judeo-Christian mythos. Obviously the first ending, where it all proves to be a delusion, suggested I was having trouble with that.

David suggested that the ending, in which built up to a big climax and then nothing happened, was somehow lacking. If I could somehow improve it, he'd have another look.

At this point, Heinlein to the contrary, I had been coming back to the story off and on for about a year. I wasn't done yet. And I was getting far from the original notion of "I can write one of these Victorian ghost stories as a lark."

I started to think in Lovecraftian terms, of a mechanistic and uncaring universe, in which there are vast forces, but no genuine supernatural, only things human beings don't understand.

The Countess Sophie-Marie Devereaux continued to evolve. One of the problems in the earlier version (and a problem of stories about ethereally beautiful seductresses in general) was making her ethereal seductiveness actually convincing. But what if she were more like a Lovecraftian Old One, a member of an immortal race of super-beings who descended from the stars aeons ago, and who have haunted all of human history, working miracles and playing frivolous games with the primitives? What if "Satan" were indeed a myth, as is "God," both made up by the aliens as their private little joke.

The title changed back to "A Servant of Satan," but now the *meaning* of that title was entirely different. I went back, reworking the Countess's dialogue, particularly in the scene where Titus and the narrator return to her chateau with the filched skull.

The climax now moved *forward* in time, with about an extra thousand words added. The Countess appears at the conjuration half-bestial, as a sphinx. She takes Titus and the narrator into a Wellsian or Hodgsonesque future, in which I got to use some neat imagery leftover from *another* far future epic I'd failed to bring off back about 1980: the last remnants of mankind, dying in mindless, sensual ecstasy, within a black pyramid which drifts across about the barren earth on lightning bolts, after the sun has gone out.

Then, back in the nineteenth century, our heroes are offered:

"The wine of immortality?"

"Or the excrement of time."

In the end, they cannot resist. The imagery (and the metaphorical skeleton of the story) is again Faustian. It has nothing to do with people deluding themselves about the vasty deep. This is all too real.

Now the quote at the front of the story (from *The Tragical History of Dr. Faustus*) is: "Her lips suck forth my soul; see where it flies!"

It flies, indeed, to the depths of Hell and the ends of time.

IV.

Looking into the folder on this story, I find five different versions. The word-counts vary: 6300, 6700, 7300, 7600, and the final one, which is 8700. That's a total of 27,900 words, of which I sold a mere 8700. Only *one* of these revisions was made to editorial "order." Robert Heinlein would doubtless have said I was wasting my time on the rest, that I should have kept on trying with the first version, no matter how unsatisfactory it might have been, no matter what damage it might have done to my reputation, on the cynical assumption that somebody somewhere is desperate enough to publish *anything*.

If they are, I'm not sure I want to find them.

The Grand Master was absolutely, dead wrong. What I got at the end was *one* good story. It had been a difficult birth, because I'd started on the equivalent of a dare to myself, and along the way my subconscious had further thoughts about the real meaning of what I was writing. I was perhaps writing before I was actually ready to write, and discovering the story only in stages.

But that's why we revise, not because we're any smarter later on, but because we've had more time to think about what we're doing, and maybe because we can look back on what we've done and realize what we've done wrong the first time.

None of are so perfect that we can get it all right the first time. Except maybe Mozart. Or Lord Dunsany. But certainly not you, me, or Robert Heinlein.

v.

Incidentally, I had to revise this article more than once, first because I forgot to say a few things, and then because, on reflection, some of the things I *had* said didn't seem quite as apt when I read them again a week later.

The French have a phrase which translates as "the spirit of the back stairs," meaning what you realize you should have said, now that it's too late and you've gone out of the room and down the back stairs.

We writers are allowed to turn around and go back up those stairs as many times as we need to.

XXIX.

DON'T GIVE UP YOUR DREAMS— OR YOUR DAY JOB

Speech Delivered at the North Wildwood Writers Conference, 2005

I have to admit that I am here under something resembling false pretenses—that is, if you think I can wave a magic wand or give you the 100% reliable formula for literary fame and fortune, you are mistaken. There is no one way. There is no magic formula.

As for the secret handshake, we don't talk about that, any more than we give out the address to that Idea Factory in Poughkeepsie that writers allude to when people ask then, "Where do you get your ideas?"

I am supposed to address the subject of Finding a Literary Agent.

I'll get to that. I promise. I may tap-dance around it a bit, but I will get there eventually.

I myself have been and in a limited way still am a literary agent. My partner George Scithers and I run Owlswick Literary Agency, very much part time, while also co-editing *Weird Tales* magazine, along with a third colleague, John Betancourt (who used to be part of the Agency, but is no longer.) We are not very active these days. We are not seeking clients. We specialized in science fiction and fantasy and mostly handle a few estates. One of the important things a literary agent does for a dead writer is just be there, so that when someone wants to reprint a story, there is an agency to sign the contract and who can be paid. (And who then passes on 90% of the money to the author's heirs.) Without this, the author's work is consigned to oblivion, at least until enough years have passed that it falls into the public domain. It is unreprintable if it is still under copyright and there is no one to buy permission from.

As agents, George and I have sold books. We sold *The Avram Davidson Treasury* to Tor books, a volume which deserves to be recognized as a landmark in American letters. But I will have to admit that the most satisfying thing that ever happened to me was when the late Lloyd Biggle Jr., already grievously ill but very much a fighter, thanked me for revitalizing his career, and said, "You've kept me too busy to die."

We didn't make any serious amount of money. We sold one collection of Lloyd's mystery fiction to a small press, a few reprints, and, more importantly, new stories to *Alfred Hitchcock's Mystery Magazine* and *Analog*. What I managed to do was get him writing again after a long hiatus. The point was not that he got suddenly rich, but that he *created more stories* and got them into print, where they might be read and might live on.

This brings me to the real, main topic of my talk, which is not entitled "How to Find a Literary Agent" but "Don't Give Up Your Dream—Or Your Day Job."

I think of myself as a *writer* first, of both fiction and non-fiction, and, lately not a little verse. I am one of you. But it so happens I have been on the other side of the fence. I am also a fiction magazine editor. It's a multi-dimensional fence with more than two sides. I have also agented. And I have done a small amount of publishing, mostly poetry chapbooks with ghastly titles like *Limericks for the Midnight Hours* and *They Never Found the Head: Poems of Sentiment and Reflection.*

Do not confuse creativity with making a living. These are two quite different things. T. S. Eliot wrote all his great poetry while working in a bank. Gene Wolfe, the pre-eminent science fiction writer, author of *The Book of the New Sun,* who might be described as the American Gabriel García Márquez, edited a technical journal called *Plant Engineering* until he retired. This is irrelevant. Clark Ashton Smith, the noted *Weird Tales* writer and poet, picked fruit and dug wells.

What the writer does is create something worth reading—something which deserves to be read. This is a private, personal act. It can definitely be learned. Parts of it can be taught. Once you have created something worth reading, then surely you have some responsibility to preserve and perpetuate what you have written. You must seek publication. Sometimes a literary agent can come in useful at this point. (I promised I would get to that. I will. I have not forgotten.)

Fame and fortune are not guaranteed, nor is the amount of

money initially paid for a story any reliable indicator of its quality or lasting interest. H. P. Lovecraft, the noted *Weird Tales* author—but he appeared in *WT* before my time, I hasten to add—is now in Library of America, which is one of the highest literary honors this country can bestow. His works are published right alongside Poe and Hawthorne and Melville. He got there well ahead of many conventionally canonical writers, such as Ernest Hemingway, and has completely outdistanced, even buried his famous detractor, the critic Edmund Wilson.

Some of the stories in that very Library of America volume originally appeared in very humble venues, some in amateur journals which paid in copies, mostly in the pulp magazine *Weird Tales*—which wasn't as great a calling card in his day as it is now. Indeed *Weird Tales* has become famous because of Lovecraft, the same reason the Globe Theatre is famous because of Shakespeare. But Lovecraft didn't know that. In fact he thought his life and career were a failure. Some of his letters are nearly as wrenching as John Keats' despairing cry, "Here is a name written on water."

But Lovecraft was doing what we all do. He was putting messages in bottles and tossing them out into the ocean—of time and of the world—in hope that some of them would one day be discovered and opened. In his case, they were.

That's all any of us can do. So much is chance. The one thing the writer can control is the quality of the message in the bottle.

Well, not exactly. He can also choose a bottle that doesn't have a hole in it, which might even float.

The most solid piece of advice I have to give to any of you is to never, never pay to be published. You *must* avoid the stigma of vanity press. I cannot emphasize this too strongly.

In the simplest terms, a vanity press is one which takes money from the author, and then prints the book. I will not say it "publishes" the book. No, it prints copies, or, in these days of print-on-demand, it makes copies available on a computer, so one might be printed if someone should actually order one. The scam works something like this: you are told that this is the way real writers do it, that you must have some faith in yourself, put money where your mouth is, and pay to get into "print." Sometimes this works through what is called "back-end vanity press," which means that the "publisher" even pays you an "advance" of some paltry sum—maybe a dollar—so you can say you got paid for the book, but, oh, by the way, they will require from you a list of friends and relatives guaranteed to buy the book. Since, with print-on-demand technology, the fifth or tenth copy printed can turn a profit, your book may never sell more than fifty copies, but still the publisher has made a profit.

You don't seriously think he's going to promote your book, do you? No, it doesn't work like that. No one takes a vanity book seriously anyway. Bookstores do not stock them. Critics do not review them. Here's why:

Recently one of the country's leading vanity presses (of the "back-end" variety) took grave exception to remarks made about them by the Science Fiction Writers of America, and replied with snotty comments to the effect that "Science fiction doesn't have to meet the same standards as *real* literature, so what do these guys know?"

So some science fiction writers decided to test the vanity press's lofty standards. A dozen of them *deliberately* wrote the very worst book imaginable, far worse than the celebrated hoax novel *Naked Came the Stranger* of some years ago. No, this book was *utterly unpublishable.* Not only was it *bad,* it was incoherent. Characters changed eye-color, hair-color, gender, and possibly species between chapters. There was no continuity. Thirty pages in the middle of the manuscript repeated. There were some blank pages, and, I believe, a repeating chapter. Global errors had been introduced via computer, to add to the level of gibberish. It was, as one real editor phrased it, "A nightmare book."

This was submitted to the vanity press, and, sure enough, accepted.

Why was it accepted? Because *no one read it.* Because vanity presses have all the editorial discernment of a Xerox machine—*and everybody knows it.* That is why the vanity author is one step *below* unpublished. One of the saddest things a literary agent ever sees is a vanity press book—usually utterly amateurish work, with a ghodawful cover—submitted to him with the request, "Now that I have published this, can you help me get a bigger publisher to reprint it?"

The answer is no. There is nothing the agent can do to help at that point except advise that the writer quietly sweep this indiscretion under the rug, never mention it to anyone, and regain the status of being unpublished. It's easy to do. Since no bookstore will stock a vanity book and no critic will review one, and few copies are sold beyond ones the author peddles personally, so, unless you tell a professional editor that you have been published by a vanity press—which point he won't want anything further to do with you—there is no reason he, or anyone, need ever know.

So don't go that route. It can delay or even end your career.

This is not to say there is anything wrong with the many off-trail, small and independent presses which exist everywhere. Particularly for such books as collections of short stories or poetry, it is not all that unusual for such a book to be published without any advance, with payment on a royalty basis only, and a sale of a few hundred copies. This can be honorable, like an off-off-Broadway production of a play. Think of it as a message in a small bottle, perhaps the only bottle available.

What you should do, when approaching or when approached by such a publisher, is study their contract and ask a few questions (or investigate their website). Who else do they publish? How are their books distributed? Do their books get reviewed. Some of my own titles, for instance, are published by Wildside Press, a revolutionary company which (for most of its books) combines print-on-demand technology with *actual publishing.* Sometimes advances are paid, sometimes not. The royalties are standard. *No* list of pre-sold copies is ever required. Wildside books get reviewed in *Publisher's Weekly.* Some, including one of mine, have been nominated for serious awards, like the World Fantasy Award. More importantly, the authors on the list are impressive. In its reprints of public domain books, Wildside does everything from Homer or Melville to Mark Twain, so I can jokingly say I have a publisher in common with just about everybody this side of Shakespeare, but the serious point is that this is a firm that publishes Paul Di Filippo and Mike Resnick and Lawrence Watt-Evans and even my client, the late Lloyd Biggle, and I can say that if it's good enough for them, it's good enough for me.

Further, there is nothing wrong or dishonorable about peddling a few copies of your book yourself. You *can* order Wildside Press books and do this, selling them at an autographing session, for instance. The reason you do this is that if you do, your per-copy share of, say, ninety cents, suddenly goes up to eight *dollars* per copy, when you get the bookstore cut. But you are not *required* to do this. The publisher really does sell books on his own. The essential difference is that he makes his money *selling books* rather than exploiting authors.

Small presses are nice, but it's not as if we don't always want more. Not that we shouldn't seek more. Let ambition spur you on. Do not be satisfied with a small success.

At the same time, do not quit your day job. Here's why. Let us imagine that in one year of writing you succeed beyond your wildest dreams. You are the envy of your writing workshop. Others would sell their souls to be where you are. You sell five stories to, say, *Al-*

fred Hitchcock's Mystery Magazine or maybe *Asimov's Science Fiction* for what those magazines pay—six cents a word. They are stories of typical length, 5,000 words. That times six cents a word equals 300 bucks a story. *And then,* in that same first year, you sell a first novel, not to a small press or micro-press, but to a real, New York publishing house which puts mass-market paperbacks in supermarkets and airports. For a typical first-novel advance of, say, four thousand dollars.

Believe me, there are paperback houses paying less than that. There is a controversy going on in the Science Fiction Writers of America right now—largely because I started it—over the definition of a "professional" publication, what can get you accredited as a member in that august organization. The problem is that too many book publishers and magazines pay far less than what SFWA thinks is an acceptable minimum standard. The organization is in danger of becoming a country club for older, more successful writers. But the newcomer who sold a novel for two thousand dollars and had it published in paperback is, to my mind, also a writer. So is the author of the story published for three cents a word. (*Weird Tales* pays three cents a word.) This work might even be better—and longer lasting—than something initially published for far more. It is folly to dismiss it.

But to go back to my earlier example, the wildly-successful writer who sold the five short stories and the novel just made $5,500. *That* is why you do not quit your day job. It does *not* follow that in the following year you will make ten thousand dollars and things will increase exponentially from there. In fact they may not increase at all. You could still have an honorable career at that level, get a lot of good stories into print, and go on to see them anthologized. You might write a novel which lives well beyond its initial publication.

Before you quit your day job, also factor in medical benefits. Now you know why Gene Wolfe, a genuinely great writer, stayed with *Plant Engineering* until retirement. Only when you find that you are *losing money* by going to your job when the time could be more profitably spent writing—medical benefits factored into the equation—should you quit your job and go freelance. Many of the best writers never reach that point. It is nothing to be ashamed of. It in no way makes you an inferior writer. Think of yourself as a folksinger. You do a lot of gigs at concerts and in coffeehouses, but you may never be as big as Seeger or Baez. Few people are. Get used to it.

The object is to produce good work. When I was nineteen I

wrote a story, which I sold to a professional anthology, which was to be part of the Ballantine Books Adult Fantasy line. Very respectable. But, alas, the series was cancelled and the story never appeared. I resold it to a "little magazine" called *Whispers,* which carried considerable prestige but paid a penny a word. I resold it a couple more times to small magazines, for a penny a word, or even less, as a reprint. It even got reprinted in Norway once. I used the story in my collection, *Tom O'Bedlam's Night Out,* which is still in print twenty years later—admittedly more because the publisher did not throw out the stock than because it was a hot seller. About twenty-five years after that initial publication in *Whispers*, the story was picked up for Marvin Kaye's *Don't Open This Book!*, an anthology published by Doubleday and Guild America, and circulated through a dozen book clubs. It reached a *lot* of people. The pay was quite respectable. At what point, then, did this story become a "professional" sale? Of course if I had not created it back in 1971, there would have been nothing for Marvin to reprint.

One of the messages I'd tossed out in a bottle had been found. What mattered is that it was worth reading.

Ah, but I am supposed to be talking about getting an agent. Again, the question is not quite the right one. It's more of a matter of *when* you should get an agent and what that agent is supposed to do. Keep in mind that the old adage is true, and the same agent isn't right for everyone. Finding the right agent is like finding the right spouse.

But I bet somebody will do it here, this weekend. Romance blossoms.

The main way you find an agent is at a conference like this one, or by asking a fellow writer or maybe an editor to recommend one. There is also a book called *Literary Market Place* where you can look up agents. (Avoid the ones who want to charge you a fee to read your stuff. Those are often scams.)

What an agent does is sell your work to a publisher. He submits it, and it's part of his job to make sure the manuscript doesn't just gather dust for several years—something which, regrettably, happens all too often in New York publishing. He takes a commission, traditionally 10% but more often these days 15%. His interests should be the same as yours. He wants to get the most money on the most favorable terms possible, because he makes his living off a percentage of your income.

By the way, if he sold your stories to *Hitchcock's* for six cents a word he's making a commission of thirty bucks a pop, which is not even worth the paperwork. He might do this as a courtesy for successful clients, but otherwise it is not worth his while.

Many people are surprised to learn that an agent is not necessary to sell short fiction. But it is true. Very few of the stories we buy for *Weird Tales* come from agents. I used to work with George Scithers on *Asimov's SF* and later on *Amazing Stories,* and it was true there too. Unagented writers sell to magazines all the time, and they get paid pretty much the same rates, because the standard magazine contract has little to be negotiated. You are not in a position to say, "I know you pay three cents a word but I think I deserve five." The rights acquired are pretty standard.

Since you may "agent" some of your own work, let me explain a few basics of what to look for in a contract. Not all of these elements will necessarily be present, but ideally they all should be:

1) It should state that the story will actually be published.

2) It should specify that you will be paid for it and when. The two most likely times are on publication or on acceptance. On acceptance is obviously to be preferred, but as long as the publisher is reliable, and *really will* pay on publication, you can learn to live with that.

3) The rights acquired will include what is called "first North American serial rights" or maybe "first world serial rights," which means the publisher wants to be the first to publish your story, either in the United States, or anywhere. But that means he gets to use it in his magazine, which he distributes however and wherever it is distributed. It does *not* mean he gets the movie rights, T-shirt rights, unlimited reprint rights, Tahitian coconut decorating rights, or whatever. The standard *Weird Tales* contract buys First North American serial rights—*i.e.*, the exclusive right to be the first publisher to publish the story in North America, in a periodical—and an anthology option, which means that if we choose to use your story in a Best of *Weird Tales* anthology, we already have permission to reprint it, but are obligated to pay you a stated amount (usually a third of the original payment) for doing so. That's all we take. Everything else remains with you.

What you must never do is sell "all rights" to anything, ever, unless it is work-for-hire, which means you are working with property (*e.g.*, novelizations of a TV series) created by others. "All rights" means you have sold the story *outright* and will gain no more income from it, even if Spielberg makes a movie or the story is reprinted in *100 Great Horror Stories About Killer Garden Vegetables.*

No respectable publisher in the areas I've worked would ever

217

ask for all-rights, but I once looked through a guidebook of children's magazines and was appalled to discover that, in that market, all-rights sales are common. It was rather like discovering that the factory across the street is a sweat shop.

Agents are actually more useful—even essential—when you start selling novels. The *easiest* way to get an agent is to sell a novel by yourself. This is actually possible. There still exist publishers—some of them—who will read a manuscript which did not come from an agent. You submit the manuscript to a publisher, they accept it, and then you say, "I will have my agent get in touch with you." Don't sign anything. Frantically, you search for an agent. Hopefully you can ask a writer friend or a *different* editor to recommend one. Few agents will turn down an opportunity like that, where the sale is already made. But the agent will earn his keep if he is on guard against the worst clauses in some contracts. After that, you and he decide if you want to continue the relationship.

If you're curious—no, it's more serious than that, important that you know this, the worst parts of contracts fall into three areas:

1) No reversion clause. That means that, even if the book is out of print, there is no way for you to get the rights back and sell it again. You have in effect sold "all rights," even if that is not what the contract said. The book is *gone.* If you're *lucky* you could end up *buying it back* when you have a better deal from someone else on the table.

2) No fail-to-publish clause. This should say that if the publisher does not publish by a set date— how long he thinks he needs, padded by a couple years—the contract is void and you get the rights back. This is also known as the run-over-by-a-truck clause. If the publisher is run over by a truck, dies, and goes out of business (possibly in that order), your book could be in legal limbo *forever* without a fail-to-publish clause.

3) A nasty combination of the "competing works" clause and the "right of refusal" clause which could shut down your career forever. If you sell a detective novel to Publisher X, it is not unreasonable for the contract to say that you shall not sell a "competing work" (such as another novel featuring the same characters) to another publisher while this deal is on. It is also not uncommon for the publisher to demand first refusal on your next book, before it can be submitted elsewhere.

But suppose "competing work" is defined so poorly as to include *all fiction* or anything else you might write, and there is no time-limit on the first-refusal clause. If the editor decides to sit on your second book *forever*, you would not be able to write and sell *anything* else.

So, yes, an agent can be very valuable. He might even get you more money. He will at the very least guard you from snares and dangers like the ones I have outlined. He might even keep his ear to the ground and find new opportunities for you. It is, after all, in his interest that you be successful. He's on your side.

But he does not have magic powers. He cannot *make* an editor say yes. A book editor says yes, not on the basis of "I enjoyed this," as much as "I can see a way for my company to publish this profitably." That can be the same as "I enjoyed this and I think my readers will too," but the two concepts are not 100% congruent. The magazine editor buys a story on the belief that such a story, if printed in the magazine, will make paying customers come back for more. There is a certain objective, Darwinian selection about these things. He is either right most of the time or he is out of business.

The agent cannot really influence this process. What you, the writer, must do, is give the agent something he can work with. That is why a recycled vanity-press book is worse than useless. It is a proven failure. Nobody wants to see it. There's nothing the agent can do. He can't sell a really lousy novel either. If the book hasn't reached a certain level of basic craftsmanship, there's nothing anybody can do. Such questions as personal taste and editorial policy will not come into play.

So, quality control is your job. You are ready to find an agent when you genuinely have something good enough for an agent to sell. When that happens, you either find an agent in the manner I have described, or else you make up a query letter and send that with a sample chapter (the *first* chapter of the book) to agents until you get somebody interested. Where possible, find out what kind of submissions the agency considers—letters, or sample chapters.

My recommendation is that if you are a first novelist, you meanwhile write the *entire book*. It is far better to be able to tell the agent—or editor—that the book is finished and available than to leave him guessing whether or not you can actually finish it. There are a lot of people who write great opening chapters who can't.

You might even want to consider another idea which may be controversial for some, and might be called the Coward's Way Out by others.

Write short stories first. I know that a short story is quite different from a novel, and the talent for writing one is not the same as the talent for writing another, but most fiction writers have both talents, to greater or lesser degrees. Think of it this way. If it takes you thirty tries to get it right, *i.e.*, publishable, would you rather spend a couple years writing thirty short stories or write thirty *novels?* If the latter, you are made of sterner stuff than I.

The point is that if you can't write ten pages of publishable prose, you cannot write a thousand. One of the other most disheartening things agents see, other than vanity press novels you're somehow supposed to resell, is a *thick* manuscript, where, once you have read the first five pages, it is clear that this person has such a poor grasp of basic storytelling technique, or even grammar, that there is *no way* this massive opus could ever be published outside of a vanity press. Worse yet, it's volume one of a trilogy. Think of the time wasted, and the trees that died for your sins!

At least if you're selling short stories before you attempt a novel, you know you are beyond that level.

Ultimately then, it's up to you. Quality depends on the writer. As they say on Broadway, you can sleep with the producer all you want, but if you can't dance, you don't get the part. You must have the goods. No amount of "fake it till you make it" will ever work if you do not. You must have something which is vital and compelling and intriguing, which people want to read. If you don't, nothing else matters.

You're writing, not because you think it's a get rich quick scheme, but because you are moved to bring into the world a work of art which will be worth the world's regard. Not that you object to getting paid for it. You are too smart to throw it away on a vanity press. Once you get that far, then an agent becomes your very useful, essential partner. Trust me. If you follow your art far enough, and develop your talent sufficiently, you and your agent will eventually find one another.

Now once this is all over, everybody go home and write.

Index

ABOUT THE AUTHOR

DARRELL SCHWEITZER is a critic, essayist, reviewer, novelist, short story writer, poet, interviewer, and editor, being the author of *The While Isle, The Shattered Goddess, The Mask of the Sorcerer, We Are All Legends, Tom O'Bedlam's Night Out, Necromancies and Netherworlds* (with Jason van Hollander), *Nightscapes, Living with the Dead*, and many others. He has been nominated for the World Fantasy Award on three occasions, and shared an award with George H. Scithers for *Weird Tales*, which he co-edited from 1987-2006. He lives and works in Philadelphia.

Made in the USA